FAILING

D0764823

A Professor's Odyssey of
Flunking, Determination, and Hope

BARBARA HONG, PH.D.

COLUMBIA
PUBLISHING
HOUSE

Columbia Publishing House paperback edition 2018. Designs are trademarks of Columbia Publishing House. Photo is a copyright of Jo Photography.

Library of Congress Control Number: 2014905262
Failing Up: A professor's odyssey of flunking, determination, and hope/Barbara Hong, 2018.
www.failingupbook.com
www.barbarahong.com

A Biography & Autobiography/Educators/Personal Memoirs
—1. Childhood Poverty. 2. Inspirational. 3. Teacher Caring. 4. Women Advocacy. 5. Immigrant Resilience.

Manufactured in the United States of America

ISBN-13: 978-0974653907
ISBN-10: 097465390X

DEDICATION

To My Husband
because you encouraged me.
To My Children
because you inspired me.
To My Teachers
because you believed in me.
To My Students
because you challenged me.

ACKNOWLEDGMENTS

*F*ailing Up would not have been realized if not for the tenacious guidance, meticulous critique, and gentle persuasion of my editors—*Sunamita Lim, Craig Holden, Sheila Black, Candice Morrow, Kevin Miller, Ellie Davis, Elijah Foster, Alexi Shirley, and Laura Chandler Vierra.* Your thorough inspections have given this untold narrative an honest and authentic voice.

My family, colleagues, and friends; thank you for your compassion and sagacity in teaching me what it means to be persistent and to embrace patience so that I may enjoy the process as much as the product. I will be remiss if I do not thank each of my students for their vital roles in reminding me every single day why I became a teacher. You are the reason I wrote this book!

To all my *Research Assistants*, you probably didn't know what you were getting yourself into when you agreed to work with this idiosyncratic professor. I could not have accomplished all that I wanted to without your promptness, dynamism, and cheerfulness when responding to all of my demands.

I believe every student crosses a path with a teacher for a reason. When teachers are willing to see an opportunity while others may see a dead end, they can forever alter the life of that student. Thank you for being mindful of that one student. Thank you for choosing to care and for showing me how teaching and learning ought to transpire.

CONTENTS

THE KIRKUS STAR
Awarded to Books of Exceptional Merit

*"An absorbing, eye-opening narrative about the value
of grit and education, sure to inspire a wide audience."*

KIRKUS REVIEW

In this stunning debut memoir, Hong (Special Education/Brigham Young Univ.-Hawaii) recounts her exceptional transformation from floundering student to flourishing professor.

Born in Singapore to an uneducated mother and an alcoholic, abusive father, Hong grew up in severe poverty. She attended school against her parents' wishes. Despite her intellectual curiosity, she consistently failed her subjects because she couldn't keep up with the fast-paced, competitive, shame-inducing educational style.

Flunking her 10th-grade finals just about extinguished her academic hopes. But one act of kindness radically changed her trajectory when an inspired acquaintance convinced her to redo the grade.

Her new teacher—who was passionate and caring—taught students instead of subjects. A friend from her church gave her the finest tutoring, much-needed friendship, and even an example of a loving home and family. After completing 10th grade with top marks, she spent her remaining school years working tirelessly, eventually earning the Best All-Round Student award.

Her passion for learning expanded into a passion for teaching; she pursued post-secondary degrees in America and began an influential career as a professor of education and international education consultant.

Hong's eloquent present-tense narration animates scenes of family strife and academic struggle and evokes an astounding range of emotions—commiseration, frustration, and eventually elation. Something is always developing, whether it's the narrator herself or the plot.

Though the memoir charts the author's intellectual growth, it also considers complex family relationships, poverty, Southeast Asian culture and education, disability, and determination. Hong demonstrates, through her own experiences, the pleasures and rewards of scholarship and effective teaching, and her account underscores how ordinary people can have life-changing effects on others.

What is Reading the Globe/Common Read about?

In 2008, Texas A&M International University (TAMIU), a Hispanic Serving Institution situated in South Texas, instituted a common reading program called *Reading the Globe (RTG)*. Because our University has an international focus, the book we select each year is set in a foreign country. Every freshman reads the book, and freshman seminar faculty integrate the book in class by integrating the universality of themes.

Who does TAMIU serve?

Freshmen come to TAMIU primarily from 130 different local and regional high schools. First-time freshmen (97%) identified themselves as Hispanic and first-generation college students (64%). Our students come to us rich with bicultural capital: strong family ties that connect two countries, sincere compassion for others, and pride in their Mexican heritage. Students also come prepared to make the most of their first-year experience as indicated in relatively high first-year persistence rates. However, like students across the nation, they struggle to persist beyond their sophomore year for multifaceted reasons that are beyond their control.

What is the role of this book?

Because our students need strategies, skills, and dispositions to persist and increase their chance of graduating from college, we decided to select a Reading the Globe book that would "anchor" students with the experiences of a narrator who modeled self-determination attributes and a growth mindset. After reading *Failing Up: A Professor's Odyssey of Flunking, Determination, and Hope*, we decided it was perfectly suited to serve as our first "anchor text."

During the transition to a college setting and the years leading to graduation, challenges often lead students to internal struggles as they question their abilities, their rationale for earning a degree, and whether they belong. Students can relate to Barbara as she struggles with repeatedly being told that she is not smart enough, incapable of making something of herself, and unworthy of dreaming of a different life. However, with the support of caring friends and teachers, Barbara begins to break free from the negative narrative that tries to ensnare her. Armed with an unwavering sense of self-determination and a growth mindset, she takes steps gradually toward achieving her educational goals.

Through this "anchor text", we have designed a freshmen curriculum to help our students develop an optimal level of self-awareness, self-regulation, self-advocacy, and self-empowerment through a growth mindset. In carefully studying Barbara's memoir, students will envision a "role model" and discover who they are, why they enrolled in college, and how they are going to achieve their goals. This first-person narrative seeks to enhance each student's resilience and persistence that no matter what life throws at them, they can prevail with a growth mindset, purposeful pursuit, and a strong sense of belonging.

Why are the proceeds going to these students?

100% of the proceeds from the sale of this book will go toward freshmen scholarships and bring students closer to obtaining a college education. You can help further this mission by encouraging your colleagues, friends, families, or neighbors to purchase a copy of this book. For more information about TAMIU or our *Reading the Globe* program, please visit us at www.tamiu.edu.

There is a crack in everything.

That's how the light gets in.

Leonard Cohen

Prologue

I sit in the scuffed and dented steel sink that takes up a quarter of the dingy kitchen in a squalid Singapore apartment. I may be four or five years old. The water is running while my sister Jennifer and I pretend to cook—we wash vegetables, fill pots, and cut pieces of paper from the telephone book as if they're chicken breasts.

Bored, we climb out of the sink and hide under the overstuffed bed in our one-bedroom flat, pretending to play ghosts so we can scare our older brothers, Phillip and Winston when they walk in.

I can hear Jennifer breathing softly beside me. I cover my eyes while peering through my fingers to see if our brothers are coming. Instead, I see a tiny square of our cement-block window. A piece of clothesline cuts across it. It's stuffed with underwear, shirts, sheets, and towels that wave in the humid, hot wind, blocking my only view of the outside sky.

Under the bed are stacks of battered shoe boxes with no shoes inside, plastic bags bulging with textiles of all shapes and sizes, and other hoarded items with no names or owners. Everything has a suffocating, damp, and lingering sweaty smell.

"I can't breathe," I cry to Jennifer, hoping we can switch position even though it doesn't help my coughing. The cobwebs are sweeping into my mouth. My breaths are getting shorter; I need air.

Two feet from my parents' bed is a bunk bed where the cracked gray paint is peeling off, layer by layer, each day. The space beneath it is also packed with more litter, fragments of clothing, and assorted trash. Where does all this junk come from?

Our apartment is so cluttered that I can't tell the difference between the living and sleeping spaces. Most of the items are either broken or antique, at least to me, but Māma (*mother in Chinese*) can't stop piling and shoving bags into every inch of space she can find. When offered a free item, I have never heard her refuse. She always has some rationale for why such and such an item will come in handy one day.

We live carefree at times. No one cares who does what as long as we don't kill each other. The only noise in the house is from Bàba (*father in Chinese*) yelling at Māma and at us. Almost everything that comes out of his mouth is vulgar and offensive.

I learn to tune out the pain by slipping under the moldy-smelling bed and escaping into dark spaces. I find the darkness a haven; like I'm carried away into a fairyland, far from the raging battles of that inhospitable place—at least temporarily. This was my beginning, in a sense, my first memory of fear and emptiness, anguish and loneliness, in search of safety, belonging, and purpose.

There were no books lying around the house. I didn't learn to read until fourth grade. Getting an education was never a priority. If anything, Māma and Bàba believed the opposite. Whenever I got a bad report card, which I frequently did, they would jump down my throat and cane me for wasting my time and their money, saying I'd be better off getting a job and contributing to the family instead.

The loftiest wish Māma ever had for any of us was to be an office clerk so we could enjoy air-conditioning while working. As far as I was concerned, that was my only aspiration too. Doing well in school was simply not on the radar for many of the kids in my neighborhood. There was only one university and only the top percentile ranked students could be admitted.

When I decided to write my story, I reflected on how the craftsmanship of a house defines the strength of its structure and whether it will withstand the winds and storms that come its way. Ideally, a steady foundation should include being raised decently; taught right from wrong, protected from harm, and provided basic physical and psychological needs.

There are some who live a more-or-less predictable life, from my perspective at least, getting from point A to point B somewhat unscathed. I envy such a life so much. I wish I could be a fly on the wall of at least one of those homes.

A cipher in a home where life is always out of sync, where there is always trouble lingering around the corner, I just didn't know, even at that early age, how long I wanted to live. Once I asked Māma if she knew when my birthday was. She brushed away my question, saying, "I don't even know when I was born, let alone you." I didn't know who I was even from birth or where life would take me.

Every day, until it was etched into my skull, were all the reminders from my teachers of who I was. Reminders saturated with the message, "You're a hopeless child!" I went through the motions of school each day, with no idea what I was getting out of it. No one talked to me, hung out with me, ate with me, or even said *hi*.

The repertoire of labels I acquired included: retarded, mute, idiot, half-brained, stupid, lazy, undisciplined, and the winner—*cabbage head*. I believed I was all these labels. After all, I barely made it through each grade.

When I flunked my most important year in 10th grade (the equivalent of US 12th grade), I was angry and disappointed, but it wasn't like I was expecting anything different. I had hoped to be the first in my family to finish high school, but that went out the window with my failure. I wanted to be the one who put a smile on my parents' faces, even if they couldn't care less about school. It is still a part of being raised in an Asian family. No matter what kind of parents I had, there was an inherent sense of loyalty I must reciprocate. I wanted to please them no matter what.

My pride was my greatest enemy. I hated losing more than anything. I had to repeat the grade, and I vowed I was only going to allow myself to be embarrassed for one year and never again fail another grade. That's 365 days, 52 weeks, 8,736 hours. That was all I was willing to handle. I would never go through another humiliation like that, ever again!

I began to turn everyone and everything away from me. I became my own worst nightmare. I still hated school, but I hated myself even more. I hated everyone. I knew how difficult my parents' circumstances were, and I was fiercely determined to escape that plight. My drive became a clever tool for me to be selfish, arrogant, and detached. I figured if no one cared about me, then why should I care about anyone else? I relinquished my moral instinct and only thought of what I wanted. I had to be a survivor.

I avoided my past because I was ashamed. I never wanted to put myself in the narrative. I just wanted to move on and embrace my present and the future. Then one day, an undergraduate with a drinking and drug problem called me out, "You're an Asian! You'll never understand. You had a good life because your parents are wealthy, you're smart, and you went to a big-name school."

What! Why would he think that's my life?

It turned out that he was not the only one with such stereotyped perceptions of Asians. Many of my colleagues and students, too, have this preconceived notion that Asians are born into a prepackaged life, filled with milk and honey and wealth. Somehow, it is thought, everything always turns out the way it is supposed to be primary due to our work ethic or some natural genetic endowment.

I decided that it was time I stopped hiding behind my own shame. I wanted to make sense of my past. There's no shame in being broken. I've been broken over and over again (not by my choice nor by anyone intentionally). Nevertheless, the struggle of the "fixing" process has strengthened me; *not* ruined me. Vance Havner[1] poignantly describes this evolution I experienced:

> *It takes broken soil to produce a crop,*
> *broken clouds to give rain,*
> *broken grain to give bread,*
> *broken bread to give strength.*
> *It is the broken alabaster box that gives forth perfume.*

The events described in this book are taken from my journals, which I have kept since I was twelve. Each account is based on my perspective of things at that point in time—some mature, some naïve, but all are intuitive recollections of events as I experienced them. If I describe moments that seem commonplace, it is because I am living a prescribed line, and for virtually all my life, that line has been defined by poverty, mislabels, abuse, and ridicule. The one thing that remains constant is my teachers—some from heaven while others from hell.

When I ask my students why they chose to become a teacher, their unanimous answer is often: "A teacher touched my life!"

There seems to be at least one teacher in everyone's journey that makes an indelible mark on us, for better or for worse. That teacher somehow shapes the way we view the class subject, what we believe about ourselves, the way we choose our career paths, and the way we view learning.

---

[1] "Broken Things," an excerpt from *The Still Water* (Old Tappan, NJ: Flemming H. Revell, 1934). Quoted in *Guideposts*, October 1981.

Although I have attempted to describe events as they happened, the accounts veer back and forth across time. This is a function of memory and its failings, as well as the missing links that inevitably exist between experiences. The journal entries were from my teenage years, while the story I'm relating began when I was much younger.

I hope *Failing Up* gives readers a first-hand perspective on what life is like growing up in a harsh, unforgiving culture of stigmatization, marginalization, and humiliation when it comes to academic performance. In this memoir, I hope to shine a personal light for educators and parents from all walks of life: A light that will encourage readers to reflect upon the effects their words and actions have on the lives of children and their future. And for everyone who has ever failed or who are failing now in any capacity of your life, I hope you'll shake off the shame and embrace failures as a way of finding who you are and what you are *really* made of. Perhaps in time, you will discover, like me, that failing can be some of life's most meaningful blessings you'll ever experience.

Part One

SPIRIT LEVEL

Chapter 1
FLATS

Home is one's birthplace, ratified by memory.
☙ Henry Anatole Grunwald

"Wake up! Wake up NOW!"

"What, Mā? I was asleep," I pry open my eyelids in protest, "it's two in the morning."

"Get up!" Māma jerks Jennifer and Phillip from side to side.

I drag my sleepy feet into the kitchen and pretend to open my heavy eyes while Winston walks in the front door after his late shift at McDonald's.

"Your Bà didn't come home again," Māma laments. "He has gone off with another woman. I can't take this anymore! A leopard never changes its spots. I have had enough!"

I try to make sense of what Māma is getting at as she summons all of us to gather by the toilet door.

Crammed between my siblings, I can barely see what Māma is doing. When I finally squeeze through from underneath, I see a round tray with five cups of cloudy white liquid filled to the brim. Māma passes a cup to each of us. Mine is so full I spill some, but she doesn't yell at me.

"Drink it up, starting from the oldest. Right now!"

I inhale to see what the cups contain. Bleach. The smell of chlorine is so strong; now I'm awake.

"Yuck, I don't want to drink this," I push it away, but Māma gives that look.

"When your Bàba sees us all lying dead on the floor, he'll be sorry! Drink it up!"

Jennifer, who's a year older than me, releases a screeching cry in rebellion, as Winston, the eldest, shepherds us into the living room, ignoring Māma's hysterical bawling. I clumsily spill more liquid on the floor.

"Never mind, don't worry about it now," Winston says. "Just leave. Quick, hurry."

On the pale blue wall, covered with chipping paint, is a picture of Jesus. Māma hung it there to remind us that Jesus is watching over us, but I'm not sure she believes it herself. While Māma tries to cling to faith, her belief wavers whenever Bàba doesn't come home.

Unruffled, Winston grabs hold of Māma's arms and gestures at her to kneel with us.

"Mā, come. Let's pray. Bà will come home soon. Jesus is watching over him, right? You taught us that." Winston soothes Māma gently like a child until she falls asleep upon the floor.

"Now I'm awake," I yawn and take a deep breath, then catch myself pinching my nose again.

Winston looks at me and points at the floor. "Clean up that spill and pour the bleach back in the bottle."

Jennifer sits in a corner on the floor with her arms wrapped around her legs, nodding herself to sleep. Phillip crawls back into the bunk bed as if this night is as normal as any other. Just another drill.

Whenever Māma gets this way, Winston, five years my senior, is the one who calms everyone and everything down. I have looked up to him as our protector for as long as I can remember.

Three or four nights later, Māma wakes us up again in the middle of the night. This time she has a pair of large black scissors, the extra-sharp kind that seamstresses use to cut fabric. She directs us to stab ourselves.

"If you stab in the heart," she says, "it'll be a quicker death."

Winston snatches the scissors by the blade, slicing two inches across his palm.

"I'll cut myself for the younger ones," he intercedes. "Don't do this to them, Mā, please don't."

Winston mediates on our behalf, and we're once again spared a mass suicide.

None of this is out of the norm. Māma often awakens us in the middle of the night, between two and four, if Bàba does not come home.

Two nights later, it happens again. This time Māma turns on the gas stove. I didn't even get out of bed. Fortunately, Phillip's sleep is disturbed by the pungent smell. He wakes up and finds Māma kneeling on the kitchen floor, distraught and sobbing.

Although I am only six, I understand that my family is unlike the others in the neighborhood. We are to bury everything within the four walls of our apartment; never to air our dirty laundry in public.

I never have a neighbor kid come over to the apartment because I don't want anyone to find out who I am and what my family is like.

෧෧෧

In 1965, five years before I was born, Singapore achieved independence from Malaysia and was struggling to become self-sufficient. Due to land constraints, the government built flats to conserve space and to warehouse the increasing low-income population.

These heavily subsidized government flats still exist today, though they have been remodeled to look more urbanized and architecturally aesthetic. These days, even upper middle-class people reside in these flats because of their convenience, community-like living, proximity to public transportation, and schools. Each community even has its own playground, parking garage, and void deck to hold events.

The Toa Payoh area, where I grew up, was one of the first waves of newer flats completed by the Housing Development Board. To accommodate the masses, a brutalist architecture was chosen. The common height of ten storeys, with twelve units per floor, defines a block. These are simple rectangular slabs with flat roofs, straight walls, and all painted white—a landscape of the modern-day ghetto. A horizontal strip of concrete balconies marks the front of the flat while the back is smeared with bamboo flagpoles of wet laundry—trousers, bras, shirts, and bed sheets—a testament to the life teeming inside.

Sometimes, when the wind is strong, pieces of neighbors' clothes fall from the bamboo sticks because they're not properly secured with clothespins. Jennifer and I sheepishly swoop the stray laundry up from the ground, often soiled and still damp, and rush home to show it off to Māma, as if they're gifts from heaven.

I know we're stealing, but there is no way to return these clothes. We can't tell, from the hundreds of bamboo sticks, to which household they belong.

From the side, the buildings are narrow, a line of identical structures that stand in desolate rows. I suppose in the US these neighborhoods are called projects, like those in New York City or South Chicago. Picture a plantation with rows of domino-like flats, narrow strips of concrete buildings lined with the occasional bit of greenery. The flooring in each apartment is a slab of gray cement. Ours is covered with two layers of linoleum—the bottom one looks dull, brown, and rotted by termites, while the top has a pink-and-blue floral design.

Our block gets hot water only when we're lucky. Most days the fluorescent lights in the stairwells work, but if they start flickering, it is only a matter of seconds before we hear a bulb burst, leaving the entire floor and stairway pitch dark. When this happens, an air of melancholy surrounds me, further deepening the emptiness and forlornness within me.

In some ways, the intrinsic emptiness of the flats covers up the chaotic lives of the people who live within—prostitutes, lounge singers, waiters, street sweepers, janitors, seamstresses, and construction workers—people who can't afford to live anywhere else.

While the adults in the apartment buildings bear no ill-will toward their children, although some do when they're drunk, they also hold no big dreams for their children. Each family aspires for nothing more than simply making it through another day.

The staircase leading to our fourth-floor apartment is littered with garbage, broken beer bottles, decomposing insects, and occasional human feces. On the off chance the elevator works, it reeks of urine and dead animals.

There's little in the way of sanitation, even less in the way of orderliness. We never eat as a family except on the Eve of Chinese New Year. Families make a point to gather for this special one-night festival. It's my favorite time of year, not so much for the dishes Māma worked all day to prepare, but for the nostalgic aura of being together like a normal family.

After the meal, we each get a red packet from Bàba with some cash inside, usually two dollars for the girls and ten dollars for the boys. This is like candy money; we can get anything we want from the stalls across our block.

Our two-room apartment is on the corner, so we have access to a small balcony area about two by three feet. The living room and the bedroom combined are 34 square meters or 366 square feet. A doorway leads from the living room to a bedroom on the right. The toilet is at the corner of an L-shaped kitchen. A large vertical sheet of heavy aluminum serves as its door. Māma must have scrounged it from the dumpster which is next to our flat. The problem is this door was unskillfully placed backward, so it stays ajar by more than a foot, allowing anyone to peer right in while you're doing your private business.

The kitchen has enough space for a single-burner gas stove, a two-foot-round, white marble table Māma inherited from her mother (the only thing she inherited from her) and two rusty metal stools. Squeezed in beside the table is a corroded three-and-a-half-foot refrigerator, another one of Māma's treasures from the dumpster. She mounted it on four unsteady cinder blocks to raise its height. This fridge has been clumsily painted over from a natural beige to cloudy white to a greenish blue and, now, an azure blue.

The only bedroom is half the size of the living room with a foot of space between the closet and the foot of the bed. We maneuver gingerly around the space to avoid stubbing our toes.

Mā's and Bà's pale sheets are worn thin with holes and unmatched patches beneath, but they feel soft. Māma reminds us the sheets were once embroidered with bright floral designs.

"Ah, expensive threads," Māma, a seasoned seamstress, rubs the silky fabric between her two fingers, "A wedding gift from so long ago."

If I squint, I can make out the faintest lines of orchid petals. They are worn to the quick from years of washing, sweating, and bodies turning, friction of both happy and sad times.

Māma caresses my back as I curl up next to her. I feel her coarse fingers stroking me gently even as she drifts off to sleep, like the way I caress Bàba's back when he's drunk. Her delicate but overworked hands prominently display a crisscrossing of thin blue veins that have surrendered to the years of heavy lifting, washing, carrying, and scrubbing. I've never seen Bàba put a plate into the sink, pick up a piece of trash from the floor, or even turn on the stove to boil water.

Soon, Māma's breathing slows down, and her hand falls off my side rib, but I'm still awake. I can hear the blaring snore, not from Māma but from Bàba. If he's really drunk, his snore is non-rhythmic, like a growling beast, oblivious to the world. However, if he's not too drunk, he sounds symphonic and gentle, like an infant falling asleep after a full meal, at least until tomorrow.

I like Bàba best when his eyes are closed. I look right into his tired ruffled face with its long eyelashes, thick nose, and exposed rotting teeth with his lips puffed and drooling. He smells like an open bottle of beer.

Why was I given this Bàba of all the bàbas in the world? Why was I born to this one? Do I look like him? Do I want to look like him? What if I became like him?

On most nights, I share a two- or three-inch, twin-size foam mattress with Winston. There are no sheets, and we rarely use blankets because of the tropical heat, and monsoon-rich humidity that is especially intense when night falls. Winston and I bruise ourselves constantly, butting knees or heads, as we fight in our sleep to get some cushion underneath our bodies.

"It's like sleeping with a twelve-legged octopus," Winston teases and hugs me.

I don't have a bed I can call my own, a personal space, or a pillow on which I can lay my head whenever I want. Each night, after some squabbles, Māma assigns someone to let me lie down with them. I don't know why no one wants to sleep with me. Maybe everyone feels grown up now. Maybe because Māma keeps calling me the *unwanted* child—I never asked her why. Maybe being the youngest I just have to earn my sleeping space.

Phillip has the top bunk bed while Jennifer has the bottom. Since Winston often works until midnight, he gets a mattress like me so, he won't wake anyone up. When I wake from what sleep I can manage, I put my mattress back in the bedroom, leaning it vertically against the wall. That's the only way we have enough room to move bodies around that sordidly hot enclosure.

The best times are when I get to sleep with Jennifer. She never likes to share, but she gives in and lets me lie next to her as long as I am quiet. This is better than sleeping next to Winston, though perhaps not as good as curling up next to Māma. If Jennifer is in a pleasant mood, she holds my hand and asks me to hum along as she whispers some Chinese songs into my ears. This is our quiet way of fun, so we don't wake up the sleeping dragon. We try to control our giggles, almost choking ourselves. We fall asleep, smiling, and grasping hands.

Jennifer is bold and speaks her mind. She's never too timid to fight for what's hers, even a bed. I wish I could be more like her. I'm always afraid of something or someone. I feel insecure, cowardly, and gutless. I dare not challenge anyone or anything. I give in all the time. At no time do I talk back, raise my voice, or defy authority. Māma says that's because I'm an obedient daughter. I don't ask for something that's contrary to what Māma or anyone says. Māma calls me the peacemaker, a good girl every mother wants. That's the ideal I live up to every time; I feel conflicted.

I wish I weren't this way.

I don't like me.

Being good willingly is one thing; being coerced into being good is quite another. I don't know who I am or what my personality is like. Why do I have to be the one who gives in all the time? I want to oppose. I want to say something. I want to win sometimes too. I don't want to be the one who gives in all the time.

As I continue to do poorly in school, I become angrier at myself. I'm done with being the peacemaker. It never pays off. Being bad at least gives me an avenue to get angry. I don't want to listen to anyone anymore, especially my stupid teachers.

When I'm not in school, the time I wake up depends on where I sleep the night before. If I sleep next to Māma, I wake up when she does, either because she's tugging on my hand to snip threads or I don't want to be alone in bed with Bàba. If I sleep next to Winston on the living room floor, I wake up to someone accidentally stepping on my hair, arms, or legs. If I sleep next to Jennifer in the lower bunk, I usually wake on my own by rolling over into the empty spot where she was. It's hard to sleep alone when I never have a bed.

On very hot nights, when even the walls sweat, Māma opens the front gate to let in some air while Jennifer and I take turns keeping the rats away from our bed. We swat them with the bamboo cane or broomsticks, but they're never afraid of us. Why should they be? Our place is almost a second home for them with all its clutter, stench, and mess clogged around every corner of the house. They have more of a permanent abode each night than I do, as if I'm the intruder and they're the hosts. Sometimes, when Jennifer curses at them, I silently thank these vermin for tolerating us in their dwelling.

Like many rural parts of Singapore, Toa Payoh has an infestation of stray cats that has spread like wildfire.

These felines never stop reproducing, and they never die. There are simply not enough vehicles to run them over either. I suspect there's a community conspiracy between these rats and the cats. Maybe the cats never prey on the rats, and the rats never get caught; instead, both wild animals have joined forces to feast off of the human provisions and to take over our dwellings come midnight.

I know cats all too well. The problem with stray cats in our block is notably excessive because of the large Malay population on the second floor. They have this esoteric fondness for felines, particularly the black, Siamese kind with the long fur coat. I don't even know if these are Siamese, but that's what Māma calls them. Each night, legions of them convene on our fourth-floor balcony, growling, trilling, yowling, and chattering, having a great night out. My hawk-eyed observation tells me they're conniving about which apartment to invade once the clock strikes midnight, and for some reason, it's always ours.

Our front door has a rusty blue gate covered in multiple layers of paint, the kind you see on an old elevator in Manhattan. The problem with our gate is that it's too crooked to close all the way, so the only thing we can do is leave it ajar, like our toilet door. When we do that, we're inviting anything lurking in the stairway to stroll right through our gate, and these Siamese cats almost always shoot straight for the toilet.

Lying half-asleep, I hear sounds from all around. As soon as we're still, the first Siamese makes its way through the gate. In a second, the rest of the gang slinks through the rickety aluminum windows and rusty gate like it's party time. If Winston or Jennifer is lying next to me, I cling to them and hold my breath for as long as I can. I shut my eyes and pretend to sleep, thinking maybe these felines have a sixth sense and they'll go about their business and leave me alone. I cover my ears, so I won't hear their blood-curdling growls, battling over whatever is in the kitchen.

Make them go away! I pray with my eyes shut so tight that they hurt. *Make* them go! *Please God … please!*

I hear more wailing as one Siamese wolfs down something odious. I never call out for Māma, not even when a large, black Siamese that's missing an ear rakes me with its claws. When I awaken, the sheet is streaked with bloody stain.

"It wasn't me," I try explaining, but Māma is angry because now she has more to wash just to get rid of the bloody stain.

I never got over the hisses and yowls of cats. The way they whine and cry like a baby drives fear through my spine. My stomach churns. My heart pounds. Call me paranoid or an ailurophobe. I can appreciate a cat's grace and agile poise, but I prefer to stay away from them. We can never coexist. We should never get in each other's way.

Ironically, I deeply admire lions. My fixation came about when I accompanied Bàba to the coffee shop each morning for his dose of Guinness Stout. I slouched over the sticky uneven table to study the oval logo on the bottle, marveling at the untamed fringe of the long mane, swaying to the wind as he charges toward what he wants. He never hesitates or stalks. He never creeps or hides. His prey has no escape now, leaving merely a faint heartbeat to pure surrender. If only I could be as gallant and valiant as the king of the jungle. His audacious confidence to conquer are formidable. He will achieve his goal.

అ✑ఒ

One Sunday morning, Māma finds out there's a seamstress in the neighborhood who needs help to watch her four-year-old daughter so she can go to work. Māma agrees to care for the child, thinking this is the answer to her prayer for some extra income.

The only nice thing about having a younger child in the house is that she has to regard me as her older sister, which puts me on a higher status now that I'm no longer the youngest. This is my first encounter with another child in my household. I'm not sure how Māma is going to treat her and me, but I finally have someone to play with.

Ah Cheng is a novelty. Everyone is excited to give her our attention. We want to hold her, cuddle her, and dote on her, but within a few months, Māma's agitation with Ah Cheng becomes apparent.

Māma is supposed to get twenty dollars each month for babysitting, but her mother never pays. The debts start to pile up. One month, then two, and then three. Māma may not be literate, but she manages to scribble some sloppy accounting on a small pink notebook for all of the back payments.

Over the next few months, the debts keep mounting, but Ah Cheng continues to be dropped off regardless. Sometimes, her mother doesn't even pick her up and she has to sleep over. Other times, we have to keep her over the weekend and even during public holidays. Soon, it becomes apparent that we are her foster family. Ah Cheng is never going to go home.

Māma is not pleased with this presumptive arrangement. Ah Cheng's mother is obviously taking advantage of us. Not only is there no additional income, but we now have another mouth to feed.

"I should have said no!" Māma regrets while lashing out at Ah Cheng. "Your mother is so manipulative and deceitful. Says she needs to work, but never pays me a single cent!"

I can't tell if Ah Cheng is embarrassed or guilty about this whole situation. She is only four or five years old. I squat in the corner of the living room, watching Māma badgering and slapping her, but I dare not do anything. I don't know if I should be on Māma's side or Ah Cheng's side. Even though Ah Cheng never utters a word in retaliation, I know she feels responsible for her mother's debts. Maybe it's her way of letting Māma release her injustice.

"If you want to blame someone, then blame your own mother. She's the one who gave birth to you and then couldn't afford to raise you!"

With great tremor, Ah Cheng bows her head as low as her neck would go, sniffing and biting her lips while her tears bleed down her pinkish cheeks.

"Wipe up those tears," Māma yells. "Don't think for once I'm going to pity you. And mop up my floor."

I walk nimbly past the commotion and step outside onto the balcony, staring at the brown patch of dead grass, something I often do to tune myself out. I resent being such a coward. Why can't I stand up for something for once? But what would that be? If I choose justice, then who is going to protect Ah Cheng? If I choose mercy, then who is going to feed our family? Still a child myself, I am confused and torn.

Six years have passed, nothing much has changed except Ah Cheng has another sister. Once again, her mother begs Māma to take care of her newborn and promises to pay up this time. Māma reluctantly agrees, giving in to her inability to say *No*.

This new baby seems to be different. She has thick, black, long eyelashes; a feature Chinese parents find exceptionally delicate. My whole family grows so fond of her like she was part of us. I even named her Sharlynn. For me, Sharlynn is like a new doll, and she feels cuddly, unlike her sister.

Something is different. The baby has a black, circular half-millimeter birthmark on the right side of her forehead. It is a Chinese belief that if a birthmark is hidden, in this case under her hair, then it's an auspicious sign.

Māma has a skin-colored mole on the right side of her upper lip, but since it is not hidden, she resigns to her fate that life is never going to be blissful. She expects herself to be in a state of constant misfortune by almost seeking after it, like the Zen proverb, *"Man stands in his own shadow and wonders why it's dark."*

Even now, Māma refuses to allow herself a millisecond of enjoyment, whether it's dining out, buying a new outfit, getting a perm, or putting on makeup. She feels as if giving in to comfort and indulging in a little luxury will negate everything she has gone through and diminish her claim to have lived a hard life. She likes to remind us that no one will ever empathize with her hardship and suffering.

Day and night, I see Māma washing piles of cloth diapers and baby clothes, but still not getting paid. With the water bill increasing and stability diminishing, I grow angrier and angrier with this injustice.

Additional children in the home are hard on younger children by nature. Not only does Māma feed these girls, but she also has to clean them, do their laundry, and pay attention to their emotional needs.

Ah Cheng grows jealous of the attention Sharlynn is getting, and so do I. I want to be noticed too. I feel as if I'm doubly invisible now with these two girls in our family. Will I ever be Māma's baby again?

"I only nursed you once," Māma recalls as she caresses my back. "I was always busy doing this or that, sewing, cooking, cleaning. No help. You had the least nourishment of all the children. You were always by yourself. Very good girl. Hardly cried, except the time when you got burned."

Māma holds up my right hand to examine the scar, now wrinkly and less noticeable.

When I was about two, I crawled around the living room to track wherever Māma went. One time, after ironing, Māma had turned off the switch but left the vertical-standing iron to cool. She proceeded to make dinner, forgetting that I would be tracing behind her. When I tugged on the cloth on the floor, the iron fell flat on my right hand.

The iron was heavy; I couldn't withdraw my hand from underneath, so I let it sit there and mumbled, not even crying. I'm not sure why, but perhaps the intense heat had killed the nerves.

Minutes passed, Māma was still cooking. I don't know how long my hand was pinned underneath the hot surface. When she finally turned around, it was too late.

She instinctively lifted the iron, but my stubborn infant skin would not unglue from the scorching surface. Māma impatiently waited for the iron to cool, staring in shock while meticulously peeling off the slimy flesh, like the thin layer of skin underneath a hard-boiled egg, willingly forgoing a few layers of the skin.

"You didn't cry loud enough; that's why I didn't hear you," Māma admits with a deflated sigh. "You just wailed and croaked, 'nnn … nnn … nnn' so no one paid attention. You didn't even have the strength to moan."

Mā beats herself up every time we talk about the mishap even though I don't recall an ounce of pain.

She presses me closer to her chest. "That was the first time I nursed you. The only time you ever had Māma's milk."

Each time I see the scar on my hand, I think only about Māma holding me close to her bosom, brushing my long black hair, kissing my forehead and right hand, to comfort me.

Māma is the sole breadwinner since Bàba drifts from job to job. The babysitting is not only depriving us of the additional income but has become a burden. No matter how Māma calculates it, we still end up being the doormat.

The mere sight of Ah Cheng agitates Māma so much that she does not allow us to play with her. Ah Cheng gets all the heat in the house because she's the older sister and the start of a bad chain of debts. The babysitting arrangement changed Māma from being a benevolent soul to an unfeeling neighbor. The worst part is I mimic Māma's tone and mannerisms toward the girls.

Both Ah Cheng and Sharlynn are only a few years apart. We eat the same food, sleep under the same roof, and get our fair share of beating and scolding from Māma, yet, my contempt and hatred become more apparent each day. I don't know why. I take a quiet pleasure in tormenting Ah Cheng by ignoring her and shaming her so I can upset her day. I want someone to pay for my anger, for the money owed us, the suffering that my family has to go through because of her penniless, manipulative, and selfish mother.

My experiences with these girls are the beginning of my search for vindication. There's no such thing as kindness in the real world. It doesn't pay to pay it forward. It's like poker. I can bluff my way into winning. I can win by learning to be a liar and exonerate myself by begging for sympathy and forgiveness afterward. God doesn't care one bit since he allows us to be the victims. I can do whatever the hell I want. I get to play mercy or justice at my own discretion. I take things into my own hands and determine I will never again fall prey to manipulations.

I am cynical about everyone and everything. I see only the faults in others. I don't trust any gestures of humanity, kindness, or generosity. I reject affection. I become my own gatekeeper and guard against anyone who tries to pry into my emotions to get me to feel something.

Māma's anger at not getting paid inescapably bleeds deeper into me. My instinctive reaction to any mis-handling is to preserve my own self-interest, even at the expense of others. I resent anyone who is wealthy or has it easy for them when it comes to making a living.

My survival mode kicks in, and I'm at war with everyone, even myself. Everyone is a suspect. Everyone is an enemy. If there are going to be winners and losers, then I must win. I gear up for a strong defense because I swear I'm not going to end up like Māma at the losing end.

I've no idea what fuels this indignation, but I take pleasure in seeing others get their share of bad luck. If people, even so-called friends, can treat my family this way, then why shouldn't I do the same? I don't want to be a bully, but I also don't want to be bullied. Every petty injustice provokes me. I just want to vindicate. I harbor such a perverse consciousness of misbehavior that I become a fugitive entrapped by my own snare.

I hate myself.

Chapter 2
MĀMA TERESA

Sometimes the things we can't change end up changing us instead.

∾ Moi

Māma was named after Mother Teresa. A doctor at a local hospital gave her the English name when she was young and was helping out there. She likes having a Christian name because it makes her sound more educated. Her given name is Joo Hiang, but everyone calls her Ah Hiang. We have nicknames, proper names, formal names, names we keep secret for good luck, and a name for official use only, like our middle name. I don't know why I'm called *Ah Hong* after my family's last name. I know Māma calls me that because she can't pronounce *Barbara*.

The Chinese regard names as a powerful foreshadowing of one's destiny—success, prosperity, health, and intelligence. In many respects, a child's name says more about the parents' hopes and dreams for the child than it does about the child. Children try to live up to what their names connote.

Winston and Phillip's Chinese middle names are about heralding an abundance of wealth. Since males are the sole breadwinners, their names are a foreshadowing of future prosperity in providing for their family. Jennifer and I were given middle names that denote gems to signify both physical beauty and riches. My name "Siew Swan" means *beautiful diamond* while Jennifer's name "Siew Kim" means *beautiful gold*. Māma had little to do with naming us since she is not literate and can't pen a single stroke.

For my English name, Bàba selected the blue-eyed, powerhouse vocalist Barbra Streisand, with a slightly different spelling. Either he was drunk at the time or it was a harbinger of how my life will be. While I don't know another soul named Barbara in Singapore, I wonder why Bàba chose a name that means foreigner or traveler from a strange land.

Bàba enjoys watching American movies and picked out our Christian names randomly from Hollywood characters, like Jennifer and Phillip. Winston, on the other hand, was named after the cigarette brand. (I can't imagine it was for Winston Churchill!)

Māma never learned to write her name, not in English at least, but with some effort, she could partially sketch her Chinese name. She also figured out some basic addition and subtraction on her own when she needed to account for the babysitting debts. For the most part, holding a pen or pencil is still beyond her. For years, Māma struggled to teach herself to write, and only in her late forties did she manage to memorize enough strokes to read some scriptural verses and pen a few Chinese characters.

Māma was born on the mountainside; that's what the section of Singapore was called, even though there aren't any real mountains in Singapore, just small hills. Her mother had a friend who lived on the other side of town called the countryside, and they visited frequently. This friend was married, but she couldn't bear any children, and she adored Māma so much.

"Why not let Ah Hiang stay here and be my daughter?" she wondered.

Māma was four, and of course, exhilarated and flattered that a stranger would want her as her daughter. She didn't mind calling her Māma too.

Māma's father had a decent job in the government housing office and could support all nine children. It seems mysterious and laughable that such a whimsical arrangement was even considered.

Māma was given away for no apparent reason. There was no payment, no receipt, and no legal documentation. A one-time casual conversation on a Sunday afternoon and, poof, Māma belonged to another family. The anecdote doesn't make any sense at all. I never felt like Māma told me the whole story.

Didn't she realize that the Sunday she was dropped off with a plastic bag of her clothes and personal items that she wasn't going to come back home?

Didn't she realize that it was not a sleepover or a weekend visit? I assume her mother said some tearful farewells to her, but maybe not.

Didn't Māma feel abandoned? Maybe she wished she had been born to her new family anyway. Don't we all wish that once in a while? I do.

I wonder what my life would be like if I had another family. Would Māma have given me away?

Over the next few days and weeks, Māma became homesick and begged to go home, but this lady said she was too busy to take her. Soon, days became weeks, and weeks turned into months and years.

A year after Māma was "dropped off," the woman got pregnant and was blessed with her own child. Over the next few years, three more arrived. Māma's hands were full each minute; mopping, washing, cooking, and changing diapers—the cloth kind. She only had experienced two days of formal schooling in her life and was kept at home. Māma wished she could learn and swears she would have been the most diligent student. I believe her just by watching how hard she tries to read the Bible. She sits in her bed for hours, even as she's aching with osteoporosis, poor eyesight, and other aging issues, just to decipher a few characters. She never stops teaching herself.

I'm ashamed that I never took the time to teach Māma how to write a word, not even a single alphabet or Chinese character. I admit I'm not good at Chinese, in fact, I hate Chinese, but she's my Māma, and I should have done more.

Whenever Māma shares her childhood stories, I have this sneaking suspicion that she was treated more like a child slave than an adopted daughter. The way she tells it, her new life was all about drudgery. She took care of all the younger ones since her new mother was the family's breadwinner. The husband, an opium addict, couldn't sustain a job. Māma ended up taking on the heaviest load and the most onerous tasks around the house.

I have never seen a photograph of Māma as a young girl. I don't know how she looked when she was little, how she dressed, what kind of activities she did, or who her friends were. I imagine that at age five or six, all she ever did was bounce a baby (or maybe two) on her hip to keep one calm and feed the other one. I could see her cooking or washing dishes while rocking an infant next to her. I could see her squatting on the floor mopping or cleaning up milk spills, never a dull moment to savor her own childhood.

When her father learned she had been given away, he was terribly distraught. Still, I don't know why he didn't just jump on a bus and bring her home. After all, the agreement was not legally binding, and the distance was less than an hour away. They knew she missed home and her brothers and sisters. They knew she was sad and being abused. They knew she was not attending school. Still, not one word about bringing her home. Perhaps the tradition is that once something, or someone, is given away, it's gone forever, lost and forgotten, so people should just move on and not talk about it anymore.

Maybe Māma didn't expect her new life to be any different from how she had lived previously, but each time she talks about her adoptive family, her eyes are devoid of life, and tears begin to well up. I'm not sure whom she resents more; her adopted family for the abuse or her biological mother for giving her away.

Māma must feel so hurt for being regarded as the lesser child among her eight siblings; the sister that no one missed, the daughter who could be given up, the child who was expendable. How could a mother give up her own flesh and blood after carrying the child in her womb for nine months and then nurturing her for years, watching her grow and crawl, walk and fall, laugh and cry? And why didn't her father, who opposed vehemently, rescue her?

Whenever I push Māma with these questions, she sighs, "Some things are better left unsaid; questions better left unanswered, and memories better left untouched. The truth is not always pretty. Why dig out what you can't change?"

ॐॐ

I grew up visiting two grandmas from Māma's side of the family. We called them both *Ah Mah*. Every elderly person is an *Ah Mah* (grandma) or *Ah Gong* (grandpa). Everyone else is an aunty or uncle. That's how we show respect, even if we're not related by blood. There is much unresolved distance in our extended family. I don't remember ever being close to any one of them.

My adoptive grandmother is a petite but strong person. She only wears the traditional Chinese one-size-fits-all blank satin pants and cotton blouse that overlaps across her chest. We refer to her as *Country Mah* because she lives in the rural part of Singapore. She is a tireless woman with her right eyelid constantly drooping limply from her weary brow, always hurrying about as if she's behind in her chores. Her energy is contagious, and everyone who speaks to her dares not defy her. Her husband died in his fifties from an opium overdose, so she had to raise all the children by herself. I've never met him, but I often saw his picture on the living room wall next to the Buddha altar.

Country Mah runs a canteen stall with one of her daughters and son-in-law, so she always has something cooking in the kitchen—an open cement floor overflowing with utensils, containers, and baskets of every kind. The kitchen area spills into the back alley, where the toilet and shower are located. The toilet door resembles a medieval dungeon door with the wide, heavy wooden block and one-inch thick iron hinges and sliding bar locks. Only a sledgehammer could knock down that thing. Because the toilets are linked to the back alley, rats and cats often stroll in and out throughout the day, sniffing for food from the kitchen.

One time, Country Mah asked me to hand her some noodles she had just fried. As I reached for the bowl, a mammoth sized, rat jumped right off the shelves and onto my face. The bowl went flying into the air, as did the pots and pans on the stovetop. Grandma grabbed a heavy bristle brush from behind the refrigerator and chased that irksome beast into the toilet. She gave it a big flush, and it torpedoed down the hole. I'm not sure it drowned because the next morning, while I was in the toilet, an identical beast jumped right out of the hole and scurried into the back alley.

I S-C-R-E-A-M-E-D and pandemonium ensued!

After that incident, I dared not use her toilet again. All I could think of was that loathsome rodent leaping out of a pit and wildly biting at me.

If Bàba beats up Māma then we have to spend the night at Country Mah's place. When this happens, I can never fall asleep until the wee hours of the morning because I'm afraid I'll be brutally attacked by rodents. When I finally do fall asleep, I have violent nightmares about the disgusting creatures.

Country Mah is still alive and strong today at age 104 and can give chase to those shameless intruders whenever they invade her kitchen.

Māma got married at twenty-four and left the countryside to move to the Toa Payoh housing flats. Now she's able to visit her biological mother and does so faithfully each week. We call her *Mountain Mah*, because she lives on the mountainside in a shack. I like visiting her because the mountainside is greener and cooler than our overheated flat.

Mountain Mah was once a slender, beautiful lady— tall and shapely with long, elegant fingers; small, slanted eye; and a tight waist, like Māma. Now she has no teeth so when she speaks, her lips smack jerkily and she spits involuntarily.

Unlike western grandmas who dote on their grandchildren, Asian grandmas are the opposite. The minute a grandchild is born, the grandma takes over how the child is being raised. They are harshly stern, nitpicky, and tolerate no nonsense. There's no pampering allowed. They consider themselves to be the disciplinarians in the family since they're the most experienced adult in raising children. Chinese grandchildren try to avoid grandmas as much as possible, at least I do.

"Ah Hong! Ah Hong!" Mountain Mah smacks her lips as she yells into the air, "Get over here now. I'm talking to you. You're grown now. You don't visit anymore. No respect. If I die, you won't even know who I am."

Mountain Mah always talks like that, as do old people in general, about dying and about being forgotten by their descendants. She is disgruntled about how grandchildren forget their roots and neglect their elders. We have mastered the art of drowning out her grumblings.

"Yes, Ah Mah." That'll hold her tongue for a few hours before she starts smacking her lips again to chasten us.

All Mountain Mah does is foretell of her death and make it sound like we have already abandoned her. Māma seizes the opportunity and reiterates, "When I get old, I'd be so lucky if one of you should faithfully visit me like I do my māma."

Then both Mountain Mah and Māma would weep and compare about how pathetic their lives are, marrying the wrong man and being forsaken by their children.

སྐྱ

My favorite time is staying overnight at Mountain Mah's shack. It doesn't happen too often. Phillip and I love to see who can spot a monkey in the nearby rainforest or chase after wild rabbits.

Our favorite activity is climbing the huge rambutan tree. This is a small, reddish tropical fruit with hairy skin and a translucent egg-like flesh that's sweet. The only troublesome part is I can never figure out how to chew the fresh part without biting into the husk of the pit. Jennifer, on the other hand, is a pro. She has a way of figuring out any challenge related to food.

Mountain Mah's farm also has an evergreen mangosteen tree. This is my favorite because they're easy to peel, but I must be careful never to let the reddish-purple skin stain my clothes, or it'll never come off. The edible endocarp is shaped like an almond and the flesh inside is tangy and juicy. Of course, Jennifer and I have a stomachache due to overeating.

The scariest part of the shack is bath time. The bathroom is a five by three feet brick wall. There's no window, only a small opening for some outside light to enter. In one corner is a two-foot-tall clay pot filled with cold water. Usually, my uncle, who stays with Mountain Mah, goes to the well to draw buckets of water early in the morning, and this pot is to last throughout the day for everyone to use.

"Conserve water. Don't use too much," Mountain Mah reminds us. "There are others who need to bathe, too. Only wash where you need it most."

It is too creepy to shower. I don't trust the water or the door. We use the same pot for brushing our teeth too.

Toward the evening, my sister and I skip to a tiny candy stand where we have to duck our heads to enter. To buy some, the boys get fifty cents while the girls get twenty cents from an aunty or uncle who's visiting. Oh, if only I were a boy.

Everyone fusses over grandsons as if they're rare gems given to only the luckiest parents. Granddaughters, on the other hand, are temporary goods stored away until we're married off for a reasonable endowment.

Among other things, Mountain Mah's shack lacks a septic system. Typically, about eight to ten families within the block are assigned to two communal toilets, two-by-three feet each. These concrete cesspools are built in the public sidewalks so families can access them. Each unit has a visible hole underground with an oval-shaped bucket that collects the waste. Twice a day, the disposal men clear the buckets in a truck and then place the same buckets back in the hole. If I'm lucky enough to catch an empty bucket, I don't have to withstand the foul smell of a full tank. However, if I need to go at the last wave of the bucket, then I not only have to shoo away multitudes of giant flies attacking me while doing my business, but I also have to pray my addition doesn't overflow the bucket. I don't know why that should matter because I'm not the one picking up that bucket, but somehow the thought of not making it into the bucket is nauseating. Other than that, Mountain Mah's place is like a vacation to me, the only kind I know.

Even in the mountainside, Māma's unhappiness is like the bad air that won't settle. She hates and loves her two mothers at the same time. She struggles to find her identity but often returns to the childhood she claims was stolen from her. I see the uncertainty in Māma's eyes. She's still afraid of being abandoned. No one in her family ever talks about her other life. Everyone treats it like nothing had happened and Māma just went away for a long summer break. No one asks about her childhood, school or servitude. There's no apology, no inquisition, no talking about it at all.

Before we leave, Māma slips ten or twenty dollars into Mountain Mah's hand. I am disgusted because we can't even afford food and here's Māma giving up our food money to a mother who has disowned her. She can't help trying to buy her way back to her mother's heart.

"Why, Mā? Why do you need to give her money, and so much? She didn't even raise you."

"You wouldn't understand," Māma reckons. "No matter how old you are, your Māma is your Māma."

She's right. I'll never understand how or why Māma agonizes to make sense of all this. I suspect now, as I have grown older and come into myself, that Māma is entangled with emotions about her own children's successes. She's thrilled, jealous, resentful, and proud of me, all at the same time. She smiles at my ability to beat the odds but also begrudges me for defining a future for myself.

"Mā, aren't you proud of me?" I beg to know.

Māma doesn't respond; instead, she hunches her shoulders and turns away.

"You are just lucky. You don't know how hard I had it. You are given everything on a silver platter. You live in a fantasy world. I gave you a life, a decent one, too, that I never had. That's why you are successful. Don't think for one second you did this on your own. You've no idea what real suffering is."

Even now, when I visit her, she compares aspects of her life to mine and does not allow me one moment to savor a sense of personal pride for what I have accomplished. She makes a point to remind each of us that if she had never married Bàba or sacrificed herself for us, then she would have been a hundred times the person she is, and none of us would have matched her.

I know Māma went through the valley of the shadow of death to give me life, and I'll forever be indebted to her. I know I didn't get to where I am today without her daily toils. Of course, I know Bàba wasn't good to her for most of their marriage. But, for one moment, why can't she just give me a little credit for my own effort? For once, why can't she stop bringing up her childhood as a comparison?

All I ever wanted is to please her. Why can't Māma be happy for me? Why can't she accept me for who I am? I want to be the center of attention for once and be acknowledged for once.

"No one had it worse than me," Māma wallows in her episodic sob stories, "so you don't have the right to be miserable."

Māma thinks I had it easy even when I try to share my struggles with her. She always has to emerge as the greater martyr. It is hard to breathe around her sometimes, and there's simply not enough room for the both of us to talk about our lives. I suspect Māma would be happier if I had stumbled more through life.

No matter how old I get, I still yearn for some motherly empathy and words of wisdom, but I can never get anything from her. I stop bringing up my battles in life. I can see her laughing in my face and mocking me. Because she's my Māma, her words pierce sharper than anyone else's and linger longer in my heart and my mind.

When I think about life and what can go wrong, I think of Māma, the child whom no one saw as she really was. She hoped things would be different when she became an adult, but they weren't. Her marriage to Bàba was a prearranged sham. She had given up the prospect of ever being free or happy.

She reminisces about the time she worked at a hospital and there was a young doctor whom she was fond of. He liked her as well, but she was already betrothed to Bàba. The irony is that for Māma, a servant child, to be promised to a man from an upper-middle class family, like Bàba, was an honor.

"You should consider yourself so lucky that someone wanted to marry you," Mountain Mah awakens her. "Instead of commiserating over your fate, you should be grateful you have a chance at a new life, unlike me."

Māma was so anxious to abandon her lamentable life that she would have married anyone who would take her. She wants to be sure she passes this same notion to my sister and me.

"If someone wants you, just marry him. Don't think too much about how you feel. You would be so fortunate to be selected."

"Marriage," Māma explains, "is about being claimed, not loved. No one can love you more than your own Māma."

Sometimes, when the noise in the apartment has settled, not that it ever becomes completely quiet, Māma shares random stories from her childhood.

"When I was small …" she begins as she threads the needle in her sewing machine. I lean forward, expecting a story of some adventure or wild mischief.

"Just before monsoon season when it's getting cooler, but the heavy rain has not come, there is an hour or two when I'm not cooking or cleaning. I climb a tree, look out across a field, and see the shack we live in. Everything looks so small and faraway. I wonder what my own māma is doing and if she's coming to rescue me."

Māma speaks of that moment with a special kind of wonder, not that she had climbed a tree and seen far beyond, but that she had been free for a brief time to be a child. That instance, time stopped, and she was allowed to be a child again and see the world outside her servitude.

Whenever Māma talks about her past, she expects me to feel sympathetic for her and to imagine her torture as she describes it. She expects me to say something to applaud her sacrifices and then crown her with praises of bravery. If I don't respond with applause, she gets agitated. What does she want from me—pity, sympathy, empathy, or admiration? Maybe everything, or maybe nothing.

I long to know what she has been through, but each time she relates her past, she takes it out on me as the perpetrator of all her sorrows. She resents my dull regards for her afflictions while sailing towards my own bright horizon. No matter what image I summon of Māma, solace is not in the vicinity.

She's doing something, day and night, night and day. Māma works wonders with those hands like an unstoppable octopus; scrubbing, cleaning, mopping, washing, making the house miraculously organized beneath those piles of junk.

She bends over the sewing machine with pins in her mouth, biting off a strand of thread, pedaling the foot-operated lever as rapidly as she can to finish an outfit and deliver it on time to secure a few dollars.

No matter how angry she is with Bàba, or how tired she is, she gets up each morning and carries on with her day. She never asks for a few more minutes to sleep in or take a day off. Bàba is the opposite. He's kind one minute, even expansive, and the next he's drunk. When he's out of it, he groans, moans, reproves Māma with vulgarities, and kicks her in her stomach, slaps her, and punches her. We never know when Māma and Bàba are going to blow up at each other. Every night and day, we gnaw our fingernails, hoping to find a place of refuge to escape whatever new plight comes our way.

In anticipation of Bàba coming home, Māma makes us pluck the roots of each bean sprout because he hates the rusty brown look, and it's the only vegetable we can afford. He considers the roots to be dirty and unnatural. All the girls in the household, including Ah Cheng and Sharlynn, sit on the muggy kitchen floor plucking away the pounds of sprouts Māma bought from the wet market. We chat and laugh and compete to see who can finish the largest pile before Bàba gets home, if he does.

Bàba always eats first, so we don't mess up the presentation of the dish, or else he won't eat. He's fastidious that way. He likes his rice a certain texture, his chopsticks placed in a certain way, and his beer at a certain temperature. If things aren't exactly the way he wants them, he throws a tantrum. The goal each night, if Bàba comes home, is to make sure he's happy.

"If he's happy, then he'll come home again tomorrow night," Māma rationalizes.

One night, Bàba sat down to eat his dinner but noticed a few brown roots from the sprouts. He got so irate that he threw the plate across the kitchen, shattering it all over the floor. He started slapping and yelling at us.

"Sorry, sorry. I should have made sure," Māma begs. "Don't be mad. It's my fault. Don't hit the kids, please, don't. Please don't."

She grabs a cloth from the sink to wipe the floor, salvaging whatever sprouts in one palm while picking up the broken glass with the other, cutting herself left and right.

"This is the only dish we have for dinner. The kids have nothing to eat now," she cries, still bleeding.

"Mā, it's ok," Jennifer comforts her, "We will eat whatever is salvaged from the floor. The floor gives an extra special flavor."

We all start laughing again as we wipe off our tears. Bàba storms out, to drink of course, and who knows what unearthly time he'll come home tonight.

When Māma is not cleaning, she is clucking happily and snipping loose threads from designer clothing—Guess, Polo, Gap, Calvin Klein, Tommy, and Oshkosh B'Gosh.

Before clothes are delivered to the retail stores, the excess threads are trimmed away so that each outfit looks neat on the shelf. For every dozen trimmed, we make about thirty cents. Typically, Māma asks for ten to twenty dozen of garments, so she can earn enough to cook one meal for us. The clothes are delivered at four in the afternoon and picked up the next day at the same time. We have exactly twenty-four hours to trim every item of apparel we picked up or else we can't get as much apparel the next time. More trimming means more food.

My sister and I snip the most. As soon as Ah Cheng and Sharlynn can handle scissors, they help, too. We compete to see who can trim the fastest. Of course, Winston and Phillip never lifted a finger for menial chores like this. They are boys.

Until I came to America, I had never heard of these brands. They were merely pieces of clothing and money for food. Now, when I see someone wearing designer clothes, it brings back memories of my childhood labor in that sweatshop. Have consumers ever stopped to think what it takes to bring one piece of clothing to the shelf?

I'm still obsessed with pulling loose threads whenever I see one hanging off someone's apparel. This is the most stable income we have, but it's not enough to keep us afloat. Māma decides to find something to sell. This is ironic because she's not a very good cook, a trait I apparently inherited.

"Burnt onions, meat, mushy, overcooked cabbage," Bàba says about her cooking, "She even burns rice."

Māma picks up some random recipe from a neighbor and starts to experiment with making curry chicken puffs. She rolls the dough flat and cuts little circles to make two halves, then stuffs seasoned chicken and curry potato mix in between the fold. The secret to a good curry puff is to fold the seams neatly so when it is in the hot oil, the stuffing doesn't fall out.

Initially, my stuffing keeps falling out, so they're not fit for sale, but I quickly get the hang of it. I need to be more agile to tuck each crease and create the uniform pleats. When the dough is ready to be fried, it takes five minutes to create a golden-brown, fresh, crispy puff. I become really good at folding the intricate pattern. The puffs may be a little rough around the edges, but they look good enough to sell for fifty cents apiece.

"Take your hands off," Māma slaps my hands. "If you want to try one, take a burnt one. No one buys those."

The aroma of the savory batter and spicy curry fills the whole apartment. I'm hungry. I am always hungry, like an earthworm digging for food constantly.

Jennifer carefully places each puff in a neat sequence, about fifty of them, and covers them with a towel to keep the flies away.

Jennifer and I are the only ones who are excited about selling these puffs. Winston and Phillip would never stoop so low as to sell food in the street. I like to sell because I love the adrenaline rush when I offer something wonderful to people and see their faces light up. It's like opening the door to a bouquet of flowers.

"Curry puffs. Curry puffs? Curry puffs! Delicious, hot curry puffs!" Jennifer recites the rhythm. It sounds like one of the Chinese songs we sing beneath our blanket.

She approaches everyone everywhere, fearlessly— on the balcony, in the hallway, in the middle of the stairs, and along the walkway.

"Here, fifty cents. They're still hot, fresh. Try one."

If the puffs aren't selling by afternoon, Jennifer drops the price to forty, thirty, even twenty cents. Sometimes, she'll throw in two for seventy-five cents. She's the best at negotiating and teaches me how to work people's appetite by persuading them to imagine biting into one of the puffs.

One time, she stops a man, probably a government official or insurance salesman, in a nice suit. I don't know why he's in our neighborhood. I hunch my shoulders and shrink back, letting Jennifer do the talking because it's actually illegal to sell without a permit. He looks into the basket and picks out three puffs, hands her two dollars, and says "keep the change." Jennifer and I stare at each other like we've just won a lottery.

"Wow, Mā is going to be so happy! We're rich!"

Seeing Jennifer happy makes me even more excited to become a salesgirl. I want to be like her and learn the art of persuasion. When I grow up, I want to go door-to-door to sell something. Imagine how much money I'd make. I am confident I can convince anyone to buy anything.

Jennifer and I beg Māma to let us eat the leftover puffs for dinner, even if they are not shaped the best. By then, the puffs are cold and greasy, but they're the yummiest things we've eaten all day.

Chapter 3
HOLLOW LOVE

Life keeps throwing me curveballs, and I don't even own a bat. At least my dodging skills are improving.
≈ Jayleigh Cape

*B*àba is an average man, five feet or so, with a beer belly. His skin is exceptionally dark for a Chinese adult, probably from patrolling under the sun. His best trait is his genial and alluring smile. In his policeman days, in his twenties, he had a relatively good physique. His voice was husky and deep, commanding at times. He had everything it takes to be an officer.

The memories of Bàba are fragmented. I can't put together a complete picture of him, even now. I look at the photos of him before he got married, before he started drinking, before he had us. Those images show a regular-looking young man with a happy life ahead of him.

Bàba is a hulking presence to be avoided, especially compared to Māma, a fine-boned and small-waisted woman. I never hear Bàba praise Māma for anything, not her looks, her cooking, or her skills, not even for bringing money home. He never looks at her except to yell, usually for something she didn't do right for him, such as his pants being too loose or too tight, that the bed sheets aren't aligned, or the hallway is too narrow. He hardly touches her except to kick her when she's down on her knees, mopping up his spit.

"Clean up now, good for nothing! Get everything clean before I get home!"

Bàba doesn't care one bit if the house is clean or messy. He's hardly home even if Māma makes us keep the house dust-free for the sake of the garments we cut. She also drives home the notion that Bàba is more pleased to come home to a clean house than a messy one.

"If we keep the house clean," Māma says, "Bàba is more likely to come home. If not, it's your fault, all of your fault."

We clean to please our anxious Māma and to calm her down as she anticipates Bàba's homecoming and, hopefully, a peaceful night.

Jennifer is the natural apartment cleaner. She's swift and has good eyes for where things can be hidden. She packs them so neatly you can hardly tell there was a pile of unwanted items there in the first place. We girls are the only ones doing the chores. The boys never lift a finger to help. I hate it that Māma never calls on the boys to do anything, not even to carry the heavy garments up and down from the parking lot each afternoon. We scrub the floor, clean the dishes, and spread newspapers to cover up piles of clutter in every corner. As long as we keep the mess out of Bàba's sight, it doesn't matter where we pile things up.

"Hurry, put all the clothes away. Quick, he's on his way up!"

We go into a frenzy when we hear Bàba parking his car and scramble to make a pathway for him to enter like he's a Hollywood celebrity arriving for the movie premier on a red carpet. Each night is a dramatic night. Our neighbors must be looking forward to our nightly soap opera to find out the latest plot developments. Māma scrambles to pick up the last strands of thread while frantically pushing the rest of the unsnipped garments under the couch. The irony is, Bàba is so drunk he never notices anything anyway. Māma teaches us to believe in miracles, and that one of these days, perhaps today, Bàba is going to be a different man.

"If you are good and obedient, maybe this will be the day God listens to our prayers and changes your Bàba."

At ten, I am paranoid about everything I do and don't do. The fear of not pleasing Māma overwhelms me, and if Bàba is really drunk, Māma gets even more upset and reaches for the bamboo cane. Then I have two angry parents to deal with.

"Why are you caning me?" I beg to know.

"I'm angry. I'm angry that God is blind to our suffering."

Māma goes on to cane me, even as her arms tremble, with tears dripping from her eyes.

There are empty bottles, ten or twenty of them, piled in a corner on the kitchen floor. At one point, we can't get into the bathroom and have to skip over the bottles to get inside. It's like an arcade game in an amusement park. Māma keeps these bottles in exchange for a few cents here and there.

When Bàba gets drunk, his speech grows faster and more exuberant, and he boils into anger and blares out vulgarities at everyone.

Māma thinks of running away from home with us, but she doesn't know where to go. We have no friends or relatives who would take us in for a night, and we have no money. Sometimes, when we get home from school, Māma won't let us inside the flat. She meets us in the hallway and whispers, "Go away, and be quiet." We know instantly that Bàba is drunk. Other times, Māma sends us away when Bàba has guests that he picks up from the bar. Māma tries to keep us from knowing who these ladies are, but we're too experienced by now and can tell by the way they dress, smell, walk, and talk that they're prostitutes.

"Go and get beer for our guests! Now! Go!" Bàba screams.

There's no law restricting the sale of alcohol to minors, but at nine or ten, it's embarrassing to run home clutching a bottle of beer. If there are no lady guests, then Māma tells us to take our time coming home with that bottle so she can try to caress Bàba to sleep. If she's unable to get him to sleep, she tells us to hurry home before he smashes too many things around the house. We have to rush back because as much as Bàba hates having no beer, he hates warm beer even more.

I don't know which is worse, having him home and drunk, with call girls sitting in the living room, or not having him home at all. Māma thinks it's better to let Bàba get drunk at home so at least we know where he is and we don't have to hunt him down at a bar or, worse, find him naked or dead in a ditch somewhere.

The smell of beer is all too familiar. That's how Bàba smells. Even with all the other odors at our flat, I can't get away from the one that identifies Bàba. I told myself never to touch anything remotely alcoholic in my life. I hate alcohol and I can't stand to be around alcoholics even more. I don't mean to be unsympathetic toward people overcoming their addiction, but Bàba wasn't trying to overcome anything; he wanted to get drunk every day and made sure he stayed drunk, never slightly drunk or half-drunk, as some may call it.

As days and years go by, Bàba's sober days become a rarity in our household. As much as I hate buying beer, I like the way the bottles look. Usually, I pick out the dark brownish-colored bottle called Guinness Stout, but a few times I buy the amber bottles or Tiger beer. I like the elegant and alluring motif on the bottle. It's a love-hate relationship. I want to know what makes a man loves this bottle more than his family. What makes a man give up his children's happiness for this bottle? Why would a man throw away everything for this bottle? Maybe I should be like this bottle, and then Bàba will pay some attention to me and love me too.

Bàba hardly brings home money from his day job as a taxi driver. He spends what little he has on beer. Māma seldom gets even ten dollars a week from him. Whatever money we have, we get it from our trimmings of those garments.

Māma has to come up with strategies to cut down the beer expense. She learns to be shrewd very quickly after she married Bàba. She keeps a bottle of beer in a remote place in the kitchen that no one can find, and then she dilutes the beer with tap water until it makes a whole bottle.

She pounds the cap back on neatly with a hammer to make sure Bàba won't suspect it's been opened. Then she wipes the bottle clean and lets it settle in the fridge. In the event that Bàba demands a bottle and Māma is out of cash, she'd dig out that hidden treasure and charge him full price for it. Māma says this will keeps Bàba from getting too drunk because he's drinking diluted alcohol. Why doesn't Bàba realize the beer tastes weaker? After all, he's an alcoholic. Maybe he knew it but did not want to confront Māma, or maybe he's too drunk to tell the difference.

When Māma runs out of every penny and can't afford any beer, she resorts to borrowing from the neighbors, a dollar here, a dollar there. If all else fails, Māma asks me to knock on every friend's door and beg for a few dollars.

"No, Māma. I don't want to ask people for money; not for beer."

"We all know what's going to happen when Bàba is desperate for a beer and does not get what he wants."

Yes, we know that all too well. Bàba is not a nice person if he doesn't get his cold beer promptly. He throws furniture, smashes dishes, and whips us with his cheap plastic belt from his half-fallen pants and brandishes a knife at any of us who gets in his way.

When Bàba finds out Māma has been borrowing from the neighbors, he gets even crazier. Bàba is a prideful person. Everything we do is about saving face—the Chinese etiquette of not embarrassing oneself in public and having a backbone. He never asks for help, especially from his own family.

"I'll never beg, not even from my own mother or sister," Bàba rants. "I'd starve to death in the streets before I asked for help! If you can't find the money, then cut more and sew more. You are useless! All of you!"

Bàba's vulgarities are a repertoire of every language utterable—Malay, Hokkien, Teochew, and English. There is no way to shield my ears.

"Kneel and pray," Māma cries, trying to comfort herself and us.

I don't know why, but I think I can only ask for one favor from God in my lifetime, so I have to choose wisely in case He decides to answer me. I'm not sure if I should pray for Bàba to come home drunk, or for him to not come home at all. I don't know if I should pray for him to stop beating us or for him to leave us. I have so many favors to ask of God. Is He there at all?

What if I pray for Bàba to die? Will God answer me?

I am my Bàba's daughter. I don't know how I could pray for anything bad to come upon him. I want to believe there's more to this man. How did a young man with such an affable smile, raised in an upper-middle class home, educated more than others in his generation, turn into the person he is—cursing, abusing, gambling, womanizing and drinking?

His eyes are dull and his jaws slack. He looks angry. He's angry at the world, at his family, at us, and at himself. Does Bàba know how afraid we're of him? At times, his face takes on a gentle look of ineffable sadness, and he reaches out to ruffle my hair or pat Jennifer on the head. We love it when he chats with Winston or jokes with Phillip. We love it when he takes all of us to a movie, like Jaws or Superman, the only two movies I ever saw with my family. These moments, though rare, are some of our most precious times.

For some reason, Phillip has had the strongest enmity toward Bàba. He received the harshest beating of us all and has never recovered from those scars, both physically and emotionally. Bàba did not stop whipping Phillip even when his nose was bleeding. One of his arms was also permanently fractured by Bàba. The two never saw eye to eye again.

Phillip turns twelve and stops talking to Bàba. Bàba stops talking to him, too. Both become strangers and enemies at the same time. They want nothing to do with each other. As the youngest child, I lost not only one, but two men in my life, at once. We are no longer a family unit. There is no family unit, just a hundred miles of separation between Bàba and Māma, and a hundred more between my brothers and sister. Even Bàba's own siblings assures us that any bàba in the world is better than our own Bàba, mourning, "the sooner he dies, the better you all will be."

I'm not sure I agree. Maybe there's another side of Bàba I don't know yet. He can be cheerful, generous, and kind. He tells stories about animals, airplanes, and politics, but mostly about cars, and these stories make me laugh so hard that my stomach hurts. He sings songs in local dialects, though I don't understand a word. I enjoy humming along with his happy voice. He tickles me, flips me upside down, and chases me around as dads do. To me, he's as ordinary a Bàba as I can ask for.

Bàba works for a time at a second-hand car dealership. In that early evening time, before the beers get into him, he tells me about the types of cars he might drive home next week, maybe a convertible, a Beetle, or even a Mercedes. These cars are usually old and beat-up, but Bàba fantasizes about being behind the wheel, and we fantasize along with him. My brothers know far more about cars than Jennifer and me, but we all get excited when Bàba starts detailing them to us.

"Imagine driving one of those elegant, bright-red-lipstick-sleek cars like Elvis Presley's 1960 MG Roadster from *Blue Hawaii*," Bàba relates from his movie obsession. "Imagine sitting in genuine leather seats with the top down. Imagine powerful engines, comfort, envy ...."

Bàba helps us picture how we would feel with him behind the wheel, Māma seated in the front with a floral scarf over her head, and all of us squashed in the back— laughing, cheering, and screaming at the top of our lungs. But these chimeras never last long. Bàba's eyes grow red suddenly. Someone says something and sets him off into a round of profanity.

"Get the hell out! Leave me alone. Useless bunch of brats!"

It's like a sudden storm; no one knows what happened, and we all try to find shelter until the unexpected tirade passes. When that happens, we give him more beer to calm him down until he passes out. That's the ploy to get some peace in an alcoholic home.

I hear Bàba moaning in his sleep, "Why me? Why me? I'm better off dead than alive. I have nothing. Nothing." Then he drowns himself into an alcoholic stupor and falls asleep.

⊱⊰

I don't know Bàba's side of the family very well, including my grandmother. We call her Fat Granny, but not in a demeaning or disrespectful way; it's just a lighthearted way of addressing someone close to you. The picture of Fat Granny I have in my mind is not particularly appealing. She looks like a traditional old-fashioned granny style and wears a matching button-up outfit all the time, blue or gray, simple and non-accessorized. What she does possess is a powerful persona. She's quite tall and large in stature, so when she speaks, her voice demands that everyone turns toward her.

Fat Granny is a legend. Relatives from Bàba's side of the family speak highly of her as the woman who founded her own empire by building a fleet of taxis. She lives in a nice, two-story bungalow with a carport and a garden bursting with red hibiscus, purple bougainvillea, and all kinds of orchids. She even has her own maid.

What makes Fat Granny extraordinary is that she's a woman. She took charge of her life when she got married and became a shrewd entrepreneur, something quite unusual for her generation. From what little I know, she was born fairly poor but married a much older, richer man as his second wife. She saved what she had and then did a very simple thing—she invested. With the profits she made, she bought more and more taxis. Before long, she owned a dozen cabs, all in her name.

Fat Granny works ferociously; the upshot is that none of her children are very close to her. Money is what brought the family together, but money is also what tore them apart. It's as easy to love a child as it is to disrupt that love at any second. Bàba was the most beloved child of all. He got everything he wanted. He never needed to utter a sound to get what he wanted. He was spoiled from the second he was born, being the oldest child and a male child. Over the years, this created insurmountable rivalry between his siblings, including the biological children of his father's first wife.

We see Bàba's family only three or four times a year. Everyone on that side of the family looks down on us and isn't afraid to let us know what they think of our Bàba. The arguments are always about money. They complain about the way he squanders his mother's inheritance through gambling and drinking before she's even gone, how willful his temperament is, and about his shameless appetite for women. Our weekend visits usually end with a negative tone, with his family saying the sooner Bàba dies, the more peace there will be in the world.

As a child, Bàba was wild and rebellious, but he was also one of the most popular and well-liked kids in school. Māma said he was very smart, and his teachers liked him a lot. He never had to study much to get good grades. He was one of those naturally gifted students. He always aspired to be in law enforcement. He was charismatic in a way that could be quite surprising to many, but these tendencies are also what got him into trouble. He had a hard time saying no to his friends, so he frequently ended up doing whatever it took to please the crowd.

As he grew older, his so-called buddies further exploited those tendencies. Bàba will still do whatever it takes to please his friends; including drinking, gambling, and womanizing. That's probably how we ended up living in the slums while his siblings live in ritzy bungalows and luxurious townhouses.

It has been rumored from estranged relatives that sibling rivalry has resulted in backstabbing, slander, betrayal, and defamation. It's all about who gets on the best side of Fat Granny for a bigger piece of her inheritance.

Bàba becomes an even greater disgrace when he refuses to quit his vices. As time moves on, his siblings reject him, and Bàba rejects them in return. We're told to dissociate ourselves from our cousins and relatives because they all have evil intents and are out to see us dead.

I defend Bàba when I hear relatives at weddings or funerals spreading rumors about him. Whenever I see my cousins, I have to ignore them because I don't want to be the black sheep caught socializing with the enemies. My parents don't get along with the relatives, but I have no reason to suspect my cousins are part of this discord. Growing up, I never play or communicate with any of them. I barely know their names. To this day, no one remembers how things reached that boiling point, but we all witness how the past generational conflicts have inevitably spilled over from one to the next.

҈

Poh Geok, my older sister, was born right after Winston. When she was nine months old, she had to undergo a difficult surgery to fix a blockage in her bowels. Due to complications, Poh Geok did not make it. Her medical record indicates the cause of death as peritonitis, a life-threatening bacterium that infects the membrane of the abdominal wall supporting the organs. Māma could not afford to bring the baby in for treatment, so the fungus spread into her bloodstream and infected her other organs, causing rapid kidney failure and liver decay.

Sometimes, Māma explains away her sorrow by rationalizing that perhaps Poh Geok wasn't as lucky as the rest of us because she wasn't given a Christian name. Bàba is grief-stricken beyond consolation when his first daughter dies.

"Don't mention her name," he laments, "Poh Geok is no longer here. Why talk of her? She's gone."

He will never speak of her again, ever. I sense the piercing pain in Māma's heart, too, each time I ask about the sister I once had. Māma doesn't want me to get to know her. Maybe she's trying to protect me from having to carry a burden of loss in my heart. Maybe she's trying to avoid remembering ever having this daughter. I don't know how she looked or what she did as a baby. It's as if Poh Geok was born and then disappeared from the family; as if she never existed. Because I never knew Poh Geok, I never had a sense of loss. Māma struggles when she talks about her, and when she doesn't talk about her.

"Come, sit here," Māma says as she lies on her bed and beckons me to listen. "Your sister is such an angel, perfect from head to toe. That's why God had to take her home. She hardly cried; she was such a good baby, so good that I never knew she was suffering inside. Imagine a baby in pain, and her mother doesn't even know. She'd have been a wonderful sister to you."

Tears of sadness and happiness roll simultaneously down her cheeks.

"Your sister was so hungry before her surgery. She looked me in the eyes … I could tell she wanted me to nurse her," Māma painfully reminisces.

"I was wearing a stupid one-piece dress, and the zipper was on the back so I couldn't nurse her. She went into the surgery hungry … and never woke up again. She wanted to drink Māma's milk for the last time, and I couldn't even fulfill her last wish. How can I ever forgive myself?" Māma beats herself up again and weeps.

⊰⊷

Before Bàba's rivalry with his siblings left him ostracized from his family, there was a younger brother, Ah Chung, whom Bàba loved and spoiled immensely.

Ah Chung was the baby of the family, so Bàba paid special attention to him. They spend a lot of time together, so much so that Māma complains that Bàba spends more time with Ah Chung than with his own family.

One week after Poh Geok was buried, Bàba was on his way home from work when he saw a commotion on Bukit Timah Road near where Fat Granny lives. He headed toward the scene to see what all the fuss was about.

A huge crowd gathered around a motorbike and a lorry transporting some vegetables. When Bàba finally worked his way through the throng, he recognized the motorcyclist; it was Ah Chung. He was lying face down on the road with his head almost destroyed, bleeding profusely from both ears. He was only twenty-three.

This tragedy sent Bàba into a downward spiral. He liked to have a beer or two before that, but Māma recalls after these two grievous losses, only seven days apart, Bàba began to drink in earnest. The misfortunes cracked him deep inside. Though I wasn't born yet, I imagine what life was like before my sister and uncle died. I picture these newlyweds with a commitment to build a life together. I imagine the joy they felt when their first son was born, followed by a first daughter. I surmise Māma and Bàba worked hard to provide for their children. What more could they ask for?

I envisage my life would have been very different, devoid of the ugliness of gambling, alcohol, profanity, and abuse and filled instead with typical childhood memories—laughter, fun, family meals, occasional sibling fights, and weekend picnics.

In 1967, weeks following these deaths, Bàba lost his job as a police officer because he misfired his gun. Thankfully, no one was hurt. Shortly after that, Bàba found himself working in a second-hand car dealership. For several years on and off, more off than on. Bàba tried to stay in this line of work, but he couldn't sustain his family. Eventually, he gave up selling cars and resorted to driving taxis. He rented one from his mother, probably the hardest thing he ever had to do. Armed with his taxi license, Bàba vowed to start anew, for his family and himself.

Bàba values his reputation more than anything else. He hates being a driver. He hates being told what to do, and now he has to listen to backseat drivers all day long.

At four-thirty in the afternoon, when Bàba gets home from his shift at work, he stands outside on the front balcony, shirtless, wearing only his loose-fitting, blue-striped, pajama pants. I want to hug him, or be hugged by him, and tell him about my day, but I dare not disturb the graveyard silence. The air around him is blue and obscure. I can't make out what he's thinking; if he's in a good mood or not, or if I should talk to him or not.

From our apartment up high, he stares down at the people walking by on the brown patches of grass and puffs away, but interestingly, never with a bottle in his hand. He doesn't like to smoke and drink at the same time, or maybe he thinks these vices should not mix. Maybe one is for ruminating, and the other is for drowning out his thoughts. When I finally work up the courage, I grab his hands. I say nothing as I lie on his shoulder, wrapping my whole self on his arm. He holds my hands gently and puts them close to his chest, as if afraid I may run away if he lets go.

We say nothing. 9|18

Chapter 4
TONIC AND TOXIC

Everybody is a genius. But if you judge a fish by its ability to climb a tree, it will live its whole life believing that it is stupid.

∾ *Amos E. Dolbear*

Māma presents the very worst that can happen to us like a spell that binds us and can never be broken. "There's no such thing as true happiness. If you're happy, there's something wrong with you … You're born into the unluckiest family. That's why you have to suffer … Everyone wants something from you. No one becomes your friend for nothing … Dreams can only bring you more sorrow and disappointment."

Since Bàba is hardly around, he doesn't advise us much—which may be a good thing. Māma speaks about the people around us as if they're all enemies, and we're prey. She instills in us not to rely on anyone or befriend our relatives. Relatives are people, too, and people only think of their own selfish interests. If anything, relatives want to see us fail and suffer more than anyone else.

I keep Māma's teachings in my heart, but I struggle silently with the conflict that if the world is such an evil place, why are some people so happy?

Māma has special names for me. She often calls me *cabbage head* or *vegetable head*. I'm not sure what they mean, but they don't sound flattering. I think she's challenging me to rise above being in a vegetated state; I'm not sure. I hope I'm more than a head of lettuce. Māma knows me best, so maybe I'm too proud, and she's teaching me not to expect too much of myself, so I won't be disappointed. Gradually, I learn to complain less and comply more. Like all mothers, Māma wants what's best for me. Why else would she stay up late sewing, cleaning, and ironing? She walks miles and miles in her worn vinyl flip-flops, delivering a glamorous dress to a nightclub singer so she can bring home some money for food. Why would a mother do all of this except to give her children a better life?

In the 1950s, the government of Singapore began to institute strict policies for planned parenthood. These efforts reached their peak in the late sixties and early seventies, the time when I was born, and continued into the early eighties. The programs went under various names. The best known perhaps was *Stop at Two*.

In a country that covers only a little more than 200 square miles, with families regularly having four or five children, the government becomes wary. Efforts to slow down the birthrate took various forms. In the year I was born, Singapore legalized abortion and offered incentives for sterilization.

Lower-income and uneducated women were offered large sums of money to have their tubes tied. Hospitals increased the fees charged for delivering babies after the second child, and the fees steeply accumulate with each subsequent child. Other punitive measures included income tax penalties, educational disadvantages for children born after the second child, poorer housing allotments, and no maternity leave for third births and beyond. Having more than two children became a heavy burden on almost every family.

Despite their dire financial situation, I was conceived as an accidental child; Māma reminds me of this every day. It's already a real hardship to feed three mouths—Winston, five, Phillip, three, and Jennifer, one, and Bàba is not bringing home any stable income.

When I turn seven, Māma tries to enroll me in first grade. She hopes I'll be accepted into the same school as Jennifer, the parochial Methodist Girls' School, where Fat Granny is a donor. Māma thinks it'll be an easy process given the affiliation. After sitting for what feels like hours in the hallway on a wobbly, wooden chair, I finally hear my name, "Barbara Hong, next." We grab our belongings and head toward the door.

"Sit," orders a stern administrative woman.

Without hesitation, she points at me and speaks in her Singaporean-English accent, or *Sin-glish*.

"Fourth child. Why apply, eh? Government says no, cannot. Control, no more children, okay?"

"Please, my daughter, Jennifer, attends this school, too," Māma pleads. "One more child, she needs to come to school here. Please try to take her."

"No, no," the administrator says with a sneer. "Not my rule, can't take this one. No choice. Try another school and no more children."

The lady doesn't even try to be discreet. She chides Māma for not stopping at two. Like Māma had a choice. How could anyone fault her for getting pregnant? I sit there watching Māma supplicate on my behalf, ashamed I was even born, as if I was expelled from school, even before I started.

Still, the administrator is unmoved.

Rejected, we lug through the hallway, passing at least one hundred mocking stares on our way out of the building. Everyone within earshot of that office heard my rejection. I hate myself for putting Māma through this.

We stroll down a flight of stairs. Māma is ahead of me, so I try to catch up. As we walk across a giant green field, she turns around and mutters something. I'm not sure if she's talking to herself or me.

"What, Māma? Did you say something?"

"You shouldn't … born!" Māma says. "I should have … you sooner. Spending all that money for nothing. Medicine didn't even work."

I am still lagging behind and can't hear what she's saying. "What did you say, Māma?" I ask again as I try to catch up.

"Never mind, medicine didn't work, not aborted," Māma says as she walks even faster. "Black market doctor said sure work, but three months later, you still came out."

I'm seven. I don't know what she's talking about or what *abort* means. I simply brush off the thought and never bring it up again, but Māma won't let it go, especially when she's upset with Bàba or me.

"I didn't want you to be born, but I had no choice; you just wanted to come out," she says in distress.

"I have to suffer whenever I get pregnant. You know your Bàba, he kicks me in the belly, even when I'm with child," Māma moans. "I knew he would beat you if you were born, just like he beats your brothers and sister."

While Māma accepts the fact that we're not bright children, she's particularly concerned about me. As the months pass, Māma attempts to explain what abortion means. I try to take it all in, never completely understanding what the emotional and physical toll entails.

"I try to get rid of you twice," Māma confesses. "You were six months inside Māma. Everything was getting so expensive, and the government says we'll get fined if we have you. I panicked. I drink bitter medicine, horrible tasting ones the back-alley, so-called physician, gave me. Who knows what he put inside?"

I listen as she talks about the potions, teas, and root concoctions she drank day and night to get rid of me. Anise seed is supposed to calm the belly, so the baby won't grow. Asafoetida, an Indian indigestion preventative, can cause a woman to lose her fetus if taken in large quantities. Teas of ashwagandha root and bitter melons are both calming drugs known to harm pregnant women, and, most powerful of all, tea of Dong Quai or Angelica is known to cause contractions strong enough to cause a miscarriage even in the latter stages of pregnancy. Other teas are strong enough to make a woman bleed heavily. I suspect there must have been several of these snake oil physicians going around promising to end pregnancies for a price.

"I took them all, every sort of toxic," Māma's eyes glances sideway.

One of the strongest medicines she drank was highly salty and acidic, and she vomited all day and night. She thought the medicine was working because I stopped kicking, but within days, I started to move again, though not as vigorously as before. She wasn't sure if that was a good sign or an omen that I was going to be born with brain damage.

"You were so stubborn and wouldn't go away. I kept drinking more medicine," she confesses, "I suffered, too; my stomach got so painful. I thought I was going to die too."

It's hard to imagine what she put herself through to get rid of me. Perhaps those remedies were nothing, only old wives' tales, because here I am. Perhaps the remedies did irreparable damage, Māma doesn't know.

That December morning, from the moment I opened my eyes and made my first cry, Māma became preoccupied with making amends to fix my brain.

"I knew what I did to you so now you must have some sort of brain damage. You'll never be normal again. From now on, you must drink everything I give you, or you'll become retarded like your brother."

Chinese people believe that if some parts of your body have a weakness, you can compensate by consuming the corresponding parts of an animal. The supernatural power of animals can correct any deficits in the human anatomy.

If I want to be fast, eat frog legs. If I want to have good blood, eat chicken blood (my favorite). If I have a weak heart, eat a pig's heart. To live a long life, drink turtle soup. Digestive problems? Consume pig intestines. The practice goes on and on. There are stalls everywhere in the streets that sell various organ soups and dried body parts. These are considered delicacies, so they're not cheap. Māma has to save quite a bit each month to brew up these "nourishments" for me.

Māma purchases organs with curative powers from local medicine men each chance she gets to make up for the intelligence I supposedly lost or never fully formed in her womb. This tonic is the horror of my childhood—dark red, almost black, a hellish brew made from the pig's liver and brains. Pigs, one of the animals of the zodiac, are supposedly very smart creatures.

"Pigs pretend to be lazy and messy so humans will feed them and take care of them. To be smart, you must eat pig's brain," Māma grunts.

Occasionally, she brews sun-dried insects and lizards, such as bees, cockroaches, geckos, and beetles, and then forces me to drink them up. I hate anything that's hot, so I put some ice cubes in the soup, which only makes Māma mad.

"I spend all this money to heal you, and you just wasted the tonic by throwing ice in it. The heat is what heals you!" Māma yells. "Now! Big gulp, drink it all at once, so it's more powerful."

Occasionally, if she has a few extra dollars, she gets the more potent herbal soup with dried seahorse, bird's nest (made from bird vomit, and most expensive), dried scorpion, and, most expensive of all, deer antler.

The man behind the counter takes a piece of broken glass and shaves off thin layers of the outer horn onto a piece of paper. The shaved portion looks like a small pile of silver threads or silkworms. Māma boils them with some sugar and a few lotus seeds if she can afford them to give it a sweet taste.

I know Māma loves me, and that's why she's going through all this trouble and expense to fix me, but as the weeks and years go by, my brain does not improve, as evidenced by my school report cards.

"All these soups and still can't study," Māma laments. "It's hopeless now. Your brain is gone. Wasted. This is blood-earned money, you know."

I want to believe the tonic is working, too, but the taste is so vile that each time I drink it, I gag. Māma says I need to stop resisting the aura so the animal spirits can work inside me.

"Will it really make me normal again?" I ask as I stare at yet another noxious concoction.

"I'm your Māma. I know how to heal you, but you must not fight it," she claims.

I look at the lumpy pig brain in a green bowl. It's probably overcooked. Even though Māma adds some clear gingery aroma and sesame oil, I still have to pinch my nose and shut my eyes so I can sip it.

"Māma, add some more flavor, soy sauce or salt or sugar, I can't drink it," I protest.

"If you can't drink it, then eat the brain, it's your choice," Māma compromises.

I gaze at the sludgy gunk, shut my eyes and take another sip. I throw up again. I can't swallow at all.

Māma comes back to check on me. "Don't be a baby. Close your eyes and gulp it down! Think of the pig's brain replacing your brain now."

"Easy for you to say, I'm the one drinking it," I rebel.

I force myself to guzzle down that ghastly soup and feel the steam streaming down my throat. Immediately, I try to picture myself a little smarter, a little sharper, a little more like the witty pig. Ironic? Yes, but it pleases Māma and makes her feel less culpable.

After several months, Māma meets someone on the market street who says she might be able to enroll me in another local primary school. "This school will take your daughter, good or bad," the lady says, "Go quickly, so you don't lose your seat."

Māma rushes home to tell me the good news. "We have a school that may take you!" she screams with joy, still catching her breath. "Quick, put on that outfit Auntie Lee from upstairs gave you. Wear red. It's good luck. Pray. We need luck now. Don't forget to comb your hair. Neat means smart, and don't open your mouth, or they'll know you're stupid."

I don my pair of uneven length blue jeans and my one bright-red t-shirt. From that day on I learn that if I'm quiet, sit still, and do as the teacher directs, I'll not get into trouble. Obedience is the most important rule in school.

I'm beaming when I get the news that the local school will accept me. Now I can finally say I'm a real student with a real uniform and have real books like my brothers and sister.

The first day of school is tense but exciting. I get up early to walk there with Māma. As a rule, all shoulder-length hair or longer has to be tied up so that not a strand is dangling off your face. Māma brushes my long black hair and ties up two buns on each side with a fluffy red band. Jennifer and I get jittery when Māma does our hair. If we move our head or body even a hair, Māma strikes us with the heavy wooden brush. This ordeal is the longest ten minutes of my morning routine.

"Ouch! Ouch!" I scream.

"Stay still. Don't move," Māma scolds.

"Sorry, sorry, don't hit me again," I plead, promising to stay still.

"Ouch! That hurts!" I wail again.

"Move again, and I'll smack you harder this time," Māma warns.

Within a few minutes, I feel the tension in my head. Māma pulls the hair so tight like I'm getting a facelift. I dare not show the tears welling in my eyes, but she notices them anyway.

"Stop crying, you're going to mess up your face," Māma snaps. "Don't you dare scratch your head or try to loosen the band."

From the minute I step into school, it's all about formality, uniformity, and conformity. We all wear uniforms from kindergarten through high school.

My first-grade teacher, Mrs. Chang, is strict. She's the no-nonsense kind, dealing with students as if we're criminals and she's a warden. After the first two months in school, she complains to Māma about how slow I am.

"Everything with your daughter takes so long," Mrs. Chang says. "Is she retarded?"

Māma is not happy with the report. It's only two months into school. She resorts to brewing more tonics for me to drink, hoping to heal me this time.

"Drink it up. The teacher will see you can learn. Good girl," Māma tries to convince me.

Though Māma thinks the medicine is working, she continues to call me "retarded" and "stupid" whenever I do the slightest wrong thing, like wiping the table the wrong way, sewing a pillow case too close to the seam, or saying the wrong word.

"I try to fix you," she says somberly, "but your brain doesn't know how to work. After all these soups, still nothing."

By the 1980s, the Singaporean government realizes that their effort to *Stop at Two* is working too well. They are now facing a declining population that, if it goes too far, will be devastating for a young nation. Later, *Stop at Two* is replaced with the cautionary slogan, *Have Three or More—If You Can Afford It.*

The upshot of this is that I grow up with the notion that I'm the generation of unwanted pregnancies. I learn to speak little, keep to myself, and act as if I don't exist. Like the persona of a zombie, I became lifeless, voiceless, and soulless.

Chapter 5

CHAOTIC ORDER

I accept chaos. I'm not sure whether it accepts me.
⮞ Bob Dylan

*M*y school is about fifteen minutes from our flat, so I walk every day. I like to pass the market and watch people buying and selling, bargaining and negotiating. Most of all, I like smelling the food, even though I can't taste it. I can't linger on the way to school because, if I'm late, even for a minute, I'll be locked out. On my way home, I browse at the stores for as long as my heart desires. I love stationery, especially the smell of brand new paper and markers. That's an irony because I can barely read or write, but I have an inclination for stationery.

I love the smooth pens and sharpened pencils, the clean erasers, the unwrinkled book covers, and the smell of writing pads. I don't deserve any new school supplies because those are reserved for intelligent students, but I love the sight of how everything looks so neatly piled and sorted on organized shelves. I even dream of being a stationery shop owner one day and building shelves to the ceiling, lined with books, like the library in a huge mansion I saw on TV. So, on Friday afternoons, I head to Ah Chek's (a middle-age man in Hokkien) stationery shop about five minutes from my block.

I never speak to Ah Chek, but I hear his customers calling him by that name. I hang out there after school for several hours, touching everything within reach, flipping through pages of blank jotter books, rotating pencils in the containers, rearranging erasers by their respective colors, and stacking writing pads to make sure they're all aligned.

I stand at the corner of the cashier table, sharpening bouquets of pencils until I get blisters on my fingers, and my hands are tired. I dust the bookshelves, so the glossy covers look even shinier.

During Christmas season, I hang out there even more until the store closes. Since it's a school holiday, Māma doesn't care if I come home late. I like to assemble the greeting cards by size and make sure each card has its correct envelope. What distresses me is when customers pick up a card, and if that's not what they want, they throw it anywhere instead of putting it back in its original stack.

As I stand by the hundreds of greeting cards on a white rectangular table, I match each card, find its pattern, and then stick a correct sized envelope in between. Subsequently, I put a rubber band around each stack so that, hopefully, customers will appreciate the neatness of things and be more considerate.

Ah Chek notices I'm there a lot, but he never kicks me out. He is suspicious that I may be stealing from him and watches me like a hawk whenever I leave the store. After a few weeks, he realizes I'm just there to hang out because I have nowhere to go after school. Besides, I can tell from the annoyed look on his face that tidying up the cards is not his favorite thing to do. I love having a pastime after school and look forward to visiting the store.

I love the smell of photocopied paper. When I hold freshly printed papers up to my nose and flip through them, I take a deep breath and let the chemical scent soak into my nose.

Māma hardly buys anything new for me. Whatever I have is handed down, which I don't mind. When the school sends out a list of supplies for the following year, I scrounge through our old stuff to see what I can find. If I'm lucky to get an old textbook, I'd bury my face in it. There's something liberating about the smell of old textbooks that I love. I wish I can absorb all the knowledge simply by inhaling books rather than reading them.

Anything I can get my hands on to write in is an incredible treat for me. I marvel at a clean sheet of crisp paper, its unwrinkled edges, plainness, and purity, juxtaposing the image of maturity, vanity, and chaos. I wish my life was a brand-new page each day, stripped of the memories of yesterday and untarnished by tomorrow's worries.

In third grade, Māma surprises me with a brand-new box of German-made Luna colored pencils. They're sitting on the round marble table when I come home from school, and the price tag is still on the box.

Luna pencils are very common, a fairly ordinary stationery item. Almost every kid has them. The box has a crescent moon that casts light over the sea beneath a yacht. Inside the small box are twelve pencils, sharpened perfectly like its advertisement. Even their names—vermilion, cobalt blue, burnt sienna, crimson lake—fill my heart to bursting. It's the first brand-new item I have ever owned. I feel so special, so loved, and so envied.

"Don't say anything," Māma says, motioning with her eyes, "or I'll be sorry I got them for you."

"Thank you, Mā, thank you! I'll be careful with them forever and ever!" I cheer. I hug Māma and go on to examine each pencil one more time.

I place the box in my school bag, so the pencils don't get jumbled up. I can't wait to show them off at school tomorrow. I have to be extra careful because these pencils will break if I drop them.

For six months, I never use any of my colored pencils. I carry them to and from school, all still in perfectly good condition, sharpened like when I first got them.

"How come you never use them?" Jennifer reprimands me when she finds them in my bag. "If you don't want to use them, then give them to me. So wasted!"

I'd better start coloring with them or else Jennifer will tell Māma as if I don't appreciate her. I develop an elaborate technique for using the pencils by coloring with only one side of the tip, so I don't wear down the entire pencil. This way, they can last a longer time. Unlike the set of colored pencils, my life is anything but orderly.

In the living room, piles of old newspapers that Māma collects from the junkyard next to our flat serve as side tables, not because they're intended as such but because there's nowhere else to set a glass of water. All the other surfaces are cluttered with broken trinkets, house-wares, electronics, or piles of clothing Māma hoards, and hopes will fit us someday. Māma saves most of these items to sell to the rummage man or peddler who comes around every two weeks. If she's lucky, she gets about two dollars.

To escape the mess and noise in the apartment, I retreat to the stairwell by the balcony. If I'm lucky, I find a spot on the stairs that is not stained with urine or alcohol spills and sit by myself, prolonging the moment when I have to go back inside.

At night, the fluorescent lights usually don't work, and I sit there in the dark praying that no crazy man will bother me. By night time, the stairs are already piled with heaps of refuse, and the stench of something rotten starts to corrupt the air.

The bigger nuisance is the plague of cats, rats, and flying roaches tearing up those mounds of garbage. I shove the night crawlers away by stomping my foot and giving the savage stare I have mastered over the years. At times, though, I stare right at these vagrant creatures, muse at the thought we're in the same predicament, and almost wish I was in their carefree state, far enough from all the woes and havoc. These stairwells become my sanctuary and refuge from the chaotic life a few feet away.

While avoiding the stray cats that look so sickly and pallid for scraps, I watch women carrying bags of laundry or groceries and prodding small children to climb the stairs. The building has an elevator, but it's almost always broken so even getting the mail on the third floor is a task. I love the anticipation that comes with it until I realize they're bills, late ones, of course, in pink envelopes.

I watch men come and go on their way to the prostitute who is our neighbor. These men are easy to pick out. They keep their heads down and their hands in their pockets, moving quickly, hoping no one will spot them.

Sometimes, I go to the hallway outside our flat to arrange the slippers, even the ones outside my neighbor's front door. For most of my childhood, little acts like these are how I assume some order in my world, even if it's temporary.

Once when arranging the footwear, I realize to my horror that one of my red slippers is missing. This is one of the many pairs Māma found in the street. I only had them for a couple of days and loved the polka dot design.

"Who steals one slipper?" I sob. "Why steal one and leave the other? Now no one can wear one slipper."

I decide to give prayer a try. "God, please help the person who took my slipper to be kind and return it to me. I promise I won't ask for anything else."

For three days, I go to every door on the entire block, searching at every doorstep and peeking through windows to find my slipper.

"It's gone. Forget it," Māma tries to console. "I found them on the street; they were free anyway. I'll find another one tomorrow. People throw things away even when they're in good condition. That's when I get lucky."

The mysterious slipper never resurfaces, and before long I give up looking.

It isn't just physical clutter that defines my home life but the clutter of emotions and anticipation. In one breath, Māma wails about how Bàba is in the bedroom with the prostitutes, but the next moment she complains, matter-of-factly, that she can't finish all her chores while he's occupied in the bedroom.

Sometimes, I walk in to find her humming in the kitchen as she makes curry puffs to sell, but five minutes later, she's weeping over the sewing machine. I don't know what to make of all this spontaneity. Is Māma going mad?

"Don't turn out to be like your Bàba. Good for nothing," she says, "He only knows how to drink, gamble and womanize, and then he leaves us all to suffer. Without me, you'd all be dead. I'm the only one giving you a life."

"Yes, Māma, I know," I say.

I can't imagine ever being like Bàba, though when he's in a good mood, it's almost better to be like him than like her.

Bàba tells about the three little pigs and the funny snorts he makes. Each time he wiggles his nose, Jennifer and I jump into unstoppable hysteria. He tells us about the beat-up cars he drives home from the second-hand shop and the tips he made selling the red Mazda with the fender dented. He boasts about the gold Mercedes with the coughing, raspy engine that's worth SIN$7,000 or $8,000 if he can get it to run properly again.

If Bàba sells a car for any amount, that means we're in for a major treat. He'd take us to the hawker stalls, and we would order whatever we want. We scoop from each other's plate to see who has the tastiest dish, laughing and teasing one another's choice.

From time to time, Bàba takes us for a drive to the airport, even at one or two in the morning. We walk around and browse through the closed stores, looking at the window displays that we can never afford. My favorite part is savoring the ambience of serenity and stillness as I hear the airplanes take off and land periodically.

I never get to sit in the front seat of the car because boys get the first choice. I'm fine with being at the back with the wind blowing through my hair. The pungent smell of salt fills the air as we pass by the East Coast Beach. Maybe Bàba will be in a good mood this weekend and take us there.

In the rare event that Bàba makes $100 (US$70) that week, he'd bring us to East Coast Beach for a succulent outdoor seafood barbecue. I love the chili crabs, and the large shrimp soaked in peppery lemon, but I hate to dirty my fingers. Jennifer spoils me by peeling the shrimps so I can eat them with a fork instead. She even scrapes the crabmeat on a plate, so I don't have to crack it with a mallet.

"You have to eat it the right way," Bàba says; "otherwise, you can't get the real taste. Suck the juice out first then lick your garlicky fingers."

Jennifer and I ignore him and continue giggling. Funny how days like this never happen twice in a row. By the next night, Bàba is drunk again, as if to make up for his sober state the day before. This time, he comes home with his pants half down, naked, staggering in from the parking lot. Māma hurries me to go downstairs and pick him up before anyone sees him.

"Get his pants on, quick!" Māma yells. "Pull up his pants, drag him upstairs!"

"How can I? He's so heavy," I revolt, refusing to move out of my hiding place.

Bàba is a heavier man now with his drinking habit, and he has a bigger beer belly.

"Why me? You always ask me," I revile. "Ask the boys for once."

"You know Phillip won't go. Winston maybe," Māma beseeches. "They're boys, and it's too embarrassing for men to be seen doing this kind of thing."

Still, no one will go.

I drag my feet down the first flight of stairs, but Winston runs up behind me, thank goodness, "Let's go get Bàba."

I kneel by the drain and try to zip up Bàba's pants, but he pushes me away.

"Leave me alone, you idiot child. I have to pee some more."

When he's finally done spraying all over the grass, Bàba wraps his arms around me so tightly that I can barely breathe. I thought he was ready, but he starts to pee again. This time, the pee splatters all over my legs.

"Oh, Bàba!" I protest. "See what you did?"

I don't know why I bother to reason with him because tomorrow he won't remember a thing. He screams vulgarities at the top of his lungs.

"What do you know about being pissed on? I work all day, providing you with food, and you complain about a little of your Bàba's pee on you? I'll pee on you some more. Huh?" He yells more obscenities in different dialects which the whole neighborhood can hear. "Whose useless child are you anyway?"

He turns and sprays himself all over me to teach me a lesson. I drip all the way up the stairs, lugging him up the flights with Winston.

We reach our fourth-floor apartment, avoiding the lift altogether in case we bump into someone familiar, or anyone. I can see passersby staring at us with their intolerant eyes and pinching their noses.

"Get him up quickly before the neighbors see him!" Māma yells from the top of the stairs.

As soon as Winston and I lay Bàba on the bed, Māma grabs a cane and hits us.

"Why, why are you hitting me?" I squawk, "I didn't do anything wrong. I brought Bàba upstairs like you asked! Look, I even zipped his pants."

It's almost a hide-and-seek game in the midst of an already chaotic scene. Māma grabs hold of my arms and legs and refuses to let go. She starts hitting me vigorously.

"You are dripping pee all over the floor, and I just mopped the place," Māma is upset, but it's not because I'm soaked in pee.

"Bà is irresponsible and did this to me. If I'm suffering, everyone has to suffer, too. What else are children good for? Who am I supposed to take out my anger on? Huh? Tell me, huh?" Māma bellows as she strikes me over and over. She finally grows tired. "Stand up now, Ah Hong. Go put your Bàba to sleep. I need to clean up this pee all over the floor."

I loathe lying down with Bàba when he's drunk like that. Māma wants me to caress him, so when he feels the goosebumps, it'll soothe him to sleep. As soon as I lie down, Bàba rolls over and puts his entire body on top of me. He's so heavy, he's squashing me, but I don't have enough strength to push him off.

"Get off of me, you're so heavy. Get off of me," I say as softly as possible hoping Māma won't hear me, but she did.

"Be quiet, don't wake him up," she warns and slaps me on my head. "Just let him lie on top of you. What's wrong with that? He falls asleep faster if he thinks you're me. Just let him touch you or do whatever he wants, then he'll go to sleep faster. I still have to wash his pants and mop the floor."

Jennifer and Phillip sheepishly crawl out from underneath the bed and sneak into their bunk bed without Māma noticing. I'm terrified of what Bàba is going to do because he thinks I'm Māma and his hands start to go all over me. While his alcoholic breath is smothering my lifeless body, his saliva drool is choking into my throat. I try to hold my breath, but that makes my heart pound even faster. There is no way out this time.

"Mā, Mā … please come!" I beg.

An hour later, Māma is done with her cleaning and reaches over to pull me out. I roll out from beneath Bàba and crawl under the bed, wailing.

"What are you doing?" Māma whispers in disbelief. "Get out from under the bed and stop sobbing. You are waking him up. What's there to cry about? Get out."

"Where should I sleep tonight?" I plead.

"I don't care. Go outside and sleep anywhere, with Winston," Māma hisses, motioning for me to leave.

"That's what men do," she gibes with overt irritability. "We, as women, have to do whatever men want. Stop thinking you're so important. You're just a woman. It's just the body they want; not you."

I feel betrayed. Why doesn't Māma hear me? Why doesn't she stop Bàba from touching me? Why does Māma allow that to happen to her own daughter? I resent the notion that I'm just a child, too young to know anything, or that I'm just a woman, worthless and irrelevant. I resent that, as a mother, she never shields me from harm, but instead, throws me into the lion's den to be shredded into pieces by the savage animal.

I feel violated, but how can I blame her for something she never understood?

Part Two
CABBAGE HEAD

Chapter 6
BACK ROW

There is nothing in a caterpillar that tells you it's going to be a butterfly.

☙ Buckminster Fuller

*M*āma drags me down the street in a frantic rush across town to deliver an evening gown she has sewn all through the night by candlelight. As we hop on the bus, the smell of perspiration suffocates me. Sticky arms and elbows rub against my shoulders and sides. The armpit stench of the bearded middle-age man makes me feel nauseous and light-headed. The noise on the street aggravates my motion sickness. I taste the vomit sprouting from my throat. This isn't going to be pretty.

"Mā, I have to get off the bus now! Now, Mā! I'm going to throw up!"

"Few more stops, swallow your saliva. Can't afford another fare." Māma tries to stabilize herself as the bus makes a sharp turn around Newton circle.

Māma is preoccupied with clasping the bag of clothing in one arm while holding tight to the handle with the other hand. She's adamant about not getting off the bus no matter what.

"Six more stops. Hold your vomit. Don't embarrass me," Māma whispers.

Five more stops.

Four more stops.

Almost there, hold on. Don't throw up.

Bus rides are hard on me because of the uneven terrain and bouncy movement, even if it's a slight jerk.

As the bus passes a busy area of food stalls, I smell the satay meat grilling. Singapore satay is the best in the world. The aroma is irresistible and overpowering, almost altering my nauseated state.

I stay up late into the night watching the middle-aged woman downstairs from our flat grilling stick after stick of skewered, seasoned meat, wishing I could have one. As the fat drips onto the burning charcoal, the sizzling sound amplifies like a hot plate of chicken fajitas. Back on the bus, my mind starts to wander, and my motion sickness begins to dissipate.

One last stop. Finally, we get off. I run to the closest drain, bend my head over, and squat down to face the moldy and insect infested acrid drain. Nothing came out, but I feel my stomach churning. My mouth is parched, and the heat is unbearable.

Ignoring my washed-out face, Māma says, "Be sure to greet Auntie politely and be quiet. If you open your mouth, people will know you're a cabbage head. Just don't talk."

As we dash through the multitudes of yelling people at the coffee shops, I whirl around and notice a vegetable vendor across the street. Piled high to the top of the giant woven container are, what else—cabbages. I still can't quite figure out what Māma means by that term. My head doesn't look anything like a cabbage, though it does resemble a brain somewhat.

Not long afterward I learned that this is a lingo for saying someone's head is hollow and incapable of thinking because the brain is missing.

I was right about the cabbage looking like a brain, but I don't know why Māma would call me that. I'm not sure if I should get upset or accept the fact that Māma knows me best.

❧

In Singapore, all students are required to wear white shoes to school, totally white—no brand names, no markings, and no labels. Those white shoes have to be kept clean at all times, even after playing in the muddy field during recess. I have nightmares about getting caned by the disciplinary master because my shoes aren't polished. My classmates get around the problem by having two pairs of shoes and wearing them on alternate days, so there's time to wash and dry one pair. Since I have only one pair, it's almost impossible to keep them clean all the time.

To avoid being caught, I steal a piece of white chalk and keep it in my bag. When no one is watching, I rub the chalk on the dirty spots and then tap off the extra dust. It doesn't always work, but my shoes look good enough to deceive the disciplinary master from afar. These scuff marks resemble my own self-deception, how I try to cover up my flaws so that no one will notice me or my stupidity.

Māma doesn't have any expectations for us, and certainly not for me. She never asks what I don't do well in school, why I resist my teachers, or why I don't do my homework. She doesn't encourage or utter anything

praiseworthy about school. All I hear is, "Study harder …
You're so lazy … Push yourself … This is all your fault!"

Hearing teachers after teachers reinforce what
Māma says about my cabbage-skull further dampens me.

"Will you ever do anything right, Bar bar la?"

"Why are you so stupid?"

"Can't you learn anything at all?"

These rumbling voices echo in my head. I can't
erase them no matter how hard I try. If anything, the
harder I try to inhibit the voices, the louder they play in my
head. It takes too much effort to get rid of these ramblings,
so the only thing left to do is to accept them.

*I'm slow. I'm stupid. I'm incapable of anything, like a head
of cabbage.*

School is mostly a blur. All day long, I hear teachers
hashing out how they're going to deal with me, like a
contagion, spreading dysfunctional learning diseases to
everyone. Teachers treat me the same way. In their eyes, I
don't stand a chance.

In kindergarten, being caned every day is an
expected discipline. I am caned for the most minute
incidents—not sitting straight up, not writing in a straight
line, not taking my book out fast enough, not answering a
question fast enough, not copying from the board fast
enough. Everything is a constant rush to beat the clock. If I
don't do it at the same speed as everyone else, I'm
considered a rebel, and rebels have to be disciplined.

"Put out your hands," Mrs. Yee, a curly-haired
teacher in mismatched clothing orders. "You have no
discipline in studying. Tell your parents you need to be
caned more often so you will study harder. I'm caning you
for your own good. You'll thank me one day."

Through the grades, I learn that I can never do
anything right. I never know what the class rules are. Why
won't teachers put them on the board? Why can't they
teach me instead of reaching for the cane? Why do I have

to second-guess what the teachers want? I'm not a psychic. Why can't someone just tell me plainly step-by-step, so I don't go home sore each day?

The bamboo stick is long, about half a yard, one centimeter in diameter, raw, unshaven, with a hook that curves around at the end. The cane has its own uncanny temperament; you never know when it's in a good mood or a bad mood. Any little agitation could provoke its temper.

Sometimes, the cane is used so much that the end splits. When this happens, it hurts the most because when applied to the skin, a double stripe will tear the epidermis. If I get home with one of these third-degree stripes, I would hurry to the bedroom and put on a long-sleeved shirt so no one will notice the scars. I become quite good at covering my tracks.

This so-called pedagogical caning is mostly used on male students. Female students are sanctioned to community service most of the time. Caning on the palm is reserved for less serious infractions, whereas caning on the buttocks is for more serious violations. The government promotes caning to instill fear to those who are thinking of breaking any school rules and to make kids study harder.

"Barbara needs to be more disciplined," says one teacher.

"She's lazy. She must be punished so she'll study more," says another.

"One more year will whip her into good shape for the real school," says a third.

In Singapore, if you're quiet, obedient, attentive, and in your seat at all times, you're a perfect student. Each day, the teacher reminds me I need to be more disciplined and to cultivate greater subservience. The role of the school is to ingrain in each of us the mindset that strict obedience to authority is the only sure way to succeed academically and in life.

Kindergarten teachers are among the harshest folks because that's the final stage of refinement before a child enters first grade. I feel as if I'm in a military boot camp my entire life, except I'm a one-recruit army training for the battlefield, fighting my very own war. I recognize it's a losing battle even before I began, but I don't know why I'm still fighting it.

At the beginning of kindergarten, I'm assigned to the back row. Mrs. Yee does not want me to steal attention from the other students who are actually capable of learning. Seated in the corner across the room, I am removed from everyone and everything except the windows. The sparrows distract me, the empty playground stimulates me, so do the swaying angsana trees. I can't hear a word anyone is saying because the vehicle noise is so overpowering.

Week after week, I sit in my corner, bored and uninvited to be part of the class. No one asks anything of me. No one expects anything of me. I'm a meandering shadow. I hate school. I hate teachers. I hate learning. I hate making friends. Nothing bothers me anymore. I simply stop trying. Kindergarten has managed to suck the native breath out of me. I'm angry with everyone, everything, even the pathetic look of the pencil. I hate every word associated with school. Even more, I hate myself.

One Saturday afternoon, when Jennifer and I came back from the playground, I'm bewildered to find Mrs. Yee, in our living room. In Singapore, it is not only unprofessional but practically unheard of for a teacher to visit a student's house.

"You're in trouble," Jennifer says. She grabs my arms and pulls me aside to conceal me.

"What happened? I didn't do anything wrong, or did I?" I try to convince myself I'm innocent, but self-doubt creeps into my mind.

Jennifer sneaks to the kitchen area to eavesdrop.

"Twenty-eight here. Forty-two, okay? Lift up your hand. How about this, loose enough?" Māma sweeps her hands skillfully as she measures Mrs. Yee, a taller than average lady with a skinny waist and long legs.

"Whew," I sigh—too soon. As I walk past the living room, I hear my name.

"Ba Bar la is such a naughty girl. She never does anything right, and she doesn't do any work. She's brainless, or is something wrong with her?"

Mrs. Yee starts to spin all sorts of stories about me. Māma nods her head in agreement, totally betraying her own daughter before she even asks me. Mrs. Yee knows I can hear every word since I'm clearly visible with my head sticking out from the sink area. Why does this not surprise me? It would be unusual if any teacher had anything nice to say about me.

I don't have the guts to speak out. I don't know why. Māma never stands up for me, especially not in front of a teacher. It's customary in the Asian culture to respect the teacher as always right. That's why they're so highly appraised and well paid.

Mrs. Yee continues to slaughter me with charges that aren't true, but I don't stand a chance in rebutting her.

"She bothers other children, makes stupid noises, and argues in class. She's so rude. Makes it hard for everyone else to learn. Why you don't cane her more?"

Māma groans under her breath and apologizes incessantly on my behalf. "Sorry, sorry, she's so disobedient." Her hands tremble as she continues to pin the hem of Mrs. Yee's silky dress, careful not to poke her.

"I'll be sure to straighten her out tonight. Sorry, sorry ..." Mā is on her knees as she takes another pin out between her lips to tighten the side seam.

Unable to take it anymore, I blurt out, "She doesn't speak English!" Māma turns and hisses at me, giving me that forewarning look of the caning coming. Defenseless, I submit to the kitchen.

"Ah, like mother, like daughter," Mrs. Yee mumbles impishly, but Māma and I hear her loud and clear.

"Barbara? What a strange name," Mrs. Yee says, finally turning to acknowledge me. "Where did you get a name like that? Who gave you such a weird name? I have never heard of anyone by that name before. It's like *Ba, Ba, Black Sheep, have you any wool* ... what does it even mean?"

She's right. I do have a strange name. When I go to the United States years later, it seems like everyone knows someone by that name, except they're a few generations older than me. I hate my name. It makes me feel ancient.

"Bàba gave me that name," I respond boldly. "He watches a lot of TV, and he likes this American singer called Barbra."

"Why would he name you after an American? You can't even speak English," Mrs. Yee stabs me with more sarcasms. "It's not like you'll ever talk to white people?"

I restrain myself just as Jennifer pulls me into the bedroom to escape another verbal plight.

W. C. Fields, the American comedian, said it best: *"It ain't what they call you, it's what you answer to."*

Mrs. Yee continues her snide remarks, assuming Māma doesn't understand, but from the look on Māma's face, she can make out what Mrs. Yee is inferring. Even so, she keeps her silence, pinning and marking the fabric. I don't expect her to defend me, but she should at least say something nice about me. I'm not a bad child.

Unsurprising to anyone, I am detained in kindergarten for another year.

Through first grade, I flunk every subject, but somehow, I still get promoted to the next grade. I know Māma is disappointed seeing that she has done everything to keep me in school; staying up all night sewing to procure a brand new school uniform for me so that I may have a good start in school.

In second grade, I get a nicer teacher, or so I think. Mrs. Lin is soft-spoken, has a pretty smile, and has long, smooth hair, like me, which she wears in a ponytail. I try to make her like me by smiling a lot, but after the first week, Mrs. Lin confirms my greatest fear. For one, I can't write my Chinese name very well, at least not as neatly as Mrs. Lin would like the strokes to be. The characters are either too big or too small, slanting up or down. It's hard to keep every stroke straight.

Out of nowhere, I feel a stabbing pain in my back, so hard I see lights. I can't cringe, or I'll get slapped again, I know that much because I have seen her slap other students before. I stay frozen as if her palm is only a wave of a feather stroking my back. I sit with my face down, tears streaming down my cheeks and onto the tip of my chin.

"Suck up those tears!" Mrs. Lin orders. "If you can't even write your own name properly, what good are you? Useless! Mrs. Chang was right about you. You can't learn, and I don't know what to do with you in class,"

The burning sensation is growing on my back as if she just tattooed her palm on my skin. The boy seated next to me tries to look away. I can't write now; my fingers are tottering, about to fall off my wrist. Why can't I remember the next stroke? My mind is blank, and my hand feels numb. Did I forget how to write my own name? Oh, for goodness sake, I'm a hopeless case.

"How do I end up with a fool like you?" Mrs. Lin says, making sure the whole class hears her grousing about why she had to slap me.

School is an imprisonment for me. I'm terrified of leaving my house every morning because I'm so afraid of making mistakes and being hit by the teachers. I don't know how torturing me physically and psychologically will straighten my handwriting.

By now, every teacher has written me off, especially Mrs. Lin. I cannot get rid of what she says of me: "If you can't even write your own name, what good are you?" I keep running those words through my head, and each time I recollect that awful flame on my back, my lips quiver. Maybe it's my anxiety that's choking me, like being stuck in a traffic jam where no cars are moving no matter how loud the honks get. My brain is paralyzed. Nothing is sticking; everything is immobilized, frozen, and deactivated. Maybe that's why I deserve to be slapped so I can wake up to reality.

Mrs. Lin looks into my eyes. "Don't you understand what the words 'study hard' and 'pay attention' mean?"

I dare not answer for fear she might slap me again for talking back. These words don't make much sense at all. What is the formula for studying hard or paying attention? Is there a secret recipe, formula or equation? Everyone keeps repeating these same commands day in and day out, but no one explains how I'm supposed to *do* it. I don't know why I'm not getting it, whatever *it* means. I just don't get it, so I do the only thing I know how; I psych myself up by repeating in my head; *I must study more; I must work harder; I must pay more attention; I must be quieter*, as if repeating these affirmations will make a difference. The only therapeutic aspect of this practice is that it keeps me from feeling the pain from the whacks.

Today's schools forbid corporal punishment, thank goodness, but teachers and parents can still verbally and psychologically abuse children. The standard of academic success in Singapore is measured by only one (high) bar— one hundred percent, not ninety-nine or ninety-eight percent. Perfection is the expectation.

This scenario is all too typical for any child growing up in Singapore's education system.[2] School performance is

[2] Knight-Hassell, Elizabeth. "Kids Share About Stress in Singapore's Local Schools." December 19, 2014. Accessed August 6, 2016.

the crux of defining who you are, what you represent in your family, how others will regard you, and what your future will hold. The standard of perfection means getting *As*, never *Bs* or even *A minuses*. Anything less than an *A* is as good as failing.

Many folks believe that the only thing standing in the way of an impeccable *A* is the child's carelessness, laziness, and lack of motivation. Hence, the child either has to be inflicted with pain, or publicly humiliated in order to achieve the grades.

By now, my inadequacy is all too apparent. Māma is right. My brain must have been fried when she tried to get rid of me. I believe it. I'm not going to amount to anything. After all, what can I expect from being an unwanted, poisoned fetus?

I become my own worst enemy, fulfilling the prophecies as foretold by my teachers and Māma. I don't know why I bother to try when I can never do anything right. It's genetic, and I can't change the way I am born. I just have to learn to live with it. Trying is just too painful.

I think about asking Mrs. Lin what's wrong with me, but I'm not sure I want to hear the answer. What if I find out? What difference would that make? Would teachers treat me differently? I need to face the possibility that I cannot learn.

"Sit still," Mrs. Lin reminds me, this time with a little more sympathy. "If you can manage to sit still, then you might pass this year."

I decide to give that a try. I sit on my hands. That way I won't move. I stare straight at the board to try and persuade Mrs. Lin that I'm making a serious effort.

It has been four years of schooling now, including two years of kindergarten, and I hate every second of it. I don't know if sitting on my hands works, but the day I finish second grade, I'm so relieved. I don't know how I stumble through these school days. I want so badly for one teacher to say something nice about me, so I can go home with something positive to report to Māma.

In third grade, I'm more lost. There are too many instructions, and everything sounds like a high-speed train. The one thing I have learned to do is to tuck my hands under the table when Mrs. Yong is talking. I don't raise my hand to ask any question. She's going way too fast. I can't catch what she's saying. I don't know how to make my ears and brain follow the speed of her mouth.

What the heck does she want?
Does she want this done in class or at home?
Does she want the odd or even questions done?

I stare at my book so hard that my head begins to spin. I peer out the window, distracted by the noise of the passing cars. I can't make out what Mrs. Yong wants. Why won't she scribble something on the board instead of verbalizing all these instructions? Everyone seems to know how to get on the right task, except me.

I scurry out of my seat to check out what my classmates are doing without getting caught. I still don't know what the assignment is, so I pretend to be preoccupied; looking around my desk or inside my backpack, sharpening my pencil, taking a sip of water, erasing something from my notebook, usually a blank page, or flipping the pages. I would do everything to show I'm doing something, so I don't look stupid.

Wait a minute, why does everyone have a partner? Am I supposed to have a partner, too? Well, it's too late; everyone is already paired up. I don't expect anyone to pick me anyway. I work alone. The last one picked; first one picked on, this is the story of my life. That's how I spend my year in third grade, constantly playing catch up and peeping over other students' shoulders.

Learning boils down to one objective—grades and nothing else. It has little to do with me as a learner. Even if I have a legitimate question, I constrain myself rather than risk being humiliated. Raising my hand connotes I'm either not paying attention or I'm being disrespectful for interrupting the teacher. If I miss what the teacher says, it must be my fault. Asking questions could reveal to my classmates that I'm not very smart, and that's the last impression I want to leave.

"Stupid homework. Stupid school. Stupid teachers!" I exclaim as I cross my legs on the kitchen floor, trying to figure out what is it I'm supposed to do for homework. There is no other space to study except the two square feet standing spot below the sink.

"Don't talk about your teacher like that," Māma chastises. "If the teacher is angry, it must be something you did wrong. Teachers won't scold students for nothing."

In fourth grade, something different happens. For the first time, I'm not assigned to the back row. Mrs. Liang places me next to a girl named, Pearl. She's the teacher's pet, I can tell. She never gets into trouble, always does everything right, is the first to finish any task, and is polite and articulate. I wish I could be half as likable as Pearl.

Even in fourth grade, I have a hard time figuring out the routines. Everything feels like a spur-of-the-moment—rushed, abrupt, and improvised. Maybe my entire class has a super psychic power to predict what Mrs. Liang is going to ask us to do, except me. I must have missed the day she sprinkled magical powder on students.

Surreptitiously, I pick up the habit of being a copycat. If Pearl takes out her jotter book, I'd take out mine. If Pearl flips to a certain page in her math book, I'd do the same. I imitate the way she organizes her desk—pencil case on the front, water bottle on the left, and pencil sharpener to the right. Pearl knows I'm copying her, but she doesn't mind.

Miraculously, within a few weeks, I begin to catch up with the class and am following along. Mrs. Liang doesn't pick on me as much as before and allows me to participate on a few occasions like erasing the board and collecting homework. I think I'm learning how to be part of the class and being accepted by my classmates.

In the jotter book, Mrs. Liang asks me to write 100, sometimes 500 times, *I will study harder … I will pay more attention … I will work harder … I will not be lazy … I will do my homework …* I have to complete these by the next day, or I'll be punished even more.

The paradox of such exercise is that it takes up all the time from actually doing the work I'm supposed to do. As predicted, I can't finish my homework by the next day, and this punitive cycle continues all over again. I try to explain to Mrs. Liang, but it only aggravates her further and reaffirms that I'm lazy.

Fourth grade is one of the hardest years in primary school because I have not developed fluency in reading yet. The tactic most teachers believe to be effective in getting kids to read well is by calling upon them to read in front of the whole class.

"Reading aloud will make you read better," Mrs. Liang says as she motions for me to come forward. "The more embarrassed you feel, the more motivated you'll be to read."

"This st-o-ry … the vi-lll-aag-e … some pee-peo-ple … out of the … woods …" I stammer and then freeze and stammer some more.

"VILLLL-AGE, say VILL-AGE. LOUDER, are you a retard? Read. Read!" Mrs. Liang interrupts me to enunciate the words. "Say PEEEE-PEEEE-PLE. Faster."

I don't know if she realizes this but shouting only makes me more nervous and being nervous makes my brain choke. I can't think straight when someone is yelling at me.

The class dares not crack up; otherwise, they might get called up to read like me, but I can tell from their looks what they think of me.

She must be stupid.
What's wrong with her?
Is she retarded or what?
If she can't read by now, she's never goin' to learn to read.

After what feels like hours of emotional torture, I finally walk back to my seat. Humiliated and demoralized, I feel like I've just been stripped naked in the middle of New York Times Square. I sit down and put my head on my desk, careful not to make eye contact with anyone.

I detest school more and more each day. Every period feels like I'm in a maze, trying to figure out how to get out of the mysterious and convoluted hodgepodge, alive.

My reading suffers even more. I avoid anything with a hint of the English alphabet—newspapers, cartoons, signposts, posters, magazines. Whether it's history, Chinese, or English, Mrs. Liang would ask me to read aloud in front of the whole class. By now, my classmates are used to it and would volunteer my name even before the teacher asks.

"Barbara, have Barbara read!" one boy shouts. His reading isn't that great either, but if Mrs. Liang picks me, then he'll be spared. I drag my feet to the front of the class, but Mrs. Liang stops me.

"Don't need to leave your seat."

What? Maybe she's going to change her mind today.

"You can stand on your chair and read. And if you don't read well, you'll stand on the table to read, announcing to the whole world how retarded you are," Mrs. Liang is not smiling, neither am I.

This is so embarrassing, but I don't have a choice. The teacher is in charge. By mid-year, I can't catch up anymore. I don't understand what the teacher is saying. History is a mystery. Art is havoc. Science is madness. No subject appeals to me. Even my mother tongue, Chinese, is alien to me.

As the year flies by, I read less and less, which only compounds the problem. In just four years of elementary school, I manage to flunk every subject. The only thing I don't fail is to live up to the prophecy that I am an idiot.

School is a spine-chilling, blood-curdling, sinister place to be. There is nothing rewarding or exciting about it. A cold-hearted, punitive institution sets out to torment kids like me.

Make no mistake; schooling in Singapore is not a luxurious undertaking but a drudgery. The key to passing, I have been told, is to comply with the regiments of drill, rote, and mechanical output. The more verbatim students can regurgitate, the better the results will be. Teachers are the knowledge powerhouses to be regarded with fear and trembling.

They are *never* wrong.

Chapter 7
A BREAK

We do not remember days; we remember moments.

❧ Cesare Pavese

*M*y primary school, unlike the Methodist Girls' School, is not exactly a top-notch establishment. It exists primarily to serve the local poor neighborhood. Our disciplinary master, Mr. Mah, is a stocky, broad shoulder man with obvious dark circles under his droopy eyes. He walks around with a bamboo cane in one hand as he surveys the hallway. He likes to stroll through each classroom, unannounced, to monitor students' uniforms and behavior.

If we see Mr. Mah from a distance or hear him coming down the hallway, we have to sit up, remain uncomfortably still, and make ourselves as inconspicuous as possible. We are on our best behavior when we pass by him at the stairways, in the canteen, by the toilets, at the carpark, or in the assembly hall. Students believe he has eyes in the back of his head. Everyone, even the most deviant kids, is afraid of him. We think even the principal is terrified of him.

Mr. Mah oversees all the student prefects—that old British magisterial monitor, disciplinarian, or guard. Prefects are the smartest, most disciplined, and well-behaved students.

One afternoon after recess, while Mrs. Liang is teaching math, Mr. Mah enters our class, unannounced.

"Sit up. Be quiet," Mr. Mah demands. He whispers to Mrs. Liang, and then she turns to address the class. "Mr. Mah is here to select next year's new prefect."

He walks down each aisle, inspecting our faces up close, then our uniforms and our shoes, and looks up again to see if we're following his eyes. He stares closer into some faces and glances past others. When he gets to my row, I try to enlarge my eyes to look more serious and bolder. I hope he doesn't see the thick chalk-patches I just colored on my shoes. I want to impress him, for some reason, so I sit up straight to make myself look taller and hold a pen to my mouth as if I'm in some sort of deep-thinking mode.

He strolls through each row and then points and says, "You ... you ... and ... you."

Me? Like ME?

Did I mistaken the general direction where his finger was pointing?

"Me? I point to my nose to double-check with Mrs. Liang.

"Yes, you, Barbara," Mrs. Liang confirms.

"All of you meet me in my office after school," Mr. Mah directs as he walks out of the class with both hands clasped behind his back.

I can't believe it! He chose me! Of all people! It's the first time I have been selected for something positive. I'm on cloud nine. I turn to my left and to my right to see how everyone reacts. A hundred thoughts rush through my mind. I bet no one saw that coming.

My life is going to be different from now onward. I'm going to get a little respect. Perchance I'll get a little smarter, too, as the other prefects rub off on me. Everyone will want to be on my good side now. Maybe I'll make a few friends too.

"Get back to class, Barbara, dreaming's over," Mrs. Liang snaps me back to reality, which means solving long division. Suddenly, I am hopeful about liking school.

ෙෙ

A popular childhood game we play is called *chapteh*. It is made up of a round rubber sole, one-inch in diameter, which has a one-inch nail sticking out of it. Three or four colorful feathers are wrapped around the nail to hold it tight. This creates a weighted shuttlecock that bounces in the air when kicked with the flat side of your foot.

The object is to see who can get the most kicks without letting the chapteh touch the ground. Many of my schoolmates are adept at playing it. I'm not coordinated and have poor gross motor skills. I can't kick the piece up in the air and react fast enough. I watch my classmates play chapteh while I stand on the side.

Kids my age seem to learn everything as they are supposed to, half the time, and effortlessly. I can't even figure out the simplest game. I can't ride a bike, play checkers or badminton, and I definitely can't skip rope. The rope is made of rubber bands strung together, usually six-feet long. I can't even make it to ten seconds before entangling my shoes with the jump rope.

When it comes to riding a bicycle, I'm even clumsier. It takes years for me to learn how to balance myself. Since my family has only one rusty-red BMX bike, and Phillip is the one who found it in the trash, the rest of us didn't get much use out of it. We have to cajole him before he lets us on it for three minutes at the most.

As a prefect now, I have shorter recess. I have to get to my designated station and carry out my duties before the others finish their lunch. My role changes from week to week. These roles include monitoring the cafeteria to make sure plates are returned to the stall after students finish eating; observing students play by the rules in the field; checking students' uniforms, badges, and shoes to make sure they're neat and in standard; and guarding hallways to maintain noise level and prevent loitering.

When it comes to observing school rules, a prefect stands and watches like a hawk even as students kick the ball or play jump rope. If someone causes any trouble; however minor, I have to write them up for Mr. Mah to inspect. It's the equivalent of zero tolerance in the US schools. So, instead of making more friends, like I thought, I make more enemies.

On days when I don't have prefect duties, I squat by the drain and stare into the filthy water. Pearl usually finds me and sits next to me for a chat. She doesn't mind her skirt getting dirty at all. She's the nicest person to me in school, or anywhere.

Pearl has a fascination with the Nancy Drew series. When we're sitting by the drain, she starts to relate a mystery, thinking I must be familiar with the popular books. I don't understand a single thing she says, but I can't bear to interrupt her, and I don't want her to leave.

I was never exposed to any pop stories or books, let alone a popular collection. Pearl is the first person who has ever narrated a fictional tale to me. I have heard Bàba tell the story of the three little pigs, but that's about all I know. Since Māma can't read, we're stuck with the random days of Bàba's soberness for any good tale.

Teachers? They don't read or tell stories in school. Reading fictional classics or fairy tales is not part of the curriculum. We don't do sharing time or read-aloud. The only thing we read are textbooks.

As Pearl relates the mystery, I'm drawn to the young amateur sleuth. I have never heard of a female superhero before, so I warm up to Nancy Drew from the start. Pearl and I pretend we're sleuths solving a murder mystery. We give ourselves nicknames, too. Pearl is tomboyish so she calls herself Dean and I am Aletha, a name I saw in a movie once. I think it sounds intelligent and powerful.

Marching around the big school field, we find little pieces of random garbage and pretend they're forensic evidence worthy of further investigation. We analyze the specimens using the tip of the pencil while making up a spooky storyline as we exchange dialogues.

Mostly, we enjoy spending time with each other, I more than her. Those investigative moments never left me. I'm still hooked on Crime Scene Investigations, Forensic Files, 48-Hours Mystery, Unsolved Mystery, Snapped, and every investigative-type series the TV offers.

ॐॐ

In the cafeteria, there are about four or five food stalls. The first sells sugary drinks like rose syrup (carnation milk mix with artificial extracts of rose flavor) and imitation pineapple juice. On rare occasion, I treat myself to a cup of rose syrup concentrate for five cents if I have saved enough from weeks of pocket money.

The second stall sells my favorite kind of broad rice noodles. Although the smell tantalizes my taste buds, I can only afford the plain noodles with a little broth, no meat. I have seen students add a spring roll, a piece of luncheon meat, a couple of fish balls, or even a fried chicken wing. I can never afford any of those extras.

The third offers mixed rice with a choice of vegetables and other dishes like tofu, fish cake, luncheon meat, and bean sprouts. The fourth has local baked goods such as pastries, cakes, and buns. I love bread, but I never bought from this stall because I can't get filled.

The last stall is every child's favorite—snacks. I often wish I could afford one packet of the crunchy treat, but I never have enough to buy both food and snack. One tiny packet of chips is five cents, but even that's too much money. What few coins I have I usually spend on my favorite noodles.

It is also common for parents of primary age children to visit during recess and bring warm homemade lunches. Typically, moms pack a three-layered aluminum food warmer to preserve the fragrance and maintain the heat, each compartmentalized with soup, some fish porridge, and a vegetable side.

Māma never comes to see me during recess because she's busy sewing someone's gown or snipping threads on the name brand clothing. Besides, it would be hard to expect her to prepare warm lunches five days a week. However, once in second grade, Māma came.

That year, I had the chickenpox. A traditional belief is not to eat anything with preservatives; otherwise, my skin will discolor and the marks from the chickenpox will darken as scars permanently. She spent hours boiling special macaroni soup with strips of chicken to ensure it was purely organic. She placed it in one of the aluminum food warmers and brought it to recess.

Māma used to sell Tupperware® to develop her sales skills, but she never made it very far. She invested in several sample items to host a show although she didn't make it to the next level of the multi-level marketing. Māma likes being the center of attention and having people come to her for advice. Being associated with a brand like Tupperware® means she is running with the Western style and modern trend. Even so, in less than a year, she struggles to sell the sample wares. It was a failed venture, and we ended up with tons of containers around the house. Fortunately, these were samples, so she did not have to pay for any of them.

Once recess is over, we grab our toothbrushes and squat by the drain to brush our teeth.

"Brush for one minute," the teacher walks along the drain checking, "then rinse out three times."

I'm diligent in brushing my teeth just to avoid Nurse Loh, the school dentist. I don't think she's a real dentist, but more like an older lady with some experience in dental hygiene. We're all scared of her because we think she derives great pleasure from our suffering and uses torment to teach us about keeping our teeth clean.

"You're in pain because you don't brush," Nurse Loh announces. "This will teach you a good lesson! Next time you skip brushing, remember this pain!"

I try not to scream; otherwise, Nurse Loh will make it even more painful by twitching the instrument deeper into the gum. She doesn't use Novocain or warn students she's about to extract something. She just pries the tooth with her cold bare hands. Each trip to Nurse Loh's office is a lobotomy in my mouth, and I'd return to my class with a mouthful of bloody cotton gauze, drooling all day.

❧

In primary school, my uniform consists of a white shirt and a blue, pleated pinafore. The two-layered uniform feels very hot the first time I put it on, but I get used to it. Keeping it clean and pressed each day is a grind, made even harder in an apartment where everything is buried under piles of hoarded items and infested with rats and roaches. I don't know how Māma does it with the clothes she sews for her clients because these garments would leave the flat in pristine condition each time. I can't say the same for my school uniform.

Māma grows weary of ironing so she starts to starch it, heavily, to keep it wrinkle-free. It's like wearing a straitjacket filled with porcupines. After two or three days, the starch wears off, and the uniform is back to shabbiness, and the little pleats are out of place. She does not have time to hem the blouse or sew the holes under the armpit and sides, so I use safety pins to keep the pieces together.

My uniform doesn't fit properly either. It's either too tight or too loose, too short or too long, too stiff or too sloppy. Jennifer, on the other hand, is the object of my envy. Māma says she's the prettier one of her two daughters. With her natural appeal and fashion taste, she has a way of making her uniform impeccable, enough to blend in with the affluent girls at her parochial school.

Unlike modern Singapore, most people aren't well-off. Many are poor like us so the special things in school are often something very simple—the decorative book covers, popular stationery featuring Snoopy, Hello Kitty, or Sanrio, or cute socks with little woolen pompoms.

I see Jennifer get ready for school; her socks rolled up to meet her crisp-looking skirt, her books covered in heart-shaped glitter paper, her pencil case filled with Hello Kitty stationery. How did she find these school supplies?

The majority of kids who attend the Methodist Girls' School come from upper middle-class or very wealthy families. Those parents are doctors, lawyers, and businesspeople. Jennifer hangs out with a Eurasian girl, named Juliana. They befriended each other on the first day of school and have been best of friends ever since.

On most afternoons after school, they meet at a common spot and go for a bite. Juliana always pays for the treats. She dines out more often than not because her mother is not home to prepare meals. Sometimes, Juliana upgrades and brings us to a restaurant in a hotel.

These pricey places come with leather-bound menus that don't have prices next to the items. I wonder how much one of these delicious chocolate cakes costs.

The server slights the chair out to invite me to take my seat and places a white serviette on my lap. The air-conditioner is blowing directly above our table and I'm feeling rather chilly. I dare not move but am glad the serviette is covering my cold thigh.

Juliana never judges Jennifer and me as being *swah-ku*, literally "mountain tortoise," someone who is not well groomed or hasn't had exposure to contemporaries. This is the first time I'm formally introduced to Western decorum and social rules of conduct in a public place.

"Hold the knife with your right hand and the fork with your left," Juliana takes my palm and presses my index finger on top of the handle, then gracefully slices the hamburger in half. Unlike chopsticks, I never knew there was a standard of etiquette for holding a fork and a knife.

"What kind of white soup is this?" I ask, eyeing it suspiciously, fearing it looks too much like pig brain soup.

"It's cream of mushroom," Juliana explains, "it's my favorite, extra thick with lots of mushrooms."

I use a silver spoon to take a sip.

"Watch out, it's hot," Juliana cautions, but it's too late, I burned my tongue.

Juliana shows us how to chew without making noise like the way Bàba does, how to greet and thank the servers, how to excuse ourselves from the table to use the lavatory, how to rest our utensils parallel on the plate if we're not done eating, how to lay the serviette when we're done, and of course, how to tip the server.

For the first time, I feel like Cinderella, coming out of the closet into a new world of balls and gowns, teacups and servants, carriages and glass slippers. I feel elegant, classy, and pretentious.

Jennifer and I share a guilty smile.

Chapter 8
OUT OF TIME

The greater danger for most of us is not that our aim is too high and we miss it, but that it is too low and we reach it.

❧ Michelangelo

When I turn twelve, I begin keeping a journal, and I write diligently in it. There are also boxes of memorabilia—cards, bookmarks, and special notes I receive from anyone. The idea of keeping a journal comes by chance when some church leaders taught me how we talk to God. I'm eager to give it a try for two reasons.

First, I get to use stationery for something other than schoolwork. Second, I get to express myself freely. I think it's a novel way to occupy myself when I have no one to talk to. Sometimes, it's the only real *person* I can engage with, an invisible friend who never judges me.

January 27, 1982
Dear Journal,

    Today is my first time writing in a journal. This morning a very strong wind blew. When I opened the door, dust flew everywhere. Bà went to register his vehicle and to check the taxi. It didn't go well; he had to pay a lot of money.

    I came home and ate my dinner after that, rested, did my homework, wrote my times table, and finished my composition on "How I spent my June Holiday," which was generally boring.

    Early morning around 2 a.m., Bà came home drunk. Every time he goes to register his taxi, his buddies get him drunk. They're so bad. Wish Bà would see that. So sleepy, but now I can't sleep because Bà is screaming and waking the whole neighborhood up. Mà is going to ask me to get him to bed, again.

My journal is a glimpse into what my daily living is like. In the beginning, I address my entries as *Dear Journal,* as if the book itself is my closest confidant, alive and ready to listen to my lamenting woes and dull complaints. Later, I address them to God or Heavenly Father. Maybe God can't be concerned about my humdrum life, but I hope He at least stays with me while I'm writing to him.

April 13, 1982
Father in Heaven,

    If Mà scolds me because it is my fault, I'll accept it, but she scolds me for studying all day and night. She refuses to allow me to turn on the toilet light to study at night. She refuses to let me use the phone. I think she wants me to fail. She says I'm using too much of her precious money to study. Father, am I wrong to want to study?

May 13, 1982
Dear God:
    Why can't I be smarter? I'm willing to do anything
to be smart. I promise I'll work so much harder. I'm willing
to try. I'm willing to sacrifice. Just tell me what to do. I want
to do what's right. I want to be happy. Are you even listening?

School is a one-way learning street. If I decide to
stop at sixth grade, there'll be no going back. The problem
is I can't climb out of the bottomless pit. In my final year of
primary school, I'm barely passing the Cambridge exam.
My results are borderline, so I'm given the choice to either
take the *express stream*, which is the usual route of four years
in high school, or the *normal stream*, which is the extended
five years. I choose the latter, so I'll be able to pace myself.
    In competitive Singapore, even if a student passes
on record, being at the lowest rank is as good as failing. In
fact, being second is enough of a disgrace. Chinese tradition
maintains that in anything we do, we had better be aiming
for the stars. Anything earthly would be a waste of time.
    When it comes to academics, the East Asian world
is harshly unforgiving. Every student is aiming for the
pinnacle, and only one winner can be at the top. If you
score ninety-nine out of one hundred on a test, the focus
will be on the one point you missed rather than on the
ninety-nine points you have earned. This dog-eat-dog
world has inevitably created a cyclone of selfishness. No
one is looking out for you except yourself, sometimes, not
even your parents. You are your own greatest competitor.
    Back to the sixth grade, where I had just flunked,
everything looks bleak. What would I do if I were to stop
school now? I have to convince Bàba to let me continue. I
want to believe Māma wishes for me to do well in school,
too; instead, I hear her join voices with Bàba, grumbling
about how much I'm spending for school and how I'm not
producing any results.

I'm confused about how Māma feels about schooling. She ingrains in us the need to get an education so we will make a decent living, but she never has any expectations for us. The way she makes us study is by caning us. I don't know if that's to make her feel better about being a stern parent or to make us feel bad about not studying hard enough.

Bàba is no different.

"I am working so hard to feed this family, and there you are throwing my money down the drain," he lashes out. "Do you know what we can do with an extra three or five dollars a month? Do you have any idea how many bottles I can buy, huh? Haven't you seen how your brothers and sister do in school? You are from the same gene! You're just another piece of garbage!"

I want to reason with him, but I dare not speak or move. I need another chance. I feel guilty and selfish for putting myself before my family in getting what I want.

"You're a lost daughter," Aunt Debra, Bàba's younger sister, rebukes. "You have lost your filial piety. Why does a woman need so much education? Look at me; I live a good life with only a sixth-grade education. You're a shame to your family."

Easy for her to say. She has money piled to the sky, marrying a wealthy man and living in a mansion he built.

Aunt Debra is right about one thing; my siblings did sacrifice their education to contribute to the family. Phillip and Jennifer are the smarty pants. Me? I am wasting my time pursuing something I'm not even good at.

Winston drops out at seventh grade and starts working in a neighborhood factory, a hot, sweaty place where he picks up whatever menial jobs he can find. He's a talker but exceptionally gifted in drawing and painting. In sixth grade, he brought home the first prize in an art competition. Māma and Bàba were so proud of him and spent some good money to have it framed and hung prominently in the living room.

School is not his forte. Winston has a hard time moving up through the grades. He starts to lie, cheat, and steal and get into a lot of trouble at school. Māma's rationale is that he's retarded. I hear people call him stupid, dumb, idiot, lazy, liar, and a thief. Winston begins to live up to these labels and uses his deficiencies as an excuse for stealing, writing bad checks, and cheating on exams. By seventh grade, he's out of school.

He works at odd jobs, mostly in factories near our neighborhood and soon finds his niche in the computer sales industry, but it is short-lived. He has since moved to Hong Kong. It's been seventeen years since I last saw my brother.

Phillip quits at eleventh grade, even though he is the brightest of us all. Unlike me, he's an avid reader. English comes easy for him. He spends most of his waking hours at the local Toa Payoh Library. We can never afford books, so Phillip stays in the library until it closes.

He is quite the exploratory child, too. He enjoys anything he can take apart. We would climb through barbed wires and neighborhood dumpster to scavenger through piles of waste, hoping to find something of value to fix. Phillip could have continued in school, but instead finds himself quite apt in the advertising industry.

Jennifer, by eleventh grade, decides she wants to become a server at a posh, gleaming, five-star hotel—the Shangri La. Her job is considered the most stable and luxurious in the family. After a year, Jennifer got promoted to a supervisory position and brought home even more money. Bàba can't stop bragging about her.

"At least Jennifer is contributing to the family and has a real job," he says proudly. "What do you do except waste money on books and school."

It's true. With the hours she works and the wages she makes, Jennifer can buy almost anything she desires—elegant pumps, fashionable dress, colorful handbags, luxurious accessories, name brand watches—things I can only dream of. The only thing I wish she would buy for me is a little more time with her.

She works seven days a week, often past midnight until three in the morning. We hardly see each other. I miss the times we used to hold hands and lie in bed singing Chinese songs together. I envy Jennifer for all the attention she's getting, at home and from her male coworkers.

Money is never on my agenda. I can live frugally by skipping meals. I usually fill myself up by drinking tap water; lots of it. That's what Māma did. I can do the same. I have no problem wearing the same clothes, pants, and shoes over and over again. I think second-hand stuff is way groovier than name brand ones because they were once valued by someone, and now I get to own them. People may look at me with disdain because I'm wearing clothing that may be unsanitary or worn by mentally-ill strangers, that's what Māma says, but it doesn't bother me one bit.

కా×

All I ever wanted was to make Māma and Bàba proud, but I'm convicted even before I stand trial. If only Māma and Bàba could hear me screaming from within. Everything I do seems to be amiss. No one cares, and no one wants to care. No matter what I do, or don't do, I'm found guilty.

Dropping out at sixth grade seems premature. I want to be the first to finish high school. I want to be the first to bring honor to my family. I want to be the first at something, anything. What's so wrong about that?

"We're worried about you," relatives after relatives would not stop offering their presumptuous wisdom. "It's for your own good. Go and make some money. You need to put your family first before your education. We're trying to caution you before you turn out to be like your father."

I don't care. Call it arrogance or pride. I like being me—well, the rebellious side of me, that is. I detest being told what to do. I'm willing to be respectful, but I'm not willing to be manipulated, not even by my blood-related (or bloodsucking) relatives. What's wrong with pushing myself to the edge? If I die, I die trying. If I fail, I fail on my own terms. I'm not going to let some two-faced, simple minded hypocritical kindred tell me what I should or should not do. If I choose to ruin my life and waste my time, so be it.

Everywhere I turn, I find wolves in sheep's clothing waiting to entrap me or watch me fall prey to my pride. I don't know how to explain what I'm feeling to Māma or Bàba. I never tell them about the bombardment I'm getting from these relatives. I know I'm already a loser. That's not news to me. What I want now is to come into my own by myself, not because someone wants me to do it.

At night, when the voices inside me are calmer, I reflect on what everyone has said and wonder if these people are sent by God as my guardian angels, trying to prevent me from hurting myself and my family. Whenever Bàba or Māma brings up the subject of dropping out of school, my heart pounds and my palms grow damp. "What's wrong with you?" Bàba demands.

"Nothing and everything," I reply.

Maybe education isn't the answer. Maybe it is a problem. I refuse to drop out, that's why I'm struggling so much. I can't tell which is worse—suffering the mockery of being a dumb kid or being mocked by my relatives for being a bonehead. I can't talk to anyone except my journal. I don't know what I need to do, what I *can* do. I'm afraid, yet I want to be courageous. I'm running out of time.

I promise Bàba that if he allows me to continue to seventh grade, I'll study extra hard. I promise to drink everything that Māma brews and not fight with her.

"It's your own life. Do whatever you want," Bàba says, much to his chagrin, as he sits on the edge of the bed with his head hanging down, "You never listens to anyone anyway. Go to hell and do whatever you want!"

I brace myself against the uneven tides and prepare to venture into yet another phase of secondary schooling. The school I am admitted into is notorious for its gangsters and bullies, but I shouldn't complain. I should be so grateful that I even have a school to attend.

My seventh-grade teachers are no different from all the other teachers I had previously. Take Mrs. Lee, for example. She teaches math. She talks to herself while writing on the board. Our job is to copy everything she writes. That's it. There's no explanation, no examples, and no homework. She doesn't make eye contact, and if we utter even a word, she would turn her neck with her glasses halfway down her nose and squint her eyes to threaten us with that look of SHUT UP—OR ELSE!

Throughout the year, this is how I sit through all my classes. I have no study help, and it's not like my parents can teach me anything. How can I study hard if I don't know what to study? I either get busy work that doesn't do me any good or overwhelming work that makes me hate the subject even more. Homework is a joke.

Sometimes I hand in something, but most of the time I don't. Even if I hand in something, the teachers don't always check it, so I don't know how I'm doing. I go with my whim each day to pick up whatever fragment of knowledge I can. I want to show Bàba that I'm trying, but nothing is making sense.

On the office door is a large display glass which publicly exhibits our grades so everyone can see and compare. Our class placements are also in full sight. I never bother to check because I know I'm not going to be placed in the A, B or even C class. I'll be in the group reserved for the lowest ranked students—the D class.

"What does *D* mean?" the headmaster asks us during assembly the next morning. "I'll tell you what it means: It means you're not trying hard enough. You're lazy. You're not paying attention in class."

It's the same old lecture. It's always my fault. My laziness, my lack of motivation, and my stupidity. It's all me. Any effort I put in is a waste of time because I can't cure my innate deficiencies.

"How come this kind of results?" Bàba is angry again. "You said better results! Get the cane!"

I go through the motion of being beaten, as usual, fewer stripes this time though. Perhaps Bàba is getting tired. His hands shake more now that his drinking has escalated. Or, has he given up on me?

Māma brews even stronger, more bitter-tasting insecticidal soup to compensate for my intellect. I don't grumble or resist; it's the only thing I can do to please her now and escape another beating.

Teachers don't seem to be bothered with kids like me. They're there to handle the behavior of students more than to teach. It is quite clear that there's no sense of urgency about helping us to pass the exams. Whatever learning I get seems to float like a feather with no destination to land.

Yeats enlightens us with this: *"Education is not the filling of a pail, but the lighting of a fire."*

My teachers are not only dampening the faint light I'm trying to ignite but infiltrating my pail with holes. Either way, I'll be promoted next year by default, so I'll become another teacher's problem. Pearl got accepted into a top secondary school, so now I'm really on my own. The fire inside of me is not burning. I don't see a flame coming; I'm fading ….

Chapter 9
FREE SPIRIT

—⟨≈⟩—

The best and most beautiful things in the world cannot be
seen or even touched—they must be felt with the heart.
⟨≈⟩ *Helen Keller*

*T*hrough all the outward madness in my life,
sometimes, an inner ray of light sparks. On the
weekends, if things aren't too crazy, Māma takes us to
church. Bàba never comes, but he gives us a ride in his
black taxi to Kitchener Road. If things aren't going too well
at home, we simply skip church. On those days, Māma
lashes out at everyone but especially herself, pinching
herself, hitting herself, or tugging out handfuls of her hair.

"If only I had died long before any of you were
born, then none of you need to suffer like I do now."

I try to hug Māma, but she refuses to be consoled.
She wants to go to church. If anything, she wants to go to
as many churches as she can. It's the only place where she

can find some measure of tranquility and refuge in her world of turmoil and strife.

We go to the Methodist church, where Fat Granny is one of the endowment members. We also go to another church on a Friday or Saturday afternoon. Since I'm the least likely to resist, Māma picks me to go with her.

The sermon at the second church is unlike the Methodist church. It's not in English. I don't understand anything the old man in the long robe and headdress is saying. There are a lot of rituals and recitations at this church. The congregation is asked to get up, kneel down, get up again, kneel down, and so on. The old man then asks the congregation to walk up row by row from the pew, and he puts a wafer on their tongue with some common cup of water. I dare not try. I'm afraid if I violate some rites, I may be cast out. Everyone looks devout and pious, worshipful and earnest. Why can't I be like that at school?

A couple of men start swinging a box of incense on a chain which emits some smell that's hard for me to breathe. Thick smoke ascends into the ceiling and then settles gradually over the congregation.

"Why … why [choking] do we … [coughing] go to so many churches?" I ask.

Māma wraps her arm around me and whispers, "The more churches we go to, the more likely God will hear our prayers. It's like the more medicine you take, the more likely you'll get better." That's how Māma rationalizes her way out of anything she can't explain.

Praying feels rather hypocritical for me. I'm angry with God for not assigning me to a better family, so why would I pray to him? Why doesn't He love me enough to give me a decent home life? Why does He want me to be miserable? Why? I think God enjoys seeing me suffer. I can't see why that is called love or why he is God.

At the end of the one-hour mass, Māma and I cross the bridge across the busy road to catch the bus home.

Behind the bus stop is a Kentucky Fried Chicken stall. Once in a blue moon, if Māma has some extra change, she lets me get a small ice-cream sundae. It's the only thing I look forward to when I accompany her to this church.

Attending church never appeals to me. The rituals are touchy-feely, long-winded, and generally boring. The sermons at the Methodist church are in Hinghwa, a dialect spoken mostly in the Fujian province, occasionally mingled with Mandarin and a few English words. I wish I could say I understand what's going on, but I don't. For two hours, I stare at the enormous clock behind the pulpit, watching the minute hand move like the continental drift on Mars. The hymn singing is the most awakening part for me because I get to stand up and stretch my legs.

Churches are all the same—mechanical. Each week, I drag myself through two hours of preaching to make Māma happy. I don't feel rejuvenated or inspired. If anything, I feel exhausted and weary and wish the pastor was not so dead. I doubt God even notices me. To Him, I'm just a child fidgeting in the pew.

When I'm ten, Bàba's sister, Doreen, brings me to another church called the Mormons or Latter-Day Saints. I come to this church somewhat by accident.

Fat Granny is very ill, dying actually. She has lung cancer because of her heavy smoking. While the adults are planning the funeral, the children are creating havoc throughout the house—running, shouting, fighting, laughing, and arguing.

Maybe the children aren't particularly close to Fat Granny, or maybe we're just being children. Anyway, Aunty Doreen thinks we need a break and to get out of the house. Thank goodness, because a lot of mourners gather around Fat Granny's bedside, pouring their hearts out, perhaps hoping for a final hour claim to her inheritance.

Māma is in the kitchen cooking and mopping, as usual, and I don't know where Bàba is. I don't recall seeing him very much during Fat Granny's last days. This estranged relationship started when Bàba's gambling and drinking habits escalated, and she refused to pay his gambling debts.

One night, he crashed into her garage. Fat Granny and one of her daughters, who was living with her at that time, called the police and had him arrested.

After three prolonged weeks, Fat Granny is gone. Aunty Doreen continues to take all of our cousins and us to the Mormon Church. For the first time, I look forward to going to church because they speak English there! Winston and Phillip also attend regularly but not Jennifer. She's never too keen about spiritual matters and is always busy doing something with her friends, especially on Sundays. I still had to accompany Māma to the Catholic and Methodist churches, twice a week, because she said so.

The Mormons are exceptionally friendly and warm, if not always outgoing and openly affectionate. If I miss service on any given Sunday, different congregants send me missives by post saying they miss me, they care about me, and that they look forward to seeing me again. These words came in beautifully designed note cards, mostly handmade and mailed to me.

As a young girl, getting personal mail is beyond special. No one has ever said such words to me. I don't know whether to be surprised, leery, or touched. I savor each word and read them over and over again, then I place them in a shoe box with all my special memories.

No one has ever said they look forward to seeing me, not even my parents, and certainly not anyone from school. These Mormons make a deep impression on me. For the first time, people genuinely care about whether I show up or not.

At that age, I don't think about religion other than I like to find an escape, and the Mormon Church feels like it's the refuge and a haven. I decide to get baptized even though I was baptized in the Methodist Church four years earlier. It's not so much the religious conviction or beliefs that draw me to these people, but the way everyone makes me feel when I step foot into that church. I haven't made much of a distinction between the different sects.

At the Mormon Church, all I see is the goodness in this world—orderliness, kindness, love, companionship, harmony, and acceptance. I see families walking through the chapel door together. These families want to be with each other. Brothers and sisters are earnestly kind to each other. Husbands and wives are soft-spoken to one another. This surreal sense of completeness, wholesomeness, and benevolence is like heaven just sprinkled a dose of fairy dust on earth. I have never seen anything like this before. In my fragmented life, the Mormon Church is the one place I'm able to mend my wounds and heal my hurt.

There are a lot of white people in this church like those Hollywood movies. I can't figure out everything they're saying even though they're speaking in English. Their mouths move so fast, and they sound so eloquent. Something else is bizarre. Depending on the time of day and what shades of clothing they wear, their eyes change colors. The most beautiful part is their natural double eyelid.

Most Asians are born without the crease, so if you want the double eyelid, you have to undergo cosmetic surgery or apply temporary adhesive to bring out that crease. Asians consider infants born with a double eyelid to be the most beautiful feature of a baby. I was lucky that way because I was born with the double crease like Bàba. No one else in the family has them. Jennifer is always a little jealous that I got the best features of both Māma and Bàba.

These Mormon people are also peculiar in the way they greet each other. They're exceptionally polite. *Thank you, you're welcome, excuse me* are not phrases I'm familiar with in my household. The more I go to this church, the more

I'm hooked on the affectionate ambience. Before long, something else begins to grow on me—God. I see my existence as more purposeful. I become less angry with him and more accepting that maybe He has a purpose for me.

At fourteen, I am eligible to attend seminary. This is not a training for the ministry but an early morning scripture study course for youth ages fourteen to seventeen. The class starts at five forty-five in the morning so we can make it to school by half past seven.

Each school day I wake up at four to get ready. Since buses don't start running until six, church members volunteer to pick each of us up. My ride comes around four-thirty. Five, sometimes six, of us squeeze together in the car and doze off on each other's shoulders right as we get in until we arrive at the church.

About fifteen youth gather in the back building of the Bukit Timah chapel. Our cohort is the first early morning seminary group in Asia. Somehow, I feel responsible to be a good role model for the incoming freshman.

Early-morning seminary demands absolute self-discipline. On most mornings, I wake myself up, though on days when Bàba is just getting home from his midnight shift, he nudges me to get up. I like that better because I get to see the gentle side of Bàba that no one knows. I know he doesn't care about seminary. He just wants me to eat the freshly steamed BBQ buns he just bought from the market. I eat five or six at one time, so Bàba knows how much I appreciate him. We hardly speak during these early-morning encounters. Bàba just stands there and smokes his cigarette—calm, sober, and at peace with himself.

My siblings don't care about why I get up so early every weekday and Māma doesn't know what I do at church. All she knows is that I am in good hands.

On some days, though, the driver overslept, and I got nervous standing in the dark street all by myself. If after thirty minutes and he still didn't show up, I took the bus, since it was after six. No matter how late I was, I never missed a class. This was the first time in my life that I learned to commit myself to something and to give my whole heart to achieving a goal—100 percent attendance.

I don't know why seminary means so much to me, but the offering of daily breakfast is quite appealing. I can't deny that for a teenager who's used to the hunger of one sort or another, the thought of food makes it all the more appealing to get myself up.

Of all the members who bring us breakfast, one couple works more diligently than anyone else—Brother Tan and his wife, Hazel. While we're in class for forty-five minutes, they're in the kitchen stirring, boiling, heating, and setting the bowls and spoons, ready for us to dig in.

Brother Tan's specialty is Chinese porridge or *congee*, which has to be prepared the night before. This is not like the porridge served in the US or England; it's not cooked grains, though it is made with rice and tastes like grits. The porridge has to be simmered for hours before it can be eaten, a process similar to crockpot dishes.

Brother Tan's Cantonese style fish porridge is my favorite, full of savory slices of fresh cod, green onion, and Chinese cabbage, spiced with soy and sesame oil. He brings in the pot in the morning, warms it up, and then scoops the creamy, fragrant congee into small bowls to cool. A bowl of congee keeps me full all day at school. I'm in heaven.

I think about how long Brother Tan must spend laboring over what to cook for all these hungry teenagers. It's not only that I have a full belly before heading off to school, but I've never had anyone care enough to do such a thing for me. For the first time, I feel I'm worth their while.

"Oh captain, my captain!" Brother Richard Ang, the seminary teacher, stands on the table, and, in his roaring, husky vocal, reenacts the scene from *The Dead Poets Society*.

117

I don't understand what all the references or metaphors mean. Later, I learned that Walt Whitman wrote the poem following the death of Abraham Lincoln and that it was about grief and hope and the promise of a changed future.

Brother Ang wears little black glasses and has a slight tummy. He grows increasingly animated as he speaks, to the point where flecks of spit fly from his mouth. He's unlike any other teacher I know. From the first day of class, I'm intrigued by his mannerism, the way he talks, the way he asks questions, the way he responds to students, and the way he makes us feel by the end of class.

He's passionate about his job. He loves to teach. He loves to listen to our stories. He loves to help us develop our testimony about God, something I'm still doubtful about.

Brother Ang has lived in America, where he graduated from Brigham Young University in Provo, Utah. He's the most educated man I know. I can hardly imagine such a thing as going to the United States and earning a university degree. He must be so smart and brave to study with the Americans.

The atmosphere in seminary is different from any other learning environment I've known. Learning is fun, inspiring, and non-threatening. I want to pay attention so I can try to answer a question or two. I want to learn even though the subject matter is foreign to me. I enjoy being a part of the class even though I'm quite new to the church.

My heart is in my mouth when I raise my hand and respond to a question Brother Ang asks. I don't recall what I said, but I know I got it right.

Brother Ang smiles and says, "That's a good answer, carefully thought out."

Wow, to hear someone, especially a teacher, tell me that I gave a good answer is as rare as hen's teeth. This is unlike any reaction I have experienced before at school. I thought learning was a one-way street where only the teacher speaks. Whatever the reason, I made that deduction, all by myself. I actually understand what he is teaching!

Maybe the question was easy. Maybe Brother Ang was being nice. Maybe I got lucky. The reason doesn't matter because, for the first time, I have a sense of what learning feels like. I want to excel and not just survive. I should give myself a little more credit. Somewhere inside of me is a learning switch that just needs to be turned on.

Brother Ang's philosophy of life is about daring to be different, each of us daring to be who we are. We don't need to conform to anyone's expectations. Be bold. Speak out. Have an opinion. Be different.

Walt Disney said, *"The more you like yourself, the less you are like anyone else, which makes you unique."*

That's perhaps the greatest lesson Brother Ang teaches me. I am a worthwhile soul—worthy of attention, worthy to be heard, worthy to be taught, worthy to learn, worthy to be happy. Heading to school each morning after seminary with this sense of self-worth and affirmation made a world of difference for me. I still struggle academically, but I dissociate my failure from me as a person. Almost like a time machine, I leap out of the old dimension into a new era. I want to be someone who is free and unconstrained by my past. I want to find me.

During the four years of seminary, I focus on improving not only my self-confidence but also my spiritual relationship with God. I learn to set goals, count my blessings no matter how small they may be, and be of good cheer no matter how chaotic life is. I try to find a better side of me, and at the same time, find another side of me that I hope to become.

Socrates reminds us, *"To know thyself is the beginning of wisdom."*

I stop finding faults about my family and my teachers and start valuing each day as a time to get to know myself and be myself. What a refreshing time for a teenager to find her identity in this time amongst turbulence, uncertainties, and the shambles of life. For once, I feel free!

At my secondary school, things get worse each week. The chasm widens between how I'm perceived at church and how I'm perceived at school. I don't have any friends. Not a single person talks to me or wants to eat with me. At least in primary school, I had Pearl. When the word spreads that I'm a Mormon, I'm ostracized even more and ridiculed every day.

"Satan worshipper!"

"Cultist!"

"Devil!"

Whether I'm going to my class, down the hallway, in the restroom, or standing at the bus stop, students mock me. I don't even know them. What's worse, my math, science, and PE teachers join in the bullying, treating me as if I have leprosy, distancing themselves from me. Within a month, everyone has nicknamed me the cultist.

All I want to do is shun people, so I don't hear their insults, but how can I avoid them? I pretend their remarks are not aimed at me and try to brush them off as mere ignorance. Strangely, it works. I care less about what people are calling me. I know they want to provoke me, but I'm not going to let them.

Jimmy Dean said, *"I can't change the direction of the wind, but I can adjust my sails to reach my destination."*

I have to stand strong on my own. This is my chance to show what I'm made of, to break out of the mold and define who I am. I cannot change how the world looks at me, but I can control how I react to the world.

The last year of secondary school is tenth-grade, and it is the final turning point for me. My math teacher, Mr. Tan, targets me more than anyone else. My class is on the third and highest floor of the building. It is the administrator's logic that the weakest students should be placed, or rather contained, on the highest floor. That way we will learn what hard work means. Classes for the brightest students are held on the first floor so they don't have to expend so much energy climbing stairs; thus, allowing them to devote more time to studying.

Mr. Tan is assigned as our homeroom teacher. I find his mannerisms strange. When he talks, he hems and haws, pausing choppily, not certain what to say, as if looking for an answer to his own question. When he gets nervous, he cracks his knuckles, pushes up his oval-shaped framed glasses, mumbles something, and then looks at the ceiling and talks to himself.

From the first moment Mr. Tan steps into the class, we can tell he dislikes us. He resents being stuck with the worst students. He thinks he's too good to teach a bunch of losers. Naturally, my religion gives him the perfect platform to target me, of all the students.

"Why are you so dumb?" Mr. Tan threw that out at me.

I have been trying to figure that out all my life. I don't say this out loud, but I wish I could. I know he's trying to get a reaction out of me, but it's not a practice for Asian students to talk back to their teacher, so I do the only thing I can— keep my lips shut.

"If your God is real, He would help you be smarter, right? But he didn't, you're still failing math."

I figure out why Mr. Tan spends so much time picking on me. The more time he spends persecuting me, the less he has to teach. Soon, the whole class knows his ploy, but no one cares if he's not teaching anyway. At some point, I see in my classmate's eyes that they take pity on me, but no one dares to say anything.

I place the *Book of Mormon* on my desk while I get ready to pull out my math textbook. Almost instantaneously, Mr. Tan's eyes fall on it. He walks over and snatches it right up.

"What is this?" he asks, holding the book up for the whole class to see. I'm caught off-guard and trapped.

"What is this?" Mr. Tan asks again. "Is this what you spend your time reading? Is that why you're failing?"

He opens the book and holds it up, rifling through the delicate pages so roughly that he tears one out. As the page floats down to the floor, he tears out more pages and flings them at me.

He throws the book at me. It hits the floor; more pages fly out. I hold back my tears because I don't want him to detect defeat.

No one says anything. Everyone is waiting to see what I will do next.

I bend over and pick up my book and put it back in my bag. Mr. Tan tilts his head to see if my eyes are wet.

"This is not a battle worth fighting," I sigh prayerfully. I need to be in control, I want to be, even though I'm the child, and he's the adult.

I reshuffle the pages into their proper places, salvaging whatever I can while holding back my tears. God will be my judge.

Part Three
A NEW PAGE

Chapter 10
MY RAIN MAN

There came a time when the risk to remain tight in the bud was more painful than the risk it took to blossom.

⤳ Anaïs Nin

My journal entry in April 1986 is written to God. I ask God to help me find hope. I offer that, perhaps, this is the year when everything changes. The world would be different if prayers were answered that way. I wish I could tell you mine was. My prayers turn from pleading with God to let Bàba stop drinking to begging I'd make it through school.

Somehow, I stagger from one year to another and make it to tenth grade. Given my secondary school's reputation, it's common practice to move students up the grade even if we don't meet the minimum expectations. Except in tenth grade, something significant has to take place. That's when we take the second national exam called the *Cambridge General Certificate of Education–Ordinary Level (O-Level)*. This exam is jointly conducted by the University of Cambridge Local Examinations Syndicate, Singapore Ministry of Education, and the Singapore Examinations and Assessment Board. Teachers can no longer manipulate the grades since the exams are sent to the Cambridge International Examinations board in Britain for grading. If we pass, we'll move on to either a two-year junior college or a three-year pre-university program.

As the spring of my tenth-grade year rolls around and the air begins to warm and moisten on its way to becoming hot and steamy, I'm nearly finished with my secondary education. Tension builds. I should have expected what was about to happen. Why wouldn't I?

I get dressed in the morning and go to school at an appointed time to pick up my results. Students stand in long lines waiting to be handed their result slip.

My turn next.

One teacher hands me an envelope, and I dawdle over to the far corner of the cafeteria to be myself. My hands are shaking as I clumsily peel open the perforated portion. I knew it wasn't going to be good. I flunked every subject except religion, where I got an *A*.

Disgraceful. Hopelessly lamentable. I have squandered four years of my life!

"I knew she's never go'in' make it," Mr. Tan mouths to another teacher who also ridicules me for my beliefs. Their words echo all the way to my ears as I stand up to walk away, hiding the envelope under my shirt. I have been in the bottom quartile since kindergarten, but I have never failed this disgracefully before. I feel cheated of an education.

Call it indignation. I don't care. Teachers kept promoting me from one year to the next regardless of whether I understood the material or not. They didn't teach much of anything but expected me to pass. I know blaming the teachers is pointless. I can't turn back the clock. Standing in the hyper-emotional cafeteria, I'm completely numb while staring at the envelope. Time stands still while everything is still revolving. I force myself into another dimension while I gather my thoughts.

Barbara, Barbara Hong, Siew Swan Hong? I ask myself. The name I'm seeing doesn't make sense. Flipping the letter back and forth, I hope I have the wrong envelope. I pinch myself to see if I'm dreaming. Maybe this will all be over when I wake up. Maybe this is all a big joke.

Out of the blue, a cold hand brushes against me, and I'm brought back to consciousness. I recognize some classmates, a few of them look upset, but most of them appear to be accepting of their results. That's probably because they didn't expect anything different from another day in school. Teachers are walking past me and looking away as if I'm invisible, but I hear them loud and clear. They're not surprised at all. They don't even feel guilty. Maybe if they did their job once in a while, I wouldn't have failed so badly.

Rumors had it that our class did the worst; only two students passed. Half of them didn't even show up to collect their results. I guess that's how predictable we are.

I can't go home now. What am I going to do? I don't know how to face Māma and Bàba. I know I'm going to hear the same old censure, *I Told You So!* I gulp a breath and run down toward the athletic field.

Racing blindly across the field, I almost knock a boy to the ground. I find myself a quiet spot and sit in the shade of a majestic tembesu tree. I wrap my legs up close to my chin and curl into a fetal position, wishing I could shrink and disappear into thin air, and vaporize.

Black ants are crawling in the dirt around me. Maybe if I were an ant, I could be crushed to the ground, and no one would even notice. Tears gushing out from all sides of my eyes. *What do I do now?*

A hundred possibilities run through my head. The clouds are raining down on me nonstop. The whole world is caving in; I'm trapped in quicksand with no way to crawl out of this mess. This was my last chance, and I blew it.

"Barbara?"

I hear my name, but I keep my eyes on the ground. "What?" I sound muffled against my knees.

"Barbara, what are you doing?" the voice repeats.

"Leave me alone!"

I lift my head out of curiosity. It's Raymond; the name people can't stop talking about since we got our results. He's the only student who scored straight *As*. What does he want from me? Did he come here to gloat?

Raymond is always surrounded by admirers and stands out among everyone, both physically and academically. He's unusually tall and has this nonconforming hairdo that sticks up in the front. Girls think that gelled hair is so cool. I have seen him around the school, but since he's from the *A* class, it's unbecoming for me to interact with him.

I don't know Raymond at all. I don't care what he thinks of my tear-stained face. This is the first time we've ever spoken to each other.

"I didn't pass," I say with a descending voice, hoping it'll satisfy him and make him go away.

I'm waiting to be scorned again, but there's complete silence. I look up to check if he has walked away, but he's still standing there. I'm confused and irritated by his lack of emotion.

"Don't be too sad, you can repeat another year," he consoles.

"What?" I reply with my eyes dilated. "I'm never coming back to this stinking school! You want everyone to laugh at me? So ridiculous!"

"Why do you care what others think?" Raymond helps himself down next to me, folds his long legs and leans back against the wire fence. "What will you do if you stop school now?"

My tears spill down my face like a dam that has just broken. I taste the salty drops as they fall from my eyes. Why can't I stop crying?

"I don't know what to do," I'm overcome with emotions. "I can't go back to school. I can't go home. Bàba will beat me to death." I tumble over my words.

Raymond stares into the open field of boys playing ball and no words. I sob again, putting my face on my knees. I see my entire future flash before my eyes, all the way to a decade from now—snipping threads, selling puffs from door to door, serving tables—nothing favorable. I dare not picture myself as a dropout.

"Not everyone is as smart as you!" I roll my eyes and offer a fake smile. Now, I sound like Mr. Tan.

Raymond chuckles. "Get up, Barbara. Let's get out of here."

I reluctantly drag my feet and trail awkwardly behind him across the soccer field and back into the cafeteria. Some girls try to grab his hand, but he shrugs and waves and walks on by. He tries to shield me from the crowd like I'm the celebrity and he's my bodyguard, and we scurry away to the bus stop.

"What are we doing? Don't you have somewhere to go and celebrate?" I ask, breathing heavily after our escape from the paparazzi.

"There's a barbecue at East Coast Beach, but I can go later." Raymond says.

"Oh, you don't have to hang out with me, I'll be fine," I say in a quivering voice.

The popular kids typically organize a gathering by renting a chalet over the weekend, but I'm never included. I only hear about it after they return to school on Monday with all their most up-to-date gossips to spill.

"You're the superstar today. Everyone wants to celebrate with you. Don't waste your time with me."

"I thought we could go somewhere instead," Raymond says, ignoring my remarks.

I feel another urge to cry, but more than anything, I hate shedding tears in front of a boy. I have learned not to look weak in front of Bàba or my brothers.

"Come on," Raymond grabs my hand.

The bus is about to pull away from the curb. The driver motions for us to hurry or get out of the way. Raymond urges me onto the bus, sneaking down the aisle to the seats at the back. It's a good time of day to ride the bus because everyone is still at work, and it's not crowded. I hate to have people notice my puffy eyes or see me with a boy. I'm not used to this. I don't hang around with anyone, let alone a guy.

"I hate this school so why would I want to return to this horrible place for another year?"

"Barbara, don't stop at secondary four, it does you no good," Raymond whispers in my ear while still holding my hand. Why is he holding on to me? It's a strange, tingly sensation, but I like it.

I'm beginning to feel awkward. I have never been physical with a boy like this before and having a stranger hold my hand is a lot to take in. Normally, I'd have brushed him away because it's a natural defense I have with touch, but I don't seem to mind with Raymond. His palms are rough, calloused, and hard. I know it's because of his athletic training and the demands of weightlifting, long jumping, and high jumping. He's a star athlete in our school and has won many medals. I've seen him race on our school sports day, and, of course, he came in first. How does it feel to be number one, I wonder?

I'm feeling calmer now. Maybe it's his hand, or maybe it's his gruff voice. I can't figure out why Raymond is always so sure of himself. Why can't I be more like that?

He's sharp-witted, ever so quick to make a joke or respond to any remarks because he knows so much.

"Why shouldn't I drop out?" I ask bitterly. "You know I'm so … so … dumb," I struggle to admit. "People always say I'm stupid, and today I proved them right."

"Don't say that," Raymond sighs, believing there's more to school than just a piece of paper with letter grades.

Results day is a stressful day for everyone, especially for parents.

"Don't your parents want you to stay in school?" Raymond asks.

"Bàba, he … never mind."

I remove my hand from Raymond's and clench both hands in my lap. My book bag, which is under the seat, slides away as the bus turns a sharp corner. I try not to fall off the seat, but Raymond grabs my hand again.

"Bà will cane me for sure," I say with a tremor of fear.

As the bus winds through the crowded downtown streets toward Esplanade Park, where the Queen Elizabeth Monument is perched over the river, Raymond and I remain silent, unsure what to make of our interaction when we reach the bus terminal.

"I just don't want you to quit," Raymond whispers into my ear. He doesn't know about my family or where I come from, but I sense he cares about me somehow.

Arriving at the terminal, everyone has to get off the bus. Raymond and I have nowhere to go, so we mingle at the sidewalk for a while, trying to figure out what this awkward emotion is.

"Want to get back on the bus and go around again?" Raymond senses my self-consciousness.

I nod, and off we go again on the bus heading back to where we had started. The return route runs through a historical site known as the Boat Quay. This place was established with low-lying aesthetic houses that have been preserved since the 1960s for their native characteristics. The abundant trees with their mystical names—rain tree, senegal mahogany, frangipani—resonate sentimental environs, contrasting the towering skyscrapers of the financial district. Men and women are dressed in pressed suits and polished shoes, something I dare not ever entertain in my wildest dreams.

As if Raymond read my mind, "Don't think only smart people get *As*. It's all about hard work. That's the secret. One more try is all you need, this could turn your life around. How badly do you want this?"

I'm not sure I want to go back to school as much as I want an education. I hate the thought of being ridiculed, but I hate failing even more.

We ride the bus until dawn. I finally tell him I have to get home or else Māma will think I'm dead. He takes my hand again, but this time it feels like a brother's consolation.

"Think of it as a do-over," Raymond leans forward and urges with a heartfelt smile. "You can erase old songs from a cassette tape and record new ones over them. You don't have to replay the songs you don't want to hear."

We don't own a cassette player, but I know what he means. It won't be easy returning to the hall of shame. I only have to endure for one year—three hundred sixty-five days; fifty-two weeks, that's all I'm giving myself to turn the tide. It'll be the threshold to a new beginning. I'll have to face my demon, Mr. Tan, and suck it up when he utters, *I told you so*. I pledge that I'll put in more than a good effort to all my studies. Doing my best is not good enough. Failure is not an option; it's the only goal.

When the lights are coming on in the big hotels and the streets are almost clotted with rickshaws, cars, and vendors, Raymond and I say our goodbyes. He gets off at his house, and I ride the rest of the way home.

We never see each other again.

Chapter 11
ACCIDENTAL ANGELS

We are each of us angels with only one wing, and we can
only fly by embracing one another.
 ~ Luciano De Crescenzo

I have a break in December before returning to repeat the tenth grade. I begin studying right away, but the time still passes in the usual blur of snipping clothes and shopping—or at least window shopping. For a big treat, Jennifer brings me to McDonald's for a soda and a small fry to share.

On weekends, when Bàba is in a perfect mood, he takes us to the East Coast beach. I don't have a swimsuit, only a pair of old shorts and an oversized t-shirt that's almost down to my thighs. Jennifer has a fancy swimsuit from a friend, Audrey, who had gained weight and can't fit into it anymore. She looks so slim and sexy in it with her tiny waistline. Bàba is still drunk all the time, but age appears to be mellowing him. Now when he drinks, he sits silently by himself all night long, mumbling words in Hinghwa, a dialect we can't understand.

He drinks around the clock so even when he doesn't take a sip, he's still drunk. He can't seem to be sober. On most days, he twitches uncontrollably in the morning when he first wakes up. He used to drink thick, dark coffee for breakfast, but when he substituted beer, the tremors got worse. I like to think the shaking is due to his age, but it's most likely from his alcohol withdrawal.

As the dreaded first day of school draws closer, I sweat at the thought of seeing teachers again. I can't stop panicking. My head is pounding with academic locutions— quadratic, apartheid, mitosis, lithosphere—terms I understand far too little. From the moment my eyes are opened, I psych myself up to remember I only have one year to close the gap of four years of knowledge.

On the first day of my return, I make my intention of renewal known to my teachers and my parents. I make sure my hair is neatly combed, my only set of over-worn uniform is ironed, my hole-filled shoes are heavily starched and powdered with chalk, and my books are wrapped protectively and packed into my bag. Before I leave home that morning, I pray so hard that this long dreadful day will transform into the start of something new.

There is not a single cloud in the sky, but the rain trees obstruct the classroom windows at seminary. I don't want to get to school too early, although I'm kind of anxious to see who's coming back to repeat like me.

After seminary, I head to the bus stop and wait for two buses to pass before boarding the third one. I hope I don't bump into anyone and have to explain why I'm wearing the same school uniform again this year.

At the entrance of the school, I feel a lump in my throat. I'm about to relive the nightmares of my life. *Please don't talk to me … please don't know my name … please don't call me.* I walk briskly to my class, avoiding all eye contact. If I can survive today, I'll make it through the week.

I'm going to make it. I have to make it. Think positive. I swallow the lump that is still in my throat.

B-r-e-a-t-h-e. Don't trip.

Finally, I make it to my classroom on the third floor. I can't believe it—it's full of people I know from last year. This is comforting and freaky all at the same time.

The first bell rings, and behold my *bête noire,* Mr. Tan, walks in. My nightmare is a reality now. I can't possibly be stuck with him again! I squeak with pain inside my throat trying to dig that clam out of it. I'm never going to make it. My heart sinks.

"You're all a bunch of failures, wasting your time here for another year," Mr. Tan announces to the whole class. Students try to rustle their books and ignore him. "You repeaters don't stand a chance. If *it* had worked, you would have passed a long time ago."

I don't know what *it* means. What had worked? His teaching or my brain?

"Barbara, why did you come back?" Mr. Tan shoots me down again.

It's a rhetorical question, a trap. I keep my composure and do not cave in to my impulse. He's not worth it.

I proceed to take out my math book.

"What are you doing?" Mr. Tan asks with that villain smile that never wipes off his face.

"Doing my math," I say politely, knowing that it's a trick question.

"Why bother? Last year when I told you to work hard, you didn't want to. Now it's too late." Mr. Tan grunts loudly to make sure everyone hears him before he turns and walks away.

A remark like that would have made me throw my book at him a year ago, but my penitent renewal of purpose prevents me from reacting to his insult.

Mr. Tan stands stiffly behind his desk and speaks in his usual monotonous and sedative voice, "Boys and girls, I'm here to tell you that Mr. Yap, the vice principal, is going to be your teacher."

I let out a loud sigh—almost audible. I hope Mr. Tan did not hear it. All the unwarranted trepidations are all gone now. *Thank you, God, for answering my prayers!*

"He's going to teach you math, you know?" Mr. Tan chuckles sarcastically, "Since today is the first day of school, Mr. Yap is busy. I'm here just for a few minutes, don't think I'm going to get stuck with you losers." Mr. Tan's face turns sour as if he just sucked on a lemon.

I don't know Mr. Yap. All I know is he's the vice principal in charge of student discipline like Mr. Mah in elementary school. He is stern and a no-nonsense kind of man. I'm never in trouble, but it still makes me nervous having an administrator as my homeroom and math teacher. It's like having to dodge two bullets at once. I'll have to both behave and do well in math now.

Mr. Yap has a humorless, poker-face persona. I don't understand what it is with Asian teachers, but they don't smile much, as if a little dimple would make them seem too nice, and students would climb all over their heads. I wonder what it would take to make Mr. Yap smile.

Mr. Yap has a right-angled figure—square face, square body, largish body mass, and oversized neck. The collar of his shirt looks like it's going to choke him every time he shifts his neck to talk. He has pronounced dark circles under his eyes. Maybe he doesn't sleep much with all the discipline problems we have in this school.

From a distance, I can see Mr. Yap walking hurriedly toward our class after what seemed like a never-ending cascade of condescending remarks by Mr. Tan.

He enters the classroom, cracks his knuckles and cranes his head to release himself from his choking collar.

"Good morning, class!" Mr. Yap says. I expect him to begin the traditional lengthy philosophical oration that every teacher gives on the first day of school on how we should behave, what we should expect, and why we should be obedient at all times; instead, he lets out a loud breath.

"Feel that breeze, everyone. What a pleasant way to start the first day of school! You're all going to have a great year, right?"

Looking at each other, we wonder if he knows who we are or perhaps he stepped into the wrong class. Someone should remind him we're the repeaters. We're not supposed to have a pleasant year. We're not supposed to be excited about a new school year. We're supposed to be embarrassed and hang our heads down. We're supposed to have a lousy year.

Mr. Yap captures my attention right away. He has animated jubilance about him when he speaks. I've never met a teacher quite like him before. As he approaches my seat, his eyes enlarge to invoke a reciprocal look back from me.

"What's your name?" Mr. Yap asks as he goes up and down each row.

"Bar ... Barbara ... Hong," I reply with a bewildered face.

Far from Mr. Tan, Mr. Yap is quite interested in us—the twenty-six repeaters. I heard no other teacher wanted to take our class, so he had no choice.

Mr. Yap is a godsend!

Mr. Yap never brings a textbook to class. He seems to have the entire curriculum in his head. He looks straight at the class when he teaches, unlike teachers who talk to the board. He's passionate about what he's teaching and genuinely interested in helping us learn. I don't feel rushed or anxious when I hear him, unlike Mr. Tan. If I don't get what he's saying, I know there are more examples coming. He rephrases the statement rather than repeat the same wordings over and over again. I swear he has a teacher intuition of my learning curve. He seems to know me as if I've been his student before. This sixth sense is hypnotic. I can't get my eyes off the board when he's talking.

It has been rumored that he's been an administrator for a long time, so I wonder when he last taught math. I don't know math, but I can tell when a teacher knows his stuff. Math may be his subject expertise, but teaching is his gift. Mr. Yap makes solving problems so effortless and logical, and he makes me want to learn something, anything from him, even if it's hard.

"Look here. Break the expression down. Write what you know and then solve it," Mr. Yap talks with us as he writes out the steps on the board.

A rhythmic flow follows how he thinks. He stretches his neck out like a crane and flaps his arms as he writes, ignoring the streaks of chalk dust all over his black pants.

"Break down the equations. Subtract one side first. Then combine the like-terms on the same side. Figure out the x on one side and the number on the other. In the final step, divide to find out what x equals. Check back to see if the answer is correct. That's it. Of course, you can do this!" He lets out a big cheer. "Math is solving problems step-by-step, doesn't matter how complicated it looks. Break it down step-by-step."

I marvel at how he can peel a concept layer by layer, backward and forward, to make sense to someone who has no background, not even the fundamental knowledge of the subject. He takes me more seriously than I take myself. I don't know how, but Mr. Yap rekindles my lost enthusiasm for anything, and he does so through, of all subjects, mathematics. He opens my eyes to embrace the excitement of discovering new knowledge, not merely schooling. I feel worthy of his attention, and so does he of mine.

"No one in this school can fully understand the heartache, anger, and disappointment that you're going through," Mr. Yap sympathizes. "Likewise, no one can appreciate your success, hard work, and sacrifice more than you do. Sometimes, *ruin is your best gift* because it allows you to rebuild no matter how damaged you are. This is your chance to show off what you're really made of. This is your year. You deserve a second chance and it's yours to take it or lose it."

Those words sounded familiar. I have heard them before from my seminary and church teachers. The question is, how am I going to get better, faster?

Mr. Yap hardly gives us homework or tests. Probably because he doesn't have time to grade them, juggling between his administrative duties and teaching loads. No student is complaining, except I know I need more practice if I am going to get good at something. Who is going to help me with my other subjects? As I continue to struggle, I'm also beginning to sense a beacon of hope. Maybe if I pray hard enough, God might send me another angel, like Raymond.

༺๛

The young women in my seminary are some kind of a wonder. Every one of them has attributes I admire—the way they talk, walk, dress, study, and treat people. They make me want to be more like them.

Julia has long, shining, thick black hair, two entrancing dimples, and sparkling straight teeth. Her clothes are always neatly pressed, crisp, and chic. Not only is she the most popular girl in church, but she's also exceptionally brilliant. Every girl dreams to be her friend. There's something about Julia that girls can't help but feel envious. Julia projects a powerful vibe with her buoyant, rapturous smile, and witty charm. When the Sunday School teacher ask a question, Julia always has her hand up and knows the correct answer. She speaks eloquently, almost with an accent, which makes her sound even brainier. She is active in sports and a super star, on and off the stage, with her natural charm in modern dance, piano, and vocal.

While I'm repeating tenth grade in a less than mediocre school, Julia is accepted into a prestigious junior college. My hope is that maybe by befriending her I can pick on her brain and she can help me out somehow.

Sure enough, when Julia finds out I'm repeating my senior year, she offers to tutor me. For free. I can't believe it—the most popular and brilliant girl just offered to spend time with me! I'm flabbergasted.

"When it's time to study, there can be no chatting," Julia sets the first ground rule. "I don't mind talking, but only after we're done with our work. If you want my help, you have to work harder than you're working now. Is that clear?"

I nod and give her my word. I try not to crack a smile, but the glow is pumping on my face. I want to leap up and kiss her, but I resist. I promise I'll work a hundred times as hard. This is an opportunity of a lifetime to have a friend and a tutor.

Initially, I thought Julia was just being polite in offering to help, but no, she was for real. She puts me on a tight studying routine from day one.

Julia is a straightforward person, and that's what makes her different from other Asian girls. She doesn't beat around the bush or try to appease anyone. She has no reason to do that. She tells me outright what she thinks and how she feels. There's no hiding from her. Some people find that offensive, but not me. She never patronizes. She states things as they are without reservation. I love that about her and wish I have that audacity.

Julia is exceptional in math, like most Asian Singaporeans. While I can use her help, I'm also afraid she might give up on me once she finds out what an idiot I am.

On the one hand, I want Julia to like me and think I'm smart. On the other, I need her to know that I'm desperate for her help.

What if she gives up on me?

What if I disappoint her and lose her confidence?

What if she tells others I'm a cabbage head?

Julia lives in a township on the east coast outskirts. Her flat is like ours except much more spacious, and it has three bedrooms. Her block is hardly new or fancy, but if I stand on her balcony, I can almost see the beach.

In the hallway are some generic plants and ferns and a rack for drying clothes like the bamboo sticks outside our kitchen. On the walls is a Chinese calligraphy and a picture of Jesus kneeling by a large tree branch praying called the Garden of Gethsemane. Inside the living room is a green vinyl couch, a wooden dining table, a color television, and three medium-size bookshelves. I have never seen a home with so many books nor have I ever witnessed someone drowning in a book like Julia does. I can't imagine ever being a reader like her. I avoid reading at all costs.

"Do you want me to work on all these problems?" I ask blankly.

"Yes, do all ten of them," Julia instructs in her usual serious tone.

If I get stuck on a problem, which happens a lot, Julia shows me the order in which I should do them with lightning-quick thinking and then ever so gently leads me through her thought process, one step at a time.

The effect of her teaching is rapid and potent. I look forward to hanging out with Julia so much that doing homework is a pleasant challenge for me, for once. I recognize my progress. It's no longer a toll to read the textbook or to memorize formulas. Even biology and history are making sense now when I stay focused on trying to comprehend what I'm reading.

In the corner of the dining room is an upright piano. To take a break, Julia plays pop songs, and we sing, grasping a brush and pretending it's a microphone. The melody transforms the house into a harmonious blend of pure jubilation, delight, and laughter. I wish I could play an instrument, any instrument, and perhaps transform my home. But for now, I'm only trying to transform myself.

Julia's father died of cancer the year before. Her mother, Queenie, works as a nurse to support Julia and her sisters, Junie and Joy. I have never met someone with only one parent, but the one lesson I learn from observing this family is that rather than being met by a feeling of loss, they're optimistically accepting of their circumstances. This is rather unsettling for me. Shouldn't they be at least a little angry with God for taking their father away from them at such a young age?

Julia's family is not particularly wealthy, but they laugh a lot. The sisters use kind words and apologize to each other for the most minute incidents. They don't scream or yell at each other. If anything, they are obsessed with praising and hugging each other, no matter how small or insignificant the accomplishment is. I can only wish in a million years that I have a family like this.

Julia and I sit at the big Formica kitchen table, where Julia's mother serves us sweet buns and lemonade from a brightly colored plastic container. Everything in their flat has a certain glow about it. Things are neatly organized and uncluttered, making it feel spacious and calm. I find every reason each time to have Julia invite me to sleepover.

Soon, Julia's home becomes my second home, and I go there every day after school. She doesn't label me even though she sees how weak I am in every subject. This acceptance rejuvenates my morale and I become a little more confident about myself.

Julia loves to find new venues where we can experience a different atmosphere to study, such as at a public park, the business district, or at places with air-conditioning like the airport or fast-food restaurants. If there's no school after early morning seminary, Julia and I stay in church and study. We have our books ready everywhere we go. As long as we can find two seats, or some floor space, we're ready to pick up where we left off. Learning becomes a natural undertaking no matter where we are or the time of the day.

If I do well and Julia is not too tired, we go to the mall and window shop. For the first time, I have a friend to hang out with, doing girly stuff like that. Jennifer hardly shops with me because she says I dress too shabbily, and I never have money to buy anything anyway. The most gratifying thing about hanging out with Julia is having strangers stare at her. She's a breath of fresh air, stunning if I may add. I don't care if no one blinks at me as long as I get to enjoy some attention just sticking by her side.

Julia practically gives up her social life to hang out with me four to five days a week. I thought she would give up on me after one week, but she is genuinely committed to teaching me. I have to put in a real effort to make sure I never take her for granted. If anything, I want to impress her, and I want her to be proud of me, even more so than my Māma and Bàba.

She also has an uncanny way of dissecting the most complicated problem into the most logical and simplistic form so I can understand. It's no surprise that Julia aspires to be a teacher, something I'd never consider in my lifetime. I want to stay as far away from school and teachers as possible. Pass my Cambridge exam is the only goal, nothing past that.

I observe Julia keenly, marveling at her power of concentration and perseverance. When she encounters a difficult math problem, she wrinkles her forehead and tackles the question like a veteran General in the army planning an attack. It's as if the stratagem was right in front of her, waiting to be unveiled.

"Yes, I got it!" Within minutes, Julia lets out a celebratory breath.

She does this a lot and steadily that sense of victorious sensation begins to rub on me. She rarely picks the easy question to solve, whereas for me, just looking at words like *factorize, the function of, the exponential model,* or *binomial coefficients* discourage me.

"Break down each word on a problem and then work on each step sequentially. Make sure you don't skip anything."

I'm tempted to check the back of the book for the answer first and then work backward to get to the same solution. Julia trains me to stay on the problem and use trial and error to figure out each step of the way so I learn to evaluate why one answer makes sense, and another doesn't. It is hard because I'm impulsive and want to jump in and solve the problem, but I discover that learning is not about speed; it's about meaning.

I never hear Julia complain about my mistakes as most teachers would. She has a way of turning errors into positive feedback.

"Look, you know that doesn't work now. See, at least you've got the first three steps correct. Try another way."

I don't feel rushed. If I do, Julia stops me and says, "Slow down, you're not taking a test. When it's time for a test, you want to work at a faster speed. For now, study them carefully and pay attention to your mistakes, then ask why you made them in the first place."

I was always taught that mistakes were terrible, and they ought to be avoided, even penalized. Julia disagrees. My ability to differentiate between what I know, and what I don't, is the point of real learning. She forces me to find my errors and to figure out what I did wrong.

Marva Collins, an American educator who taught in impoverished Chicago schools, said, *"If you can't make a mistake, you can't make anything."*

I can listen to the teacher all day long and still be clueless as to what she's trying to teach. Listening is not the same as learning. Julia understood this precisely. She uses my errors to assess my learning and her teaching. For the first time in a long, long time, I'm able to make sense of the way I learn. I use a concrete way of deconstructing problems, equations, or terms, that helps me to analyze which steps I did correctly and where I need correction. Like a light bulb, I used to be plugged into a broken socket, but now, I am in a live outlet. I feel the electrifying surge in my understanding of math, and I'm loving it!

Julia's sheer excitement in learning is infectious. Sometimes, when I'm ready to knock off for the day, she shakes her head and says, "No, we're going to keep going, another half hour. You can do this." She's not joking when she says I need to put in a lot of effort to pass the Cambridge exam. I need to be more steadfast, so I begin another page of word problems.

Julia has another beautiful talent when it comes to appraising performance. Like a baseball pitching machine, she never stops reassuring me when I do something right.

"See, you can do this! You did it! It's all you."

She speaks with such composure and genuineness, her smile stretching from ear to ear. Julia doesn't give empty praise for the sake of it. If I don't do well, she has no qualms about telling me. But if I do well, she never misses a chance to let me know it was all me. She doesn't take credit for anything, not once. I think she sets herself a target of a hundred praises for each day we study together. I know she is trying to help me build a sense of self-efficacy that I can accomplish something on my own. She wants to convey that I'm capable of learning even though something may appear hard or foreign. Slowly but surely, I believe I can do the math, and I can learn anything I set my mind to.

In over a decade of schooling, this was the first time I understood math. On one level, Mr. Yap helped shed new light on math. On another level, Julia reinforced this light by practicing carefully with me. It was like putting two and two together. I'm able to catch a glimpse of how the mathematical world works, and I love it!

It sounds so simple, and perhaps this is the thing about good teaching combined with hard work. Quality teaching should be simple. No concept is ever too hard to understand if the teacher knows how to deliver it.

Good teaching = quality teaching = caring teaching.

Mr. Yap and Julia did not just teach math, they taught *me*. My learning, not the curriculum, was their priority. They were empathetic teachers. They knew I was discouraged, beaten, shamed, and confused, still, they were willing to walk each step with me and allow me to pace myself.

Math has always been the most intimidating subject, or maybe Mr. Tan was, yet when I was able to solve the problems, I felt like I had just conquered the world, a sensational boost to my morale that I can learn anything. I realize this is not scientific in any sense, but I'm grateful that Mr. Yap and Julia taught by their intuition instead of by dictation.

By mid-semester, I was at the top of my class. Granted, it was my repeat year, but I never dreamed I could reach such a point in my life. For the first time, I was doing well in all the subjects.

If there's one lesson I have learned, it is that relationships matter, people matter, and feelings matter. In anything we do, we ought to begin with a relationship of trust. Not only were these angels passionate about their subjects, they cared about spilling that passion over to those they taught. When teachers can tune in to students' emotional and learning needs, they're more likely to pay attention to what is being taught. Empathetic teaching endows teachers with the natural responsiveness to reach individual students. This dynamic relationship spontaneously synergizes both the teacher and the student to engage in authentic discovery, going back and forth as self-reflectors on both ends.

As the school year comes to an end, I eagerly look forward to returning to pick up my envelope, the one that says *Cambridge General Certificate of Education*. My cold hands shake a little, but as I open the envelope, it reveals a perfect score. I passed every subject with distinction, including math!

I was a fragile piece of sackcloth, coarse and unrefined, woven in roughness and irregularities. But with the touch of a few masters' hands, I was carefully threaded and woven into a fine tapestry. I can go on to a three-year pre-university at Townsville Institute, the equivalent of the eleventh and twelfth grade in the US. Now that the hard part is over, how am I going to convince Bàba to let me continue with more schooling?

Chapter 12
MINDS OF MY OWN

A weed is a plant that has mastered every survival skill
except for learning how to grow in rows.
≈ *Doug Larson*

"*D*ad, I want to go to pre-u. I promise to make you proud." I plead with Bàba for days, but he won't give me an answer.

It's hard to reason with someone who is perpetually drunk. Like talking to a zombie, he won't remember by the morning. I turn to Māma and she agrees to let me continue on the condition that I pay for my supplementary fee, buy only one set of uniform, and wear the same pair of shoes for the next three years.

Pre-u begins as a blur of faces, classrooms, and places to go. Townsville Institute is no Promised Land and it's not like I become an intellect overnight. I still don't know if I'm going to make it through the next three years.

All I have mastered are two key skills—persistence and focus.

Townsville is an hour away from Toa Payoh. The only way to save money for my bus fare is to practice fasting again like I did in secondary school.

Getting to school involves a lot of waiting and is somehow melancholic. I get on a bus to get to the subway, then transfer from the subway to hop on another bus, then walk for another half mile before I reach school. Returning home is the same. I hate this routine because it cuts into my studying time. I hate it more because of four boys—Jin, captain of the group, and his gang Fred, James, and Andrew.

A group of girls also spend their days trying to impress these boys. Discernibly naïve, these girls wear their skirts so short and tight, I don't know how they walk or sit. They would lean over the bench at the bus stop or pace in front of the boys giggling to get their attention.

The irony is that these boys are not particularly interested in girls. In Singapore, it's more popular to stay unattached than it is to be a couple because it is considered uncool to be seen with girls while hanging out with your buddies. Whereas for girls, it is more flattering to have a boyfriend, especially when he is in the popular gang.

I never sit on the bench at the bus stop for fear of wrinkling my ironed skirt, or worse, dirtying my only uniform, so I stand to one side with my nose in a book. These girls like to strut around the bus stop like peacocks, enticing the boys to notice them. That's fine with me, except I'm their bait. What they want is to provoke me so the boys will poke fun at me.

"Ba-ba-la," Andrew pokes at my name in his brisk Hokkien dialect. "What's wrong with your shoes?"

I blush a fierce red. My shoes are scuffed and obviously old, if not in shreds. I ignore him, but Fred follows up.

"Somebody is maaaaaad. Somebody is madddd."

"Leave me alone," I say with my teeth clenched.

Now that Andrew has everyone's attention, everyone is staring at my shoes and sneering about my being down at the heels. The girls whisper something to James that makes him burst into loud laughter. The boys and girls ripple with amusement when, in the course of insulting me, someone says my face looks like a raccoon— dark circles under my eyes from staying up late studying.

"We're just trying to chat with you. Why are you so quiet all the time?" Jin seems faintly surprised.

I realize he isn't making fun of me, but in his clumsy, boyish way, he's trying to be my friend. Jin behaves the most gentlemanly of them all. I later heard from the girls' gossip that he likes me. I'm not sure if this is another one of the pranks they are pulling or is it for real. He teases me because it makes the other girls giggle, and in turn, makes him popular. Whatever it is, I'm numb to everyone at school. I don't hate them, nor do I like them. I'm fine with being alone and being called a weirdo. I am different, and I'm used to it.

My school days are filled with a thick air of malaise about my scuffed-up shoes, my dingy ankle socks, my protruding teeth, my mutant butt or my flat chest. My mother does it, too, frequently pointing out my buck teeth and flat bottom by comparing me to Jennifer, whose teeth are perfectly straight like a poster at the dentist's office. The butt issue is a big one in the Chinese culture. Having good curves mean you are fertile; thus, increasing your chances of finding a husband.

"Why are you always studying?" asks Lina, a former classmate from my repeat year. "Golly, take a break please for goodness sake. Where do you think you're going to end up studying so much?"

I bite my lip hard so I can't answer her and pretend to be absorbed in my book. I've learned not to react to rhetorical questions because there's no end to it, thanks to Mr. Tan.

"I heard you're the loudest lizard in school," Andrew persists. "Let me hear you hiss, lizard. Hiss, hiss, hiss!"

Lina and Andrew chuckle, "Yeah, no man would want to come close to her. I mean just look at her."

I turn my head to avoid showing my tears while feigning interest in reading my notebook. I swallow a lump like a fat piece of chicken breast stuck in my throat.

"What's the matter with her?" Alice asks as she nudges Fred. "Do you think she's crying? Oh, we see tears. She's human. She can cry."

"At least she's not hissing. I think I like the lizard sound better," Andrew cuts in.

Rrriiiinng … Saved by the bell, I walk to the bus stop and stand in my usual corner, ducking everyone.

Across the street, I noticed a new sign: Thrift Store. OPEN.

What on earth is a thrift store? I have never heard of that before. All I know about the pale blue building across the street is that it's a school for retards, as my teachers call it or MINDS—Movement for the Intellectually Disabled of Singapore.

When we're not performing well, teachers would throw out sarcasm like this, "If you fail, you should join your brothers and sisters across the street."

Once the teachers set the tone on how these people are to be regarded, it becomes a habitual joke for students to tease one another about moving in with our "siblings" across the street. Needless to say, I'm one of their targets.

"Barbara, are you sure you're in the right family?" Fred references me, "Maybe you were born across the street by accident. We need to send you back."

I turn a deaf ear to his remarks.

Andrew interrupts, "I'm not sure MINDS would take her back, Ba-ba-black sheep."

I stare fixedly at the sign. James mumbles something to Jin about never setting foot in that building because the kids could be contagious.

Māma said we should never touch a person in a wheelchair because we can become paralyzed, too. Also, never get too close to people who look abnormal because they can infect you. I don't think mental retardation is contagious, but what do I know. I have seen some of these children before when they come across to our school to use the field. They're different, but I don't know what it is.

"What's wrong with going in there?" I poke at Jin, "I'm going to check out what is a Thrift Store."

He's taken aback because I finally talked to him for the first time.

"Barbara, you're out of your mind!" Fred snaps, gazing at me with a look of horror. "You could catch something from them. Aren't you afraid? They're cuckoos inside there."

Lina giggles with a hint of sarcasm. "Don't be stupid, Barb, but I guess you can't help yourself."

I guess I can't.

"You know what? Let her go in there," James jeers. "Her look may scare them into being normal again."

"Well, if I don't show up in school tomorrow, you'll all know why," I say as I head across the street.

"Hey, wait a minute!" Jin calls after me, but it's too late, I'm already darting through a gap between two cars.

I follow the sign and walk up to the second floor of the main grayish-blue building. As I turn left, the words *Thrift Store* are written in red on the windowpane.

The little room is slightly larger than my living room and has a huge L-shaped wooden trestle table piled with dresses, shirts, pants, suit jackets, skirts, belts, socks, shoes, ties—all neatly sorted out. I'm not sure what's going on, but people are browsing through stuff left and right and making small talks. The place isn't nearly as terrifying as everyone makes it out to be. People are exceptionally polite to each other and speak in soft, gentle voices. It's as if I just stepped into a funeral home. The place resonates with an aura of kindness and serenity, something I'm not expecting.

I hear a noise from behind and see a woman who looks familiar. Her short hair is pulled back, and she's wearing a gray suit with a white lace blouse buttoned to the neck. She also seems a little disheveled.

"Are you here to help?" she asks, not waiting for my answer. "Mary will show you what to do. I have to run now, but it's nice to see you here."

She shakes my hand vigorously, and then off she goes. I have seen her before, but I can't remember where.

"So, you're the new volunteer?" Mary asks while standing over an ironing board wreathed in a cloud of steam.

"No, I mean, sure ... yes, sure. I'm Barbara. I saw your sign outside. I go to school across the street."

There's no reason for her to be impressed by this. Townsville is just the newest pre-u in the city.

"I'm the store manager," Mary says, somewhat sardonically as she points to the sign behind her with her name and title on it—*Manager, Thrift Shop*.

Mary is an unusually tall woman with a serious-looking face and short gray hair. She supervises all the volunteers as well as the higher functioning kids who can help out at the store. These children learn to make simple transactions, like counting money and bagging items, but mostly they're there to help fold clothes.

I remember where I have seen the first lady who shook my hand. She's a sister from the Mormon church. I think her name is Min Lian. She's the best-dressed sister at church, in her proper dark suit and crisp white blouse.

When Min Lian returns, she smiles warmly. "You are the girl from church, yes?"

"Yes, I ..." I want to say more ...

"Barbara is a volunteer from the school across the street," Mary introduces me. "Today is her first day."

Min Lian beams. "Wonderful, we can always use more hands around here, and the kids love new volunteers. We're going to get to know each other very well."

Min Lian graduated from Toronto, Canada with a degree in psychology. Now, *that* is someone I want to emulate. I don't know what a degree is or what that kind of achievement entails. All I know is everyone wants to talk to her. Maybe it's her friendly personality, but I suspect it's also her intelligence.

"You can help fold," Mary points at a door with a beaded curtain that has an *Employees Only* sign above.

Some of the clothes have a faint musty odor of mildew. Some are torn or have holes in them, but from a quick glance over the piles of clothes heaped up here and there, I can see some are quite new looking and need only some ironing. After about fifteen minutes, I settle into the routine and am no longer thinking about those boys' remarks. I peer out through the windows and see my bus pulling away. I imagine Jin and James craning their necks to see if I'll come rushing out so they can say I have been inside a mental institution.

"You can help Tian over there." Mary points to a young girl, about ten or twelve, with short fringe hair, wearing a Peter Pan-collared blue blouse. She has the smoothest face I have ever seen. Her dress is a little scruffy, but her red polka dot slippers are adorable, like the ones I lost when I was little.

Tian smiles back and keeps on smiling. I take a step closer, and she smiles even more. Although Tian looks like any normal kid, she hasn't spoken a word since she was born. Mary says Tian has been a resident of MINDS since she was three.

I motion for Tian to imitate me folding clothes, something I'm quite good at from folding those snipped garments. I show her how to button up the shirts, tie the laces around the dresses, and pile them up. I repeat myself each time so she can follow along. All afternoon, Tian and I work in perfect synchronicity. I love to sort things, probably it has something to do with my obsession with being organized and neat after being haunted by a hoarder. Over the next several months, I work with Tian, and we look forward to seeing each other in the afternoon.

During my third week, I meet another boy, Ming. I can't quite pinpoint why, but he scares me a little. He behaves so differently than the others. Ming has an intellectual disability and Tourette's syndrome, which is why he has trouble speaking and controlling his movement.

"Ming is a quick worker, almost tireless," Mary says. "He has a lot of energy and stops only to let out a short barking noise from time to time."

I have no idea what all that means, but I become very curious about Ming and Tian and all the children living there. I'm intrigued by their behavior and what's going on in their heads.

What do they know that I don't know?

Why do they act the way they do?

What are they trying to tell me?

For the next three years at Townsville, I actively volunteer at the thrift store. This is perhaps my way of escaping the popular gang because I no longer need to take the bus at the same time with them. I love splitting my time between school and running across the street. Some afternoons, I'm so engrossed that I barely notice the time.

"It's time to go home, Barbara," Min Lian motions me with her watch.

I haven't told Māma about my volunteering activity. I have been lying about staying late to study with my friends—another lie because I don't have any friends.

One of the best parts about volunteering is that every so often, Mary and Min Lian would bring treats for everyone—almond cookies, warm chicken buns, barbecue pork, won-ton, fried spring rolls, or something I crave but can never afford. I never pass up free food, especially if I have to skip lunch to save for the bus fare.

Skirts are fifty cents, shoes forty cents, t-shirts twenty cents, hats, oh how I love hats, are only ten cents, and sometimes, even free if they have been sitting around for months. Most of the donated items are not in good condition, but a few of them are quite decent. I looked for donations from the American people because these items are generally in better shape, almost new and even brand name, like the clothes I snip back home. These are the best treasures because I finally get to wear one of those brands instead of sending them back to the manufacturers.

Min Lian and Mary keep one or two of the nicer, less worn out items of clothing for me and only charge me fifty cents each. I feel so spoiled to have "newer" clothes in my scant collection, and I like the novelty of choices as I pick out my Sunday clothes for church. At times, I decline what was reserved because even fifty cents is still a lot of money. Besides, Māma has this notion that wearing clothes that had been worn by handicapped people is contagious and I could catch whatever disability or diseases they may have. Whenever I bring home an item from MINDS, I hide it underneath a pile of hoarded items and pretend I found it there. Māma barely remembers what she has in those stacks of junk anyway. I don't know of any Singaporeans who would conceive of the idea of wearing other people's clothes, except Jennifer and me.

A neighbor on the first floor of our block was born blind, but she can play cards like nobody's business. I don't know what psychic power she possesses, but when she brings the cards close to her eyes, she instantaneously places her bet, as if she sees what's coming. I don't know a single thing about cards but judging by the commotion, I'm guessing this lady must win a lot, driving everyone crazy and making them curious at the same time.

Māma warns us to never look a blind person in the eyes, or we can go blind too. She also exhorts us never to trust anyone who wears sunglasses because they can't look you in the eye. Māma is full of old wives' tales that I find most absurd now, but at that time they made perfect sense, and I never questioned Māma's wisdom.

One of the best bargains I find is a crisp white blouse made with custom buttons running down the front. It has sharply designed cuffs, slightly puffed sleeves, and somewhat of a Victorian style. The hem is trimmed neatly, and the sides precisely aligned. The cotton fabric is soft and has a luxurious feel to it. Totally my type.

I take the blouse, walk to a fluorescent light in the corner of the room to examine the stitches and notice a red spot on the front, but it is hardly noticeable.

"You like that blouse?" Min Lian asks.

I shrug with a hint of excitement in my eyes, "Yes, kind of, but …"

Before I can utter the next word, Min Lian snatches it up, quick as a bullet, and says, "Go on, take it. Here, go. No need to pay."

"Are you sure? Thank you, thank you. Thank you!" That's all I can say. I hug the blouse beside my face like a child getting a brand new doll for the first time.

The white blouse becomes one of my most-loved articles of clothing. It fits me perfectly and I feel rich. I don't really know what that's like, but I feel snotty. I never realized a piece of second-hand clothing could have such an effect on someone. I see why Jennifer enjoys spending her hard-earned money to buy one piece of nice clothing.

"That's why your sis looks like a movie star, and you look like a maid," Māma reminds me when she sees me wearing the white blouse over and over again. I become so attached to my blouse that I rarely wash it because I don't want to wear it out.

Over the next few months, I save enough to buy a pleated, blue-and-white, polka dot skirt—I'm crazy about polka dots. I also got a silky red dress that I can wear to church and a pair of polka dot slippers like the ones I lost a decade earlier. I know I'll never be as stunning as Jennifer, but I feel a little elegant, graceful, and almost glamorous.

James and Lina and the bus stop gang can't believe I have been going across the street. I hear their catcalls each time I run over there after school.

"Barbara is catching their disease; she can't even hear us now!" James makes sure I hear him loud and clear.

I hear the other kids laughing behind my back. I feel hollow where my stomach should be as if I might faint. But once I cross over and open that door and hear the bell tinkles, I feel relieved again. Min Lian comes to greet me.

"Good afternoon. Hard day at school, huh?"

As a job placement officer, Min Lian helps youth with disabilities find jobs and learn to live more independently. She teaches me about how to treat people who are different.

"We can all learn from these folks if we first try not to judge," Min Lian counsels. "These boys and girls are as worthy of our love as anyone else, maybe even more."

Min Lian becomes like another older sister to me, and much closer than Jennifer. I sometimes imagine that she was Poh Geok, the sister who died before I was born. Maybe God sent her into my life to watch over me.

Chapter 13
WORK IN PROGRESS

It is better to have a heart without words than words without a heart!

⮞ John Bunyan

MINDS becomes a big part of my after-school activity. I learn to work with people of all backgrounds and ages. I challenge myself to talk to strangers and assist the residents with their day-to-day routines, like brushing their hair, cutting their nails, washing their faces, or just holding their hands and sitting down, doing nothing. If Ming becomes agitated and starts flapping his arms, I calm him down and comfort him. I become quite good at making Tian laugh as we stack piles of musty smelling clothes around the table. The highlight of my day is when one of us finds some random things, even money, in the pocket of a donated article.

For some reason, I am entranced by anything nautical—anchors, three-stripe collars, red-and-white buoys, steering wheels, blue-and-white striped ribbons, sailor knots, and so forth. I look for these items, hoping something nautical gets buried in those piles.

I'm becoming more conscious, or rather, more aware, of who I am and what I want. I embrace my weirdness, flaunting it in the faces of my schoolmates. I don't care about anything except studying and being myself. Gradually, my grades show signs of significant progress, and I feel, in some ways, that I'm off to a good ending. It's not always as clear and simple as it sounds though.

The other students ostracize me, but I'm used to it. Their rejection is probably a result of my own behavior. I reflect on the intensity of my dislike and distrust of people. I don't care what my schoolmates say or think about me, not because I'm strong, but because I'm too prideful. If I wanted to, I could have befriended them; instead, I shun everyone out of my life so that no one can hurt me. The effect of this exclusion is becoming more pronounced as time goes by, to the point that my teachers begin to detect my awkwardness around people. I don't know how to be polite or kind to people. I don't know how to be empathetic or sympathetic. I'm obnoxious, haughty, and egotistical.

After lunch, my economics teacher, Madam Foo, a stern-looking, no-nonsense woman, pulls me aside.

"Barbara," she says with growing concern, "you seem like a nice girl, but you're too arrogant."

"What?" I don't even know what that word "arrogant" means. "Why? Me? How?"

"You're not very nice to your classmates. Like the other day when Janice had the stapler, and you needed it, you blurted out, 'Who took the stapler? I need it now!' without considering her feelings."

I dare not say a word. I'm overcome with shame. I look down at the floor as she continues.

"You're rude, and you need to change. You act like you're more superior because you think you're better than anyone else."

I have no idea that's how others think of me, and it hurts, especially when it's coming out of a teacher's mouth. I knew Madam Foo had not been very fond of me ever since she found out I was a Mormon. Her husband is a Presbyterian minister, and she has been trying to convert me to her church ever since. I have politely declined her invitation at least half a dozen times, but she sees it as her mission to *save* me from a cultish practice. That's beside the point. She's never this blunt with me. This confrontation seriously awakens me. If a teacher has to point that out, I think it's time I take a hard look at myself.

I realize I don't like this *me* at all.

Pearl Bailey, an American Actress, once said, *"There's a period of life when we swallow a knowledge of ourselves, and it becomes either good or sour inside."*

I'm a hypocrite. I have to change. I want to know how I can be kinder and behave more civilly, talk more politely, and not be that overbearing and smug girl. Such behaviors are not in keeping with the tenets of my new-found faith. I have to take some drastic measures quickly.

My only real friends in Townsville are the Muslim students. For some reason, we connect better. I never ask them, but maybe I'm not very nice to them either. They have been patient in accepting me into their circle and even offer to sit with me during recess. These are the only friends I have. I don't want to lose them. I need to let down my guard and allow people in my life. I have built a wall so high and thick since elementary grade that till now, I am the only one behind it. No one wants to climb through that wall to be with me, and if I'm not careful I may end up very lonely.

I have no one but myself to blame. I have gotten so used to being alone that sometimes I feel I can make it better on my own. That's my pride speaking, but the only person losing here is me. This is my last chance to make amends. The conversation with Madam Foo sinks deep inside me. I feel more of a failure than at any other time. It's painful to admit it, but she's right. I'm beginning to feel abandoned by everyone, even the teachers whom I try so hard to please.

I'm at the MINDS store after school when Min Lian asks, "What is it, Barbara? Something's troubling?"

"I'm not sure. Have I missed everything I'm striving for in my life?"

"Don't be too hard on yourself. Life is forgiving. You need to let go of the past and let God embrace you."

I nod, but I'm still troubled. I go home and crouch under my blanket in Jennifer's bed and soak myself in some sad Chinese music. I thought I'd be happy once I started making steady progress in school, but life had thrown odd emotions at me that I was not prepared to process. I'm going through the motions of schooling but missing the whole process of learning. I don't want to just study, study, study and not get educated at all. I need to be ruffled and pushed out of my comfort zone. I need to do something that makes me feel real joy, authentic happiness, true love. Do any of these even exist?

Meanwhile, at Townsville, something new is happening. Mrs. Tan, the head of the English Department, dressed in her usual business-like and démodé blouse and skirt, makes an announcement during the general assembly.

"After much work by members of the English department, we've decided to start the first debating team."

A mixture of moans and cheers flood the assembly hall. Some students are excited about the initiative, but the majority boo it.

The subject of debate stirs wild excitement in Singapore and is considered prime-time TV. Only the smartest and most articulate students get selected to be on the elite team. Understandably, Townsville can imagine few things more *haute monde* than starting a debate team.

Mrs. Tan gestures for the rowdy crowd to settle down. "Shhhhhh ... I know you're all very excited. Remember, only the top students will be selected."

The second-floor classes will be the biggest challenge because these students major in literature, meaning they are college bound, whereas those of us on the third floor major in commerce or vocational bound.

"Do you think we can beat them?" I ask Nora, a short, bubbly Muslim girl who sits next to me.

"Beat them? You must be joking! We don't stand a hair of a chance."

"Maybe we can if we have enough practice," I respond smugly.

As soon as I say it, I wish I could swallow my words. This hubristic nature is getting to me again. What is it about my addiction to winning? I don't care what comes flying out of my mouth, but I have to say it with such pomposity. I can't stand myself, but I can't stand losing even more.

Back in class, Mrs. Tan nominates four students, and then the entire class votes on it. I am one of them! I can't believe it. I thought I had been blacklisted after that stapler incident. I'm stupefied and secretly flattered, but I have no clue what to do.

Our team includes two of my Muslim friends, Zulkifli or "Zu" and Nora. Zu appears to have an overdose of growth hormones because he is larger than the average kids his age but the wittiest. He has a jocular, good-natured banter about him. Nora has an eloquence about the way she modulates her voice. She can almost convince you of anything because of her prolific cadence in public speaking.

Finally, we have Alvin, the socially awkward guy who entertains the class with his out-of-context jokes. He's easygoing and very adaptable. Alvin seems to be the go-to guy for anything technical. The team is set, or so I think.

As four oddballs, we have no idea what the teacher or our classmates see in us. I hope they didn't vote for us so they could make fools out of us. I'm not about to let that happen to the team or to me. Sometimes vain confidence can be helpful.

The way the contest works is that we debate the other classes on our floor first. If we make it through, we move up to challenge the winners from the second floor. Incredibly, our team begins to rack up wins. It helps that our competitors on the third floor don't put in as much effort as we do so it isn't hard to beat them.

Our team spends many afternoons after school at a nearby community center researching, practicing, writing, and contending to see how we can come up with one-line zingers to sting our opponents.

It's so exciting to see our efforts pay off. We don't just beat the other teams; we have landslide victories every time. Next week, we move on to compete against the second floor in the best of three competitions. After two weeks, every class is out of the game, except us. Now it's just the oddballs against the four literature majors.

My knees shake as I listen to the cheering and booing in the front row. Mrs. Tan announces the final results over the PA system. I can barely contain myself. This is going to be a lot of pressure. If we lose, it'll be as expected. But if we win, it'll look like a fluke. I don't know how we're going to compete against this caliber of wizards.

Mrs. Tan announces the final topic: "*The head should rule over the heart.* We're the opposition team."

You wouldn't think such a simple sentence could arouse such endless discussion, but it does. We gather immediately after school at the usual spot in the community center and hash the subject inside out. Alvin, who prides himself on being a rationalist, presents a compelling argument on how and why this is true.

"Men use their heads more, and women use their hearts more," he contends, "it's obvious that it's safer to rule by the head than by the heart. We're sure to lose now."

Nora doesn't look convinced, and neither do I.

"Alvin, in every argument, there's always a loophole," I assert. "We must find the flaw and use it."

Alvin shoves his books in his bag. "Everyone knows the head is more important. We're doomed. This is an unfair question."

No way. I refuse to believe we're going to lose. The head should *not* rule over the heart! We have come so far, beating five classes in the last month. Surely *that* says something about defying the logic of the head.

We believe we can win. We must win. I won't accept failure since the start of the debate and it sure is not going to happen in this final round. We put in hours every afternoon to prepare. I pray and hope that we won't make fools of ourselves. No matter how we're going to stumble, we must at least land on both feet and do our class proud. What does that tell us? Our passion is stronger than our brains combined. We're not about to give up on this last question no matter how uncertain things appear.

"We stand a good chance for a fair battle," I reaffirm. "Now think, think, think. How can we turn the argument around in our favor?"

I do what I can and write out the research for each team member. I go through all of their pointers to make sure we're all on the same page. Every day, we read, write, dispute, compare, argue, and role-play. We eat each other's lunches and drink each other's soda. We laugh, we yell, and we get on each other's nerves. These are unforgettable afternoons and evenings, and we feel ready to take on the opposition team.

On the big day, as each team walks onstage in the assembly hall, the roar of applause soars through the crowd. We sit tall in our seats and brace ourselves for the battle of our lives as the voices of the underdogs. We want to prove everyone wrong.

As the moderator calls my name, I'm nervous, anxious, and excited all at once. I try to hold myself together and deliver a well-rehearsed argument full of audacity and eloquence.

"Our heart … is the center of our soul … Our heart sees more than our head or … even our eyes. Our heart listens, whereas our head only hears … often what we want to hear. When we listen to our head more than our heart, we're more likely to make mistakes and hurt someone or get hurt. If we let the wisdom of our heart guide us, we are a better people overall."

The crowd cheers.

"It's a far more superior ethic to let our heart tell our head how to live. Anything short of that, and we're not true to ourselves. Our head gets clouded with too much logic, too many predictions, decisions, motives, worries, rationalizations, and judgments. Just look at the blunders men make when they don't ask for directions." The crowd roars again in support.

The audience laughs. The opposition team can't hold themselves back, and they laugh, too.

"Mankind has, in the past, allowed logical inclination to rule over moral intuition. That's why people suffer, children get hurt, and tyrants abuse. Life is dangerously uncertain when left to the head. If we have to choose one organ over another to sustain our lives, I believe we're better off choosing our heart over our head."

With full gusto, I argue every opponents' points. I can hear cheers from my team on the side of the stage.

And then it happens. Our awkwardly shy and unglamorous commerce major team defeats the all-time literature class.

We did it!

"Oh my, Barbara, once the four of you got started, there was no contest. You all spoke with so much passion, definitely from the heart. Congratulations!" Mrs. Tan declares the winner.

Each team member receives a trophy engraved with our names. This is the first time I have ever won anything, the first time I have ever held a trophy, and the first time I'm publicly recognized. I can hardly contain myself.

Weeks following the debate, the four of us are still treated like celebrities on campus. Our schoolmates on the third floor cheer us on for having beaten the snobs. Even the teachers begin to regard us in a new light. Of course, the second-floor losers refuse to concede even months after the debate. I don't think they ever will.

I have never experienced such triumph. I understand now what it means to be a positive leader, to listen to each other, and to enjoy the fruit of teamwork. There is a sense of solidarity, purpose, and resoluteness.

Following this event, I become obsessively competitive. Whatever I'm doing, I want to be number one. I crave that primal sensation of being on top. I don't care what others think, say, or feel. If I lose, I'd stay up all night tossing, struggling, and wondering why I didn't win and what I could have done differently. Sometimes, I go on for days and weeks, ruminating over my stupidity for not foreseeing what led to my failure. I want to surpass everyone else, and I can't be short-changed. If I don't get one-hundred percent on an exam, I'm upset with myself and everyone else, even those who have nothing to do with it like my neighbor who lets her cat out too late at night.

More than anything else, I hate being defeated. I yearn to be a champion all the time and to be on top of the world. It is all about me, me, me. This fixation on winning, of being in control, and a compulsion for conquest comes to define my daily life. I'm tortured mentally and physically, but I cannot help it.

Rick, my classmate, becomes my sole competitor. We have a love-hate relationship. We admire each other's nerdiness, but we also compete for the top grade in every assignment and exam. Everything is a competition between us. We're friendly, yet we hate each other's guts. We keep our eyes on each other like a hawk for fear of being sabotaged. As the saying goes, "Keep your friends close, but keep your enemies closer."

It's Friday afternoon, we walk into the assembly hall and notice two plaques installed conspicuously above the doorway. One reads, *Top Student of the Year* and the other, *Best All-Round Student of the Year*.

The odd thing is, no names are engraved on it. It has empty boards, about five in each column. Rick and I are thinking: *That could be me!*

Rick puts his right hand below his chin as if solving some mysterious crime. "We could be the *first* ones on that plaque. Which one do you want to be?"

I knew exactly which one—the *Best All-Round Student*, of course! I can't settle for being the *Top Student*.

I want to make history in this school. It's a lousy school, but still, I want to be the first in something grand. I pretend I don't want either, but I think we both know what each other is after.

Three years in Townsville is not the easiest time. I am more determined than ever to study hard. My eyes are fixed on that one plaque. Whenever I get discouraged, I would envision my name engraved on that first line of the rectangular brass plate and get myself up from the floor.

Three months passed. Then one morning, during the flag-raising ceremony, Mr. Raj, my homeroom teacher, walks up from behind me and whispers into my right ear. I can't quite catch what he says because of his strong Malay accent.

"What, sir?"

"Congratulations. You've been chosen," he says and then hurries to the back of the line for the national anthem.

"Chosen …? For …?" I follow his eyes with a wrinkled forehead, hoping the disciplinary master doesn't notice me while all the students are saluting the flag.

"Best … Student!" Mr. Raj tries to mouth the words again.

"What? Best what?" I'm trying to read his lips.

Wait, did he say what I think he just said? I can barely believe my ears. "Seriously?" I stop singing the anthem. I can't remember the pledge. Standing motionless, it feels like the longest morning ceremony ever.

When it's finally over, Mr. Raj walks up and proclaims in his strong Malay accent, "Yes, '*Best All-Round Student.*' You've been selected by all the teachers. Congratulations!"

"You are an outstanding student counselor, won the first debate championship, and stayed in the top three position every year …" Mr. Raj continues even though I am in an obvious state of shock, not even blinking.

Four weeks later, for the first time in eighteen years, Bàba sets foot in my school. The only other two times he has ever entered a school were to bail Winston out of the principal's office for lying and when Winston was forced to drop out of seventh grade. Māma dragged me along that day because she was afraid Bàba might make a scene. I'm not sure what she thinks I could have done if he burst out.

As I lead Māma and Bàba to their seats in the assembly hall, the smell of alcohol wafts through the air like I just walked into a bar. Bàba has never taken Māma out on a date for ages, so they look awkward with each other in public.

My name is called. Feelings of the jitters and uneasiness overpower me. I find my way up onto the stage, tripping on a step, almost two. This moment is going to make Māma and Bàba proud, at least that's what I hoped.

After the ceremony, I try to initiate a conversation, but Bàba simply brushes me off.

"Let's go, I have a shift to do," Bàba says as he turns around and staggers toward the parking lot, lighting a cigarette.

Not a word? I'm perplexed. I have waited for this moment since kindergarten to hear Māma and Bàba utter something positive about me, maybe even be proud of me, but nothing. A hundred emotions race through my mind. I long for heartfelt praise. I deserve it. I earned it. At least that's what I think. Even a "good job" would suffice, but zip.

Today is my day I made something of myself because of my diligence. Why can't I get a little attention for my effort? I've made it this far, and there's nothing they can say to make this day a little delightful for me? I don't understand.

Maybe they are happy, but I want to hear it from Māma and Bàba. Maybe I'm trying too hard to get their attention. Maybe everything was for naught. Maybe I will always be the unwanted child.

Chapter 14
DEFINING ME

————— ✦ —————

Never mind searching for who you are. Search for the person you aspire to be.
≈ *Robert Brault*

$\mathcal{E}$ ven after attaining good report cards, winning competitions, and earning recognition for my efforts, something doesn't feel right. I still feel unfulfilled. Winning satisfies me, but this sensation quickly vaporizes, leaving me craving for an even greater dose of high again. If winning is supposed to be a constructive endeavor, why is my gratification so short-lived and episodic? Shouldn't this so-called satisfaction be more durable and perennial?

I sit on these uncomfortable thoughts for weeks. I can't believe something worth striving for could be so volatile and erratic. I begin writing in my journal more earnestly, conversing, rather than complaining, to God about what I need to do to sustain my happiness.

Min Lian and I become close as we spend more time together at MINDS. On weekends, I sleep over at her place, and we chat through the night about everything under the sun. I continue to attend church diligently each Sunday in the hope of squeezing as much inspiration from God as possible on what I ought to do with my life.

Out of nowhere, I have a glaring awakening that I should not be striving for wins; I should be aspiring for change—changing from the inside out. When I'm being competitive, all I care about is winning, getting the prize, often at the cost of personal detachment from others. I want to turn my competitive edge into ways to improve from within. I should be less concerned about what the world thinks and more about what I want to get out of myself. Centering on nurturing my personal traits, characteristics, and temperament should be my goal rather than waiting for an outside force to define my own happiness.

"Try not to become a man of success, but rather try to become a man of value," said Einstein.

All my life, someone has been telling me what to do, what not to do, and where I should or should not go. I'm tired of letting others take charge of my feelings and my happiness. I do not want to be afraid of failures, criticisms, or disappointing someone. I want to be in control of my life when I embark on a challenge. Whether or not I make it out alive, it's my call.

Winning can feel grand like being chauffeured around and everyone acknowledging you, but you never own the ride. Don't get me wrong, I'd feel quite important being driven by someone, but I'd rather drive my own car and see the world on my time. I want to be the one behind the wheel and find my own destination even if it means getting lost once in a while or taking a detour. At the end of the ride, I get to decide if I have arrived or if I want to go on further.

Everything I have done so far has been to please someone else—my parents, my teachers, my friends, my church leaders, even the staff at MINDS. I have made every effort to do well in school, but now that I have attained the highest honor, I don't know what else there is to pursue. Instead of enjoying the fruit of my labor, I am worried about losing my place to someone else. The paradox is that my whole life, I thought the goal is to be number one, but as soon as I've reached the pinnacle, I begin to question if that's what I really want in the first place.

The problem with a competitive mindset is that it assumes there have to be winners and losers, whereas an ambitious attitude allows winners and losers to coexist because no one is replacing anyone. Being ambitious empowers me to become whomever I want to be without the fear of being no one. I don't want to be chasing after destinations and never getting anywhere. I actually want to get to a place and know that I've arrived.

I'm tired of being defined by grades, report cards, trophies, or recognition. I'm tired of worrying whether I'm going to be beaten by someone or not. I want to be in charge of my own journey. I don't want to care anymore if someone wants to race against me or ignore me. If a hundred people beat me to the finish line, I want to be fine with that, and just keep running until I cross the finishing line.

The purpose of any pursuit should be about finishing my own race and not about who gets there first. The only person I should be competing with is *myself*. I shouldn't need anyone to keep track of the time for me. My journey is my business and I want to direct the course myself.

Once I turned my mindset to being ambitious, I became less focused on defeating others or feeling defeated, but more concerned about improving myself and enjoying the journey. If I fall, and I surely will, I only allow myself to cry for twenty-four hours and then I get right back up. I learn to not let pride ruin the opportunity to inspect myself. I try to figure out what went wrong and what I can do differently the next time. I adjust my plan and restart my track again.

With this new insight, I see myself, and everyone around me, as finishers rather than as competitors. I set a vision to claim my own majestic journey and not worry if there's any cloud overshadowing me.

∾∾

It has taken me sixteen years of schooling to finally say I know how to learn. I can't help but feel that God is guiding me on my new ownership to life. He may be the Creator, but I am the author of my own book.

Picture a high school graduation ceremony—everyone of us dressed up in caps and gowns, our families bearing lucky cakes and flowers, and photographers snapping away. Wouldn't that be lovely?

Graduation at Townsville is perfunctory. I go to school, stand in line, grab my certificates, as I did in sixth and tenth grades, say goodbye if I bump into anyone, and go on my way. At Townsville, it was not a celebratory day at all because most of the students did not pass.

Being the first one in the family to finish high school, Jennifer brings me to McDonald's to celebrate. It feels rather strange hanging out with Jennifer again because we haven't done this for a long time. We no longer play in the sink or hide under the blanket to sing Chinese songs.

"What are you going to do now that there's no more school to attend?" Jennifer pokes at me.

"Well, I have been thinking ... I'm going to serve a mission. I mean, not right away, but when I'm eligible in three years at twenty-one."

"What? Serve a mission? Where are you going to get the money? You think Bàba is going to let you do that? What about Mā?"

Jennifer goes on and on without giving me a chance to talk. Her eyes grow so wide that I don't think any camera could capture her expression of befuddlement.

"Barb," clutching her hand to her chest, "be serious and grow up! You're not thinking of spending more money you don't even have, are you?"

"Of course not, I'm not using any of Mā's and Bà's money."

"Maybe you can work as a clerk first and see what you'd like to do later," Jennifer solemnly advises, "going on a mission is a waste of time and money. One and a half years is a long time."

She reaches across the table and whispers in mock horror, "Or, come work with me at the hotel. You're not as klutzy now."

Jennifer is flattering me to dissuade me from going on a mission. She asked me once to help out for a big wedding, and I thought it would be fun to see what working as a server was like, so I agreed. Oh boy, was I wrong!

I had to carry a tray full of food and serve drinks to hundreds of wedding guests. I did handle a basket full of hot curry puffs but holding a loaded tray of glassware is a different story. At one point during my walk through the tables, a male guest tugged on my right hand.

"Excuse me. Urhhh, get me a martini on the rocks." The man smelled like he was already drunk.

"What?" I asked. "What rock do you want?"

"Martini on the rocks, idiot!"

I felt a hundred eyes staring at me.

"Come on. *Wa-lah*! How could she work here? Don't even know what's the common drink. So stupid."

"Sir," I said, "how about orange juice? I can get that for you. It's better for you anyway."

"What? This is a wedding. I'm going to drink all the free liquor I can. Get my drink or I'll have you fired."

I had no clue what he wanted. As I proceeded toward the bartender, a server treading behind me caught her foot on the carpet and tripped and a fresh pot of hot jasmine tea spilled all over me!

"Ahhh, oh, so, so hot, hot, hot, hot!" I yelled.

Jennifer rushed toward me from fifteen tables away. She lifted me up in my soaked pants and scurried me through the kitchen door so people wouldn't stare at us.

I made eighty dollars (US$50) for an eight-hour shift, not bad for one hellish night. It was the most money I had ever seen, but I never wanted to be a waitress again.

"You have to be nice to be a waitress," counsels Jennifer, "Let's face it. You'll never survive. You have to please people all the time, and you're simply not a pleaser. You're too direct."

"Do Mā and Ba know you want to go on a mission?" Jennifer resumes her persuasion on why I shouldn't go.

"I haven't told them yet," I choke. "I don't know if they'll let me. I'm always going against their will and everything I want to do costs money." I look at my sister and gulp a mouthful of soda.

"Brain freezzzeee!" I giggle and splatter some Sprite on myself while ignoring the glances from the other diners.

Embarrassed, Jennifer pretends to turn her head around as if she doesn't know me. She does this whenever we bump into each other on the bus ride from school. She refuses to acknowledge me when she is with her friends. Unlike when we used to hang out with Juliana, Jennifer is now more conscious of my public awkwardness and she has an image to maintain.

We don't always see eye-to-eye when it comes to school and church. Jennifer was baptized the same day as me back in 1980. I was ten, and she was eleven. Since then, she has never been active. I don't know why, perhaps she had to choose between God or her peers.

"You know what?" I surprised Jennifer, "I want to pay my whole way for my mission. I know the church will help out, but I want to do this all by myself." Jennifer stops listening to my delusionary fantasy and wanders her eyes around for something more realistic to focus her mind.

The church will support anyone who wants to serve a full-time mission but can't afford to pay the full cost. Since the majority of the members in Singapore are the only converts in their family, it's common practice for the church to pay for whoever wishes to serve. It would be outlandish to expect non-member parents to support their children on a mission that costs around US$7,200.

"That's tons of money, you know?" Jennifer rants.

"Well, I have two years to save that amount," I say before I realize the words are out of my mouth.

Jennifer is quiet for a long time, thinking I must have lost my head.

"If I want to serve God, I want to do it all the way, with one hundred percent of my money. I don't want to rely on anyone. Will you help me find some jobs?" my doggy eyes beg.

My ambitious drive could be my curse and my blessing. I can't shake off the idea of being the first missionary in Singapore to pay all her own way. I guess I still crave after the feeling of being the first. I work myself into a state of optimism and imagine one step closer to being officially called, "Sister Hong."

Make money. That's what I need to do. Jennifer's suggestion of waitressing crossed my mind a few times because I know I'll get tips from overfed diners, but I want to raise money by some other means. I still think of myself as too klutzy to be a server. I have to look for other jobs.

There's a flower shop in Toa Payoh Central that I often pass. The owner, Aunty May, has a lot of business and is always busy. Sometimes, she leaves the store unattended to deliver flowers to nearby locations.

"I can help to watch the store and sweep the floor," I say eagerly, hoping to impress Aunty May.

"Ok, you can help me for a couple of dollars. I'll come back quickly." Aunty May dashes out with her bouquets and vases across the street.

I study the charts on the wall and start memorizing the floral names. Some of my favorites are sunflowers, daisies, lilies, and most of all, tulips.

Before long, I find myself picking up the unwanted cuts from the floor and putting together a corsage or boutonniere. Sometimes, there are even enough random flowers on the floor to put together a simple bouquet. The owner likes my creations so much that she displays them in the refrigerated shelf.

"Wow, you have an eye for arrangement, even the ones that are thrown on the floor," Aunty May marvels, "you never know what can be created out of scraps that no one wants."

I like to think I have a gift for seeing beauty in things that others regard as trash, like second-hand clothing.

Maybe one day I can be a florist like Aunty May. I love the smell of the flower shop, the crispy tissue papers, the fresh cellophane, and the final touch of the silky ribbons. Most of all, I love seeing the smiles and surprised looks on people's faces when they receive flowers.

Another job comes my way when a church administrator asks if I'd be a custodian for the administration office at United Square, about ten miles from my house. Five days a week, I take a bus and walk to the church office. I wipe down the tables and computers, arrange the stationery, empty the garbage, mop the floor, vacuum the carpets, and clean the toilets. At the end of the month, I made $100 (US$70), the most I have ever seen.

I don't enjoy physical labor but I'm not sure if I dislike the monotony of the job more or the loneliness of being by myself at work.

Out of the blue, a brother from church hears that I like making crafty cards, so he presented me with a Japanese book to try out for my birthday. I go crazy from the moment I open the book. These are not just ordinary cards but light-induced, three-dimensional, *kirigami* pop-out Japanese art. They require acute dexterity in handling a box cutter, or the whole card will not stand upright. For someone who has been trained from young to be immaculate at snipping threads, this is the perfect indulgence.

I start to make cards for every occasion and take custom orders from church members, sometimes up to fifty cards per week. There are all sorts of models to work from—famous skyscrapers, a basket full of flowers, optical illusions, grand pianos, tulips, sunflowers, animals of every kind, and my favorite of all, two ballerinas dancing on a platform.

The major problem with making these cards is the huge blisters on my right three fingers. I have to be laser precise and slice each line steadily nonstop. By the time one card is finished, my hand is sore, and my fingers are numb. Sometimes, one card takes twenty to thirty minutes to slice before I can release my fingers and feel the blood flow through my palm again. Within a month, my fingers are raw and bruised with cutter imprints like I tattooed on them. I can hardly hold a pair of chopsticks or write, but my cards are spectacularly unrivaled.

I salvage makeup kits that my sister no longer wants and use them as pastels for shading and coloring. I scavenge Māma's old buttons, lace, ribbons, and patches of leftover clothes as ornaments. I beg my sister to bring home unwanted cake doilies from work to use as backgrounds on the card. Any random articles around the house become part of my art toolbox collection. Though I make less than two dollars an hour after covering the costs, it's a hobby I enjoy wholeheartedly compared to cutting threads or selling curry puffs. Beyond the pain there is something rewarding about seeing a little figurine materialize out of a flat sheet of paper, like resuscitating a life.

"At this rate, Barb, you're never going to save enough for a mission even if you break your fingers!" Jennifer jibes.

She's right. Jennifer is always the practical one who keeps us down to earth. Fortunately, I find a new way to make better money by tutoring kids after school.

"What? Become a tutor? What exactly can you teach?" Phillip ridicules, knowing that's not my cup of tea, not even remotely close, especially in a high-pressure society like Singapore.

Everything I know about tutoring, I learned from Julia. I imitate her mannerisms, to the point of taking on her speech pattern, appraisal of the students, angular handwriting, grading standards, and mindful feedback. I try to make sense of how these kids may learn a concept by putting myself in their shoes, something I know all too well.

I discover that I do have an inclination for teaching and am quite good at it, surprising even myself. What's more is that my students are making great strides and the parents are very pleased. My client list keeps growing each month and the money is good.

Unlike the Western world where children go to school to learn, in Asian countries like Hong Kong, Japan, South Korea, Taiwan, and Singapore, most children enter school ahead of their grade level with parents strong-arming them through over-scheduled tutoring on weekdays, weekends, and holidays. This is why tutoring is such a lucrative business.

On average, parents can spend between six hundred to a thousand dollars each month on tutoring per child, depending on whether they are individual or group sessions, elementary or secondary level.[3] The irony is that these kids are probably already the top achievers. They're not struggling in school; their parents just want them to get ahead, way ahead of their teachers and everyone else. That's the price children pay for being raised in a competitive society.

Walk into any bookstore in Singapore, and one will be captivated by the spread of assessment books piled halfway to the roof, starting as young as preschool. Parents are obsessed with coercing their children to practice the workbooks day and night. No wonder Asian kids don't fret when it comes to testing—it's a habitual part of their daily routines.

కౌన

One Sunday morning at church, an American family sits next to me with their four beautiful young children. I noticed them when they were introduced a few weeks ago. After church, Jana asks if I'd babysit her four children for a few hours each day so she can run errands. Of course, I agree because I have been fascinated with these American kids since I joined the church. Not sure if I can actually handle one, let alone four, ages between eleven and six-months-old.

Jana's house is like a mansion even though it's a typical townhouse. There are no huge houses in Singapore due to land scarcity. When I step into Jana's place for the first time, the physical grandeur is overwhelming. I'm afraid I might get lost if I start wandering around.

The "mansion" has an upstairs and downstairs, like a castle I have seen in some Barbie doll catalogs. The dark

---

[3] Nayak, Shivali. "'The Best Education System in the World' Putting Stress on Singaporean Children." ABC News. January 05, 2016. Accessed August 14, 2016.

wood floor has a spacious living room with a black upright piano and a black leather couch. The windows, almost nine-feet high, are framed with curtains—pink, green, lavender, and blue florals. There is even an air-conditioner in every room, including the kitchen, laundry room, and bathroom—something beyond me.

In a corner underneath the stairs, there is an entire space dedicated for the children to play! They have Barbie dolls, remote-control cars, airplanes, at least twenty stuffed animals, and every early childhood toy imaginable. Even baby Jasmine has a room of her own with a wooden crib and bumper all around to cushion her. I've never witnessed such gentle care and coziness toward an infant.

The most appealing part is the bathroom—or the fact that they have more than one! The laundry area has a washer and a dryer, something I've never seen in my life and didn't know how to work it.

When I'm at Jana's place, I pretend it's my future home. I take great pride in caring for the place and the people within. I clean, dust, wipe, and mop whenever I get a chance even though that's not what I'm paid to do. It's an honor to take care of my fantasy home where I can escape to three times a week.

Babysitting this family is more of a blessing than a job. I pretend I'm coming home to *my* kitchen with a refrigerator filled to the brim with food. I have *my* very own piano, *my* own bed, *my* own walk-in closet, and most of all, *my* four children—Elozia, Jal, Zachary, and Jasmin, rushing to wrap their arms around me. Funny how, some twenty years later, I subconsciously named two of my children Jasmyn and Zac, but spelled differently.

"I love you so, so much," I whisper to Jasmin as I rock her back and forth, back and forth, back and forth. "You're so beautiful. I love your eyes, your lashes, your nose, your smile, your everything …"

I love looking into Jasmin's big brown eyes and kissing her on her cheek and forehead and pretend she's my baby. As Jasmin falls asleep, I hold her close to my bosom and give her one gentle kiss before laying her down in her maple rosewood crib. I check on her every few minutes to make sure she's sound asleep, but also because I want to see her one more time.

The seven months of babysitting turns into a life-changing experience for me on how to care for children and eventually raise my own. I love being around this family. Each time I walk into their house, there's a sense of calmness and tranquility, something different from the home I knew. The one thing I'm not used to is the soft-spoken nature of this household. I never see Jana spank her kids or call them names. She uses words rather than a bamboo cane to express how she feels. I never hear her yell or use vulgarity. Conversations are dignified and respectful. These are rather dramatized scenarios as if they are scripted for a fairy tale.

Unlike Māma, Jana handles each situation without having to yell at or threaten the children. I observe keenly as she handles the chaos and pays attention to every word uttered from her mouth. She is in such control of her temperament that the children, without exception, readily comply.

Maybe Jana is just being polite because I'm there, but that can't be true day in and day out. Maybe it's her patient nature and not the situation. No matter how chaotic the children are—and trust me when I say these boys and girls are typical of their age, rambunctious and energetic, the only kind of tone that comes out of Jana is ever so soft, unflustered, and affable.

When the kids run up and down the stairs, spilling juice on the just-vacuumed carpet, Jana calls out their names and placidly invites them to settle down. "Zachary, be careful with your cup. The juice is spilling on the carpet."

I want to emulate Jana's composure, even if it means learning a new way of life, the American way, or maybe the Mormon way. Each time I leave her house, I find myself wishing my family could be a little more civilized like hers.

"Hey kids, want to make some brownies?" Jana asks as she wipes up the peanut butter and jelly spilled on the counter.

"Jana, may I watch how you do that?" I ask. I have no idea what brownies are or how they taste, but it sounds chocolaty, and I love everything chocolate, especially the dark ones.

Jal jumps right back on the kitchen counter while Elozia grabs the eggs from the refrigerator. Zach tries to snatch an egg, too, but he drops it on the floor.

"It's alright Zach," Jana chuckles. "Elozia will clean it up. Go wash your hands." Jana chortles at the chaotic scene while grabbing a mixing bowl and a spatula.

I stand there and watch. Zach drops pieces of eggshell into the batter as he learns to crack an egg, and Elozia cleans up the mess on the floor.

"I want to stir, Mommy. Let me, my turn," Jal calls out and snatches the spatula from his mom's hand as he pulls the bowl closer to him.

"Oh, okay, hold the spatula like this and go around slowly like this." Jana tries to show him, but Jal brushes her hand away, and the mix goes flying all over his shirt as if he has just woken up the batter monster. Now Elozia has more to clean up. Poor girl.

"I can do it myself, I can," Jal insists with a shirt soaked in brown powder and sugar.

Jana is the most patient mother I have ever known. The way she talks to her children, no matter what the crisis is, makes them feel loved and reassured. Even I'm a child again when I'm around her—adored and pacified.

At Jana's house, I'm reliving a childhood I never had. The aura is saturated with children's laughter, wholesome dialogues, gentle apologies, and incalculable returns of *I love you*. For the first time, I see the possibilities of breathing love into a home.

My only problem with babysitting is that I'm overly protective. I do not let them go outside or do too much physical activities in the backyard. Everything takes place within the walls of their house. They don't go to the playground, watch TV, or play ball. I am the most humdrum babysitter.

While at Jana's, I develop a fixation with the daily news. I don't know what that's all about, but I suspect it started when I was on the debate team and had to know everything that's current. I look forward to getting the local newspaper Jana subscribes and immersing myself in what's going on around the world.

Back home, if I ever read a book, it's for the sake of a test or fear of being embarrassed by the teacher. Even then, I read only what the teacher assigns, not a word more. Gradually, my compulsion for learning becomes a serious undertaking. I read just about everything—politics, finance, legal, business, sports, health, science, yes, even obituaries. I had no idea that notices of the deceased were even published. I browse through bits and pieces of news as I keep an eye on the children. Soon, Jana's place becomes a sanctuary of knowledge for me, more so than books can teach. I want to know everything there is to know.

৵৽

On a warm spring day some twenty months later, I walk to the nearest branch of the bank to deposit that month's earnings. When the teller hands me my account book with the new balance, I'm over-thrilled to see five figures before the decimal point. I have saved over US$7,000! I can't believe I'm going on a full-time mission at last! Now I just need the blessings of Māma and Bàba.

Winston presents me with a pink towel that has my name embroidered in a calligraphy style. Min Lian takes me to the market and helps me find a suitcase so large that it would be forbidden under today's airport regulations. Jennifer shops for every toiletry she can think of. It looks like she emptied the store. Then, of course, I need skirts and blouses, which I get from MINDS.

Māma and Bàba know that nothing is going to change my mind. I'm twenty-one and I'm going to do whatever I want. In that cramped and cluttered flat where I fought off hideous rats and ghastly cats and the elbows of my brothers, now I try to fight off tears as I say goodbye.

Jennifer puts a chiffon blouse in my hand. "For you. It's very expensive," she whispers so Māma will not know.

Māma has tears in her eyes as we wave goodbye. Bàba too, though he tries to hide it.

As if in a fairy tale, everything happens as planned. I board the plane to Manila for my one-week orientation at the *Missionary Training Center*. The MTC is sort of like boot camp, though nothing harsh. Its focus is to prepare us to teach about God and Jesus Christ and to serve the community with all our heart, might, mind, and strength.

As the plane takes off, I scrunch my face, feelings of excitement, relief, and fear all flooded in at the same time. My first time on an airplane, soaring into the unknown, embarking on what will prove to be the most trying but poignant experience of my life.

Chapter 15
THE GIFT OF SELF

*Our opportunities to give of ourselves are indeed limitless,
but they are also perishable.*

→ *Thomas S. Monson (Mormon prophet)*

When I land at the airport, the Mission President of the Manila Missionary Training Center (MTC) and his wife come to pick me up. I'm the last one to arrive that day. When we enter the two-story bungalow downtown, about fifty other missionaries are already there, all dressed in their Sunday best, eagerly awaiting instructions on what the next week is going to hold.

To help us stay focused on our mission, the headquarters has outlined very specific rules in a pocket-sized white booklet known as the *White Bible*. Each day, there are things to do, schedules to follow, and rules to obey. Our first instructional session is going through the handbook and all the rules by which we have to abide. No exceptions. Anyone who breaks the rules at any point in the mission will be asked to leave. The mission is a serious place for serving God. It's an intense crunch time to understand the purpose of why we're here.

"Sister Hong," the Mission President calls me over to his office, "I wish to present you with your official missionary badge. Welcome to the mission field."

I'm finally an official missionary! I never thought this day was possible. I am finally doing the very thing I want to do without anyone telling me. It feels empowering to put on this three-by-two-inch black badge as a reminder of what it takes to achieve one's goal even if you start with nothing. Today is my first day in the field and I am determined not to be distracted except to serve God every second of every minute for the next eighteen months.

As prescribed in the handbook, I wake up at six to get ready for my individual scripture study at six-thirty and companion study with another missionary at seven-thirty. There's no time for chatting or lounging around. Every minute I'm on God's errand.

At the training center, we wake up to a typical breakfast of fish, eggs, rice, vegetables, and then more fish, and eggs, rice, and vegetables for lunch and dinner. I struggle with the taste of the adobo, especially when it's cooked with fish, but I get used to it quickly. I'm grateful for whatever meals they provide, at least I'm not starving like I did back in Singapore.

The missionary cohort is divided into groups of five or six. We role-play teaching each other about the gospel. Each of us is also assigned a companion like we are going to experience in the field. We look out for each other everywhere we go, and I mean *everywhere*. We're never out of sight of our companion, even when she's in the restroom. We stand by the door and wait.

Each group has an instructor, usually a returned missionary from the same area, to teach us and to give us some tips on what they have learned while on their mission. He leads us in all aspects of the training. Unlike the leader of a typical boot camp, the instructor is kind, patient, and empathic, and demonstrates what a representative of Jesus Christ should act like in public.

All day long, we study. We do not do sightseeing or tourist activities. We're reminded constantly that the Missionary Training Center is not a place for socializing.

"It's our time to prepare to serve God," as our leader says, "every minute is God's time, not yours."

Having been through four years of early morning seminary, this expectation of self-discipline and scriptural mastery is not new.

We pray a lot—before individual scripture study, after individual scripture study, before companion study, after companion study, before each meal, before class, after class, before group lesson, after group lesson, and before bedtime. About ten or more times a day, not counting all the quiet moments I plead with God to help me through the training.

By the end of the week, it's time to say goodbye. We write in each other's journal, sending off well wishes as we fly out to our assigned areas. I didn't think it was going to be so difficult to part after one week, but my Filipino friends have become my family.

After returning from the Philippines, I am assigned to Petaling Jaya, a major city in Malaysia with over 400,000 residents. Historically, the Malay Peninsula has been a rich trading ground, a place where East and West meet and mingle over farming and shipping routes. There are rain forests and mountains, beautiful beaches, and flowers everywhere: hibiscus, bougainvillea, birds-of-paradise, and orchids of every shape and size, especially on rubber trees.

Malaysia is comprised of Indian, Chinese, Arab, and Southeast Asian influences. It's more diverse than Singapore with Malay being the dominant language.

There's also a good mix of Christians, Buddhists, Hindus, and atheists—like in any community, with sixty percent of the population being Muslims. This diversity means that customs and regulations matter greatly in keeping the peace of each sect. As missionaries, we have to be conscious and sensitive in appreciating each other's beliefs and practices.

"Sister Hong!" an American male missionary exclaims as he reaches out to shake my hand. "Are you ready to embark on your first assignment to Malaysia?"

"I sure hope so!" I fake a smile to conceal my nervousness. One week of orientation in Manila isn't near enough to prepare for this arduous journey. I feel a vague sense of anxiety over whether I'll be a successful missionary. I assume these seasoned missionaries has been in my shoes and yet they made it somehow, so I hope I will, too.

"Well, let's get on the road. We don't want to miss the show." His companion drags my overstuffed suitcase into the back of a white van. "This will be the best time of your life!" he exclaims with excitement. I hear returned missionaries say that a lot, but I still hasn't quite grasp what that expedition entails.

My flight to Manila was my first time on an airplane, and now I'm taking my first train ride. I can hardly catch my breath. Sitting on the train by myself, I'm overcome by the most painful nostalgic feeling for my family. Being on my own is harder than I imagined. Even if I did not love the place, I called home, I miss being with people I call my family.

Up to this point in my life, I have always wanted to escape from the entrapment of my scrawny, mangy, suffocating flat. I hate the sweaty stench, the nights of Bàba's drunkenness, and the bloody cats. Now that I finally leave home, by choice, to do what I have set out to do, I feel somewhat guilty and ambivalent.

Am I doing the right thing? Should I have left? Am I just running away from something or running toward something?

I'm having second thoughts. I took all this money I have earned and put it toward my own selfish goal instead of giving them to my parents. The novel sensation of being free is invigorating but stepping into another life for which I feel underprepared is petrifying.

After what seems like an endless ten-hour ride, I finally reach Petaling Jaya. From the scratchy window panes, I see a crowded station with passengers hurrying off somewhere. I lug my bag onto the platform and glance around for someone with a black name tag like mine.

"Hi, Sister Hong!" A young Elder, an assistant to the mission president, notices me from afar. He walks over and shakes my hand with a firm grip or the missionary handshake. "Let's get you to your apartment. The other sisters are waiting for you."

Each week, we plan our schedule by filling out a blue tri-folded planner for everything we want to accomplish, right down to the half-hour. There's no idling time. My trainer, Sister Linnie Tan, and I are out of the apartment by nine in the morning, again, based on the mission rules, and back by nine at night. If there's any time we're not teaching, we're talking to people on the street.

Even before my mission, I have been told to *lock my heart*. We're not to waste our time with matters of the heart. Keeping all the mission rules is essential to my success. Locking my heart pertains as much to worldly stuff as to dealings with the opposite sex. I am to think less of my desires and needs and more about serving others. Even though being a full-time missionary has a lot of dos and don'ts, no one is breathing down my neck. I know I am on a spiritual errand, so I am immensely conscious of how I use every minute of my time.

After about three months, I'm assigned to labor in Ipoh, Malaysia's fourth largest city. The town's claim to fame is that it used to be the tin-mining capital of the world. The landscape around it is marked with the scars of open-pit mines. The town has stagnated over the past forty years or so, and as a result, the downtown is still occupied by many of the old Colonial-era buildings. The railway station, for instance, is a masculine white building that, through the steadily falling rain, looks like a decrepit palace.

The park in front of it is lined with palm trees that rustle in the wind and rain. It's the kind of city where generations of a family stay and never leave to go anywhere. I find the people contagiously friendly and the *Ipoh Ho Fun* unparalleled to any noodles I've ever tasted.

I try to see the goodness in others and don't judge people by the clothes they wear, the vehicle they drive, the way they speak, or their general dispositions. Naïvely, I also envision that strangers will be delighted to meet me because I have something important to share with them, but that's not the case at all.

As the weeks trickle by, being a missionary begins to be excruciatingly hard and often unrewarding. I have never seen more people change direction faster than when I approach them. I have never heard more people tell me "I'm running late for an appointment" than when I ask for two minutes of their time.

My black name tag, which reads, *Sister Hong*, has a lot to do with this avoidance. It's not like I look like a nun, but I guess it's easy to mistake the title of *Sister* to be such. My old-fashioned, run-down clothing probably contributes to that notion. If people have nowhere to escape, like in an elevator, they would stare at their feet or up at the roof, anxiously waiting to dash out the door once it opens.

I'm shunned ninety-nine percent of the time, but I find comfort in the American writer, Wayne Dyer's words:

"The highest form of ignorance is when you reject something you don't know anything about."

Each Sunday at church, I walk past a corner classroom to remind myself: *"If you come to a point when it's too hard to stand, try kneeling."* Prayer becomes my daily dosage of a spiritual vitamin boost; it heals, mends, re-energizes, and bolsters my feeble heart to carry on. Sometimes, I want to shout from the mountaintops—or, more accurately, at the bus stop where I proselytize.

"Why? What am I doing here? I'm here for you, God. Why is it so hard to talk to these people? Help me out here! I'm desperate!"

Even the physical aspects of the mission are difficult during the long days on the street under the hot equatorial sun. I often feel hungry, though this is as much my fault as the circumstance. I'm reluctant to spend the hard-earned money to buy anything. There are times when my stress level is so high that I wish for a packet of chips or a piece of sweet to curb my cravings, but I dare not spend. I'm afraid of running out of money before my eighteen months is up. I do the only thing I know, which is distract myself from the thought of food like the many nights I had to do growing up in Singapore and forced myself to go to sleep starving.

I have never prayed so fervently than I do during my mission. "Oh, Heavenly Father, please, help me help these people … open their hearts … help me be humbler … teach me to listen … bless my family … lift my spirit …"

My supplications become more earnest and more desperate at times, but the inner voice comes back with even greater reassurance, "You're about my business. I will take care of you. Be still and know that I am God."

There are exceptional moments when someone is pleasant enough to stop and listen to what I have to say. "Tell me more … I have been looking for an answer for so long. Look at all that's happening around the world. Do you think there's a God? Where did I come from? What is the purpose of life? Where will I go after I die?"

There are also times when people look so promising and eager to hear the message and then, out of nowhere, decide to stop. "I'm not interested anymore." "Stop calling me." "I want nothing to do with you or your church." "You're a cult, leave me alone!"

It's not easy to take rejection because I regard my mission very personally. Each refusal feels like a knife stabbing through my arteries. On the positive side, I learn to be more patient and accepting of others and to allow everyone to exercise their freedom. I learn to respect the rights of others, and, most of all, to believe that God is mindful of each one of His children.

After getting to know someone personally and hearing their stories, I feel close to them, as if we've been friends for a long time. Then, all of a sudden, someone decides to ignore my calls. I find it hard to reconcile that hurt. Each time I have to recover from such a rejection, I search within myself to see how I can be more empathetic and in tune with the spirit to understand their hearts. The gospel is about love, kindness, patience, and gentle understanding. I cannot share the message of love unless I love them first. Even if they reject me, I must still love them unconditionally as Christ would.

Toward the end of my sixth month, I gain a new awareness about people. Rather than set a goal to convert people into the church, I take this opportunity to help people improve themselves. The gospel is about happiness so if I can help others make better choices in their lives, I know they will be happier.

I learn that a subtle but important distinction exists between being religious and being spiritual. Being religious entails obeying rules and showing the outward demonstration of faith, whereas being spiritual is about internalizing a degree of connectedness to our inner self that is deeper than an outward expression.

Buddha taught: *"Just as a candle cannot burn without fire, men cannot live without a spiritual life."*

I see my role as helping people find the inner voice within themselves. This inner voice can come from a belief in a divine being, but more often than not, it's something that emanates within one's moral and spiritual conscience, also known as the light of Christ. I learn from first-hand experience that it's impossible to go through life alone. All the sufferings, abuses, poverty, mental illnesses, addictions, loss of loved ones, betrayals, and disappointments are for a reason—to build my resilience and my faith that I'm not alone. How else would I have made it so far?

No amount of wealth or status can bring me more inner peace than the knowledge that I am watched over by a divine being. There comes a time when I must seek another avenue to release my earthly state of mind, away from the daily humdrum and manic chaos. I need to know that a supernatural power is there to strengthen me, comfort me, and pick me up when I stumble through life's uncertainties. I can't escape the madness around me so why do it alone? All I need to do is reach out for his hands to take the wheel and continue in my journey.

As much as the mission is for me to serve God, it's also for Him to open my eyes. I am worth more than what I thought. I may have failed but I am not a failure. I want more out of myself than what I'm constantly being measured against—grades, money, winnings, or popularity. I don't want to run around life's minefield without a spiritual compass. That is dangerous, exhausting, and most definitely, meaningless. My faith has altered my belief about myself, and now as a missionary, all I hope to do is extend this experience to others as well.

Plato wisely puts it: *"We're twice armed if we fight with faith."*

At night, when I'm down on my knees pleading with God to sustain me for another day, I see moonlight shining on one of my popup cards—a grand piano. I wonder how a small ray of moonlight, over some 200,000 miles away, can revive a piece of cardboard into such a vibrant silhouette. I brought this card with me because of the painstaking effort it took to cut each key on the keyboard. This is a constant reminder that I must allow the touch of the Master's hand to play the tune of my mission.

I get off my knees, and my eyelids flutter shut as I marvel and, oddly enough, feel flooded with gratitude that I get to be a missionary today.

On Mondays, missionaries write home. This is part of the rule. Though my Chinese is weak, and Māma's literacy is limited, I try to convey a few simple words, hoping she'll get the gist of what I'm trying to tell her.

Mā,

My mission is good.
I'm healthy.
Every day busy teaching. Walked a lot.
I miss you.

I love you, Mā.

Love is something Asians hardly express openly, at least not in words or gestures. Missionaries only call home twice a year, typically on Mother's Day and on Christmas, so writing is the only way of letting her know I *do* love and appreciate her. I know she must be worried since the day I was born, if I'll survive the toxic she has ingested in her attempt to abort me or the damage done to my brain.

Amid my absence, Bàba, unbeknownst to the rest of us, sold the taxi, which was the last of his inheritance. He used the money to buy our family a new flat in Serangoon, a greener neighborhood that's farther out in the suburbs from Toa Payoh. Even though the new flat is modest and has two toilets, the whole place seems sullen, lifeless, and weary.

Jennifer, Phillip, and Winston are living on their own, so no one hardly comes to visit. Māma and Bàba stop yelling at each other, but I'm not sure if they're at peace or happier because Bàba can't drink now due to his declining health. Standing by the balcony smoking twice as much, he seems sober and quiet most of the time. Māma, on the other hand, continues to keep up a frantic pace, keeping the house tidy, mopping, wiping, and dusting. I don't why, but they stopped talking to each other.

Eventually, my time in Ipoh comes to an end, and I spend the final months serving in Singapore, proselytizing in neighborhoods I have known my entire life. As I get ready to end my mission, I have no clue what my following crusade will be.

"What's next, Sister Hong?" Brother Ang, my seminar teacher, asks "You have only three months left on your mission. Have you given any thought to college?"

"Me, college?" I suppress myself from laughing out loud, "What a ridiculous thing. I was lucky to have made it through school, Brother Ang. College is for intelligent people. I don't even know what that entails."

I had begun to enjoy studying when I left Townsville, but college is too far-fetched. No one in my family would even imagine that.

"I can't see myself in college. That's for smart kids, and the rich ones probably."

Brother Ang is silent, forcing me to think and eventually break the silence.

"I also can't picture myself working. I'd make a good florist or something along that line."

Silence.

"Look, how about I continue making cards? That hobby earned me enough for my mission, didn't it? I can make a living out of this trade."

He chuckles to embarrass me for my naïvety.

Jennifer left her waitressing job at Shangri-La a few months ago and is now a secretary at a temp agency in midtown.

"I can work with Jennifer at her temp job agency," trying to convince him to drop the matter. "Surely, she can help me find a job with all those hotel connections, maybe even an office job!"

From my youth, all I have ever heard Māma say was that she hopes one of us will work in an office with air conditioning and have a personal cubicle. I don't know what that would take, but Jennifer certainly made Māma's dream come true.

I pretend to have convinced Brother Ang and he stops asking me. As if Brother Ang can see through my mind and heart, he gives me a sharp look and with candor says, "I thought the mission gave you more confidence."

"I ... I *am* confident," I stammer a little but quickly catch myself wavering.

"You're capable of surprising everyone around you, and you're also capable of surprising yourself," he says.

My cheeks burn. I'm still not used to praise.

I attempt a joke, "Well, I wouldn't like to sit in an office all day long anyway. I like what I have been doing—talking to people and teaching. Is there such a combination other than being a teacher?"

Brother Ang paces up and down, his hands clasped behind his back, trying to find a way to put his thoughts into words.

"Listen, what you need is a new place to bloom, somewhere you can spread your wings, somewhere you can exceed yourself."

I thought my mission was exactly that, but I guess not. It's a rite of passage into adulthood but not something that defines my potential. I feel there are a lot of holes in the small boat I'm in right now, and I'm going to drown back to where I started unless I know where I'm going to paddle next. I'm not sure I should leave my family again. I have been away for one and a half years already. I feel thrilled to venture into the next phase of my life, but also immensely guilty for leaving my family again.

Who wouldn't want to have a fresh start? But sometimes, it's more of a fantasy than a reality. There will be a lot of reproofing if I were to leave again. I can't go wherever and whenever I desire. That's considered irresponsible.

"Have you consider attending BYU in Hawaii?" he inquires with hesitation, not knowing my family's circumstance.

I have overheard conversations about Brigham Young University in Hawaii for years but never paid attention to it because I have no intention of pursuing further studies. It is common practice for young adults who completed their mission to attend the church school. Over the next couple of weeks, Brother Ang, backed by Min Lian and my mission president, continues his campaign to persuade me to apply for BYU–Hawaii.

"And the young men are cute and smart in America," Brother Ang's wife, Julie, chimes. "You might find a nice boy. You don't want to end up being an old maid, do you?"

I blush ferociously because I'm still on my mission, and dating is the last thing on my mind. I find it hard to believe that any guy would hang out with me long enough to become serious. While many of my friends from my mission are already making plans for family life, I can't picture anyone loving me enough to want to marry me. Māma has made it a point to remind me that I'll be so lucky if any man even notices me.

"Look at your flat chest, deflated butt, and crooked teeth," Mā derides me blatantly from head to toe, front to back. "No sane man would dare to walk next to you, let alone marry you. You should be so lucky if he's blind."

I don't know if BYU–Hawaii is the answer. I don't know if there's such a thing as the right man or the right place for me. Should I give myself a shot at BYU–Hawaii?

School is more of a last resort than an aspiration, or maybe, an escape to erase my past. My head is telling me studying is not a thing for me, but my heart is begging me to take on the challenge and discover a new beginning. What do I have to lose? If all else fail, I'll return, in shame no doubt, and start my life back up again. I've done that before throughout my life. I submitted my application and awaited the decision.

At my mission apartment, while I sort through my luggage and get ready to return home, I try to wrap my mind around the idea of going to America. All I can picture in my head are teachers hitting me and humiliating me. Why would I subject myself to my greatest fragility in front of those American professors? They'll probably laugh at me and then expel me after one semester. Not to mention, what will Māma think if I decide to leave Singapore again?

As the last month of my mission winds down, I still haven't heard back from BYU–Hawaii, but I am content that I have devoted the past eighteen months to serving God. I continue to agonize over the grueling possibility of having to go back to school, handing in homework, and taking exams.

It is a Sunday night, and all my companion sisters are asleep. The small apartment seems tranquil. I look out the window from my bed to observe the dark sky, wondering if I'm one of those tiny specks swallowed by the massive space. Can I ever shine through the dark clouds or am I always going to stay hidden? When will it be my time?

I have never seen any pictures of Hawaii. In my mind, the only image I have is of myself, Jennifer, my brothers, and the rare days Bàba takes us on an outing to East Coast Beach. We're wearing old t-shirts and jumping into the waves while Bàba watches from the shore with a brown beer bottle in his hand.

I picture a single palm tree standing out from the yellow-flowered frangipani and the rain trees that flood the streets. The leaves sway gently in the wind, and each time they lift themselves, the light shakes out around them. It's paradise. An odd feeling fills my chest—a calmness that I can only describe as surreal. What would it be like to be a tree? Would I simply wait for what is harsh and accept what is good and let the wind blow me wherever it may?

Proverbs 3: 5–6 comes to mind: *"Trust in the Lord with all thine heart and lean not unto thine own understanding. In all thy ways acknowledge Him, and He shall direct thy paths."*

I don't want to be a brick wall forever, cemented to a building and grounded permanently. After twenty-two years, I want to break free and break away. If I don't do it now, I don't know when I am ever going to break through these clouds.

Part Four
FOUND

Chapter 16
AN ISLAND OF LOVE

In any moment of decision, the best thing you can do is the right thing, the next best thing is the wrong thing, and the worst thing you can do is nothing.

~ Theodore Roosevelt

A second flight will take me even farther afield than the Philippines. I see America this way—men are cowboys who ride horses over vast plains of tall grass (based on Bàba's favorite character, John Wayne), women in chic brand name clothing (like those I snipped), fair skin, wavy blonde hair, electric blue eyes, and long, curly eyelashes. Asians like to call Americans *white ghosts* because their skin is so fair that they look ghostly.

White people is still a foreign concept. My overall impression of Americans is that they are well-read, savvy, ingenious, exceptionally magnanimous, well-mannered, sometimes far too honest, and mostly jovial. I see myself as being far below these white ghosts in every aspect. I also have this image of Americans living in Barbie-like Cape Cod or British style Victorian houses with well-kept lawns, a wooden swing set, a collie named Lassie, and everyone sitting by a dining table eating dinner together. At least that's how the TV portrays them.

As the plane thrusts into the sky, I picture myself going upward beyond the skies toward the unknown. People say it's a brave thing to embrace new adventures in your life, but that's a lie. I'm not brave at all, I'm scared to death. I have no idea what I'm in for and what I want to get out of it. I don't even know what *it* is.

To distract myself, I pick up a magazine in front of my seat and flip through the pages. I always thought the highest mountain is Everest but it's actually Mauna Kea on the Big Island. Very cool. It rises from deep under the waves to reach a final height of 33,500 feet above the ocean floor. Hawaii comes from the word, *Sawaiki,* which means *homeland.* It's the only state in the US that's composed entirely of islands. Its picturesque landscape bound by the panorama beaches is the most breathtaking thing I have ever seen. Its magnificent amber sky emits an unruffled serenity that's both aesthetic and tranquil. Because it's a land of volcanoes right in the middle of the ocean, even on the hottest days, there's something feminine and majestic about the islands. Perhaps it's the intuitive waves, the surging cacophony of the ocean hitting the rocks that keep people so buoyant and rejuvenated.

I arrive at the Honolulu airport on a humid Saturday afternoon. As the gentle breeze blows in my face, the fragrance of plumeria fills the briny air. I am reminded of the frangipanis back home, a genus of same tropical tree. I can't believe I'm in America! Land of super-everything—supermarkets, super highways, super-sized meals, and superheroes.

I dive through the baggage claim, embarrassed that I have the biggest piece of luggage ever invented. Being the practical Chinese I am, I have to economize. Good thing there aren't any restrictions on baggage size. Jennifer and Mā stuffed the bag with everything imaginable even though they have never been overseas before. No matter how I argue, they're convinced that I'll not be able to find anything in the rural, remote part of North Shore, Laie.

"They don't have anything like this over there," Māma says, pointing to the shampoo, hairbrush, bobby pins, paperclips, and ballpoint pens.

"She's right, Barb," Jen adds. "What are you going to bathe with, brush with, or write with? Toilet paper?"

From sanitary pads to hair accessories, toothpaste, toothbrush, and every daily amenity, Jennifer makes sure I have one of each at least.

"Don't run out of pens and erasers, White Out, scotch tape, staples, or thumbtacks," she says, "make sure you have at least a year's supply."

My host family, the Matsuzakis, welcomes me with open arms at the airport. Their son, John, just returned home from serving a mission in Singapore, so he arranged for me to stay with his family for two weeks before I check into the dorm.

The Matsuzaki family is the textbook case of the aloha spirit—contagiously friendly, generous, kind, and happy—unlike any groups I have ever met. Initially, I feel uneasy about having people hug and kiss me on my cheeks whenever they greet me. Māma's distrust of people has set me on an overly cautious mindset about meeting people who are nice.

"If people are nice to you, they want something from you," Māma warns, "Never trust anyone. Watch it, nine out of ten times, people are con artists, ready to take advantage of you. If you're gullible, you'll fall for it."

But soon, I learned that Hawaiians are just organically friendly. They want nothing more than to radiate their love to others. I don't, for a moment, perceive the Matsuzakis as con artists. It's true that sometimes their more-than exuberant personality, asking "How are you? Are you enjoying yourself? What can we do for you?" makes me want to shrink into myself like a tortoise, but that's their aloha spirit, they can't help it.

Dinner at the Matsuzakis' is a family event. Everyone helps prepare something. Whether it's cutting, chopping, pouring, stirring, cooking, setting up the table, or placing the napkins, everyone has a role to play—a scenario that never happens in my home. Māma never lets us help with any cooking. She insists that she's the only one who knows how to cook in the family. I have never once turned on the stove in that kitchen to boil water or an egg. Thank goodness for my missionary training, I have learned to cook a dish or two. Here at the Matsuzakis, the kitchen is a lively zoo, filled with laughter, teasing, and merriment.

The Matsuzakis introduce me to the best food in Hawaii—Spam musubi. Essentially, it's fried Spam with sweet soy sauce laid over white sticky rice and wrapped in seaweed and a layer of fried egg. Unlike on the mainland where people sell baked goods for school fundraising, Hawaiians sell Spam musubi! This is the only kind of meat we ever ate growing up, and I love it! Māma would fry the luncheon meat with a mixture of onions and potatoes over diluted ketchup as the sauce. It's one of my favorite dishes. Those were the good days when Bàba would eat Māma's cooking without throwing the plates at her or us.

On weekends, the Matsuzakis take me to the beach and feed me Hawaiian barbeque and local Japanese tempera. I can't believe the one thing Jennifer forgot to pack for me is a bathing suit, so I sit on the bench in Waikiki and watch everyone else swims. For some reason, I associate the beach with sadness, loneliness, and faraway horizons. The combination of palm trees, the cool breeze, and familiar laughter make me feel I have abandoned my family and come to enjoy a new life for myself, like the prodigal daughter except I don't have any inheritance to squander. Somehow, I didn't feel as guilt-stricken when I went on my mission, but Hawaii is different. It's way too distant, too carefree, and all too heavenly from everything I have ever experienced thus far.

I'm hyperventilating. I try to calm myself by distracting my mind with the rhythmic ripping sound of the mesmerizing waves. What if I made a wrong decision? What if I should have stayed? What if I don't make it? What if …? What if …?

૭∾๑

It is hard for me to say goodbye to the Matsuzakis when I move into the dorm. I pull my sweater tightly around me and drag my oversized luggage to Hale Two, room 209B. The dorm appears much bigger than I had expected. The freshly painted room has maroon carpeting, a pale pink desk, two twin beds, and two narrow white closets, one of which is all mine.

For the first time, I have my own space. There's no need to put my mattress away. I have my very own desk, my own writing space, my own closet, my own bulletin board, my own pillow, and my very own bed.

After the Matsuzakis leave, I finally have a moment to myself, but ironically, I'm not happy. I feel lonely and alone without a roommate or my family. I force myself to unpack my oversized suitcase and make this place my new abode for the next four years. A package of steel wool pot scrubbers flies out. I can't believe Jennifer packed so much inside this bag. I find sponges, spools of sewing thread of every color, slippers, tissue paper, a travel iron, a cassette tape player, cassettes of Cantonese, Mandarin, and country songs, and more redundant stuff.

I giggle to myself, and then tears start streaming. My emotions are mixed. I can't believe I'm finally here, in college, starting a new life and embarking, once again, in the world of schooling—something I had consciously avoided. I can do this! I have to do this. There's no turning back. I look around the room, still in disbelief that I have made it to America! I have to stop unpacking for a while. My heart won't stop pounding, like the waves hitting against the rocks, disrupting and rebellious.

Oh God, why am I here? Why am I feeling guilty? Oh dear, is this a big mistake? Why can't someone hold me and reassure me?

I feel so alone.

I walk over to the mirror behind the door and sit down on the carpeted floor. I can't remember the last time I cried. I haven't had the chance to be alone and pour my heart out since my mission, or maybe longer. It has been too many years of buried tears imprisoned inside of me, and now all I want to do is release each drop. Bawling like a toddler, I watch myself in the mirror, bursting into tears. I'm not sure if these are tears of joy, sadness, relief, or trepidation. I haven't figured it all out yet. Exhausted, I lay on the floor, still unsure if I should claim the bed yet.

After a few minutes, I get up. I unpack a stack of taped items and found my journals, the ones I hid under the mattress before I left on my mission. When my family moved to Serangoon area, Jennifer found them and carefully taped them up so the edges wouldn't get bent. Oh, my thoughtful sister!

I flip through the pages; a piece of paper flies out. I recognize Jennifer's handwriting immediately. It's a letter from her. It's unusual in my culture to express affection openly, let alone write down how we feel.

"I love you, Barbara. Take care of yourself and don't forget your family back home. Love, Jennifer."

In twenty-three years, it was the first time Jennifer expresses how she feels about me. We have never said that to each other before. I don't quite know how to react. I'm deeply touched.

It's the first time a family member has ever said they love me. I know Jennifer would never have spoken those words in person, not in a million years, but I know she means them. I sob again, even heavier this time. I look at all the stuff Jennifer has packed for me and shove it under the bed for now and just savor the sweet note from my big sister. I think back to our times together playing by the sink and pretending to cook. The times we squatted on the front door of our flats cutting, trimming, and sewing into the wee hours of the night. The times we fought and argued and made up. Oh, how I yearn to have one more day with Jennifer, even if it's a lousy one.

My roommate has not checked in yet, so I have the whole room to myself to pour my heart out. I didn't realize how much I have taken my family for granted. Leaving home has put a sentimental dent in our kinship. I'm not sure how I'm going to make it through the week, never mind the semester or the years ahead.

I go downstairs to check out the dorm television. *The Wizard of Oz* is playing. It scares me a bit because it feels like a dream I had once. It is the moment when Dorothy goes to Oz, and suddenly the world is brighter and more colorful than she has ever imagined—freer, more amazing, and more beautiful—but she misses her simple home.

The first week of school is a blur of shaking hands, learning names, and finding places on campus. I also have to find a job. The campus is full of freshmen unloading, unpacking, and standing in lines—for books, identification cards, food, and registration. I try not to stare at everything and every person, but I can't help it. I have never seen Polynesians before, and I don't even know which part of the world they're from.

At that time, BYU–Hawaii enrolled students from fifty-five countries. Today, they have students from over eighty countries. It is the most diverse university in the US. Everyone looks so peculiar—Hawaiians, Samoans, Tongans, Fijians, Micronesians, and many others I can't even figure out. I didn't know that these islands existed. This was the first year a Mongolian student was enrolled on campus. Studying with all these foreigners will be the rarest experience in my lifetime. I can't wait to get to know what they are like.

I was accepted into BYU–Hawaii as a sponsored student, which means I don't need to pay any tuition, but I have certain contractual obligations. These include living on campus, eating in the cafeteria, staying as full-time status, maintaining my grades, and working twenty hours a week in specific jobs, particularly at the Polynesian Cultural Center (PCC).

The PCC hires a good number of students, so their employment covers most of their tuition costs. The Church envisions this as an avenue for the Pacific Islanders and students in surrounding Asian countries to obtain an education. I don't know of any Singaporean or international students who are not on sponsored status. It's basically a free ride to a four-year undergraduate degree.

My advisor, JoAnn Lowe, is the most genuine, docile, and petite lady I have ever met. When I say petite, I mean literally the daintiest lady on planet Earth.

She stands at 4' 7" and probably wears children's size clothing. I know she's much older by the photos of her six children displayed on her filing cabinet. JoAnn also has the most irresistible radiance in her countenance that combusts through her smile. I have never seen a woman capable of having so much love and patience for every student she advises.

While sitting in the hallway waiting for my appointment, two things happened that would change the course of my life. One, a cute couple walked in the doorway. I later learned that the man was the son of the University President, Aaron Shumway. The lady with him was his fiancée, May. This couple was an example to me of what falling in love is like. I see them walking around campus holding hands, going to the movies with her white puffy pillow. He is as respectful as a gentleman should be, and she is as affectionate as a lady could be. My heart takes a picture. I hope someday I deserve someone who would love me like that.

The second thing is I spot a mustard-yellow flyer on the bulletin board. *Hiring—Research Assistant. Twenty hours per week. Education Major. Proficient keyboarding skills. Senior standing preferable.*

What on earth does *keyboarding* mean? What does senior standing mean? What is an education major? All I know is that Asians primarily study business, computing, finance, accounting, hotel management, engineering, and science—careers that are perceived to secure better earning potential. I read the flyer over and over again. The harbinger of change beckons me to inquire about it.

At the end of the hallway, I see an office door— *Education Department*, and tiptoe toward it.

"May I help you?" Mona, the secretary behind the desk, dressed in a traditional Hawaiian muumuu, asks.

"I, uh, that job, on the flyer, uh, research assistant, uhhh," I slur. "Can you tell me more?"

Mona can tell how nervous I am and responds with a warm aloha smile. "That would be Brother Jackson, but he's not here yet. Would you like to take a seat? He should be here any minute."

That sounds weird. Am I supposed to address professors at the university as *Brother* and *Sister* as we do at church? I'll have to get used to that.

The atmosphere probably explains it all. Everyone is so friendly, smiling all the time, and polite. Maybe it's the contagious aloha spirit mixed with the spiritual mission of the institution that transcends the typical academy of higher learning. What a contrast to the schools in Singapore.

"No one has applied yet," Mona says, "Brother Jackson just put up the poster yesterday. Are you an education major?"

I clear the frog from my throat. "No, no, uhhh, not really. I haven't decided yet," I pretend I know what that major is.

"I'll wait for him here," I reply.

Just as I'm about to sit back down, Mona says, "Aloha, Brother Jackson, there's a student here waiting to speak with you about the research assistant position."

My palms grow wet, my muscles tighten, and my eyes dilate. This whole ordeal of being interviewed by an employer, who is also a professor, is daunting.

"Good morning!" Brother Jackson greets everyone and then turns to me. "Come right in."

My heart thuds wildly as I tiptoe behind him. His office has a huge desk on the side wall with books and journals piled to the ceiling with titles like *Exceptional Children, Disorders, Disability Study,* and *Special Education.* I cringe inwardly. I don't know what these terms mean. Oh, please don't ask me about special education.

Brother Jackson is rather large in stature, almost six feet tall. When he sits, I have to stretch my neck to maintain eye contact with him. His voice is equally deep, loud, and booming, a little gruff but still affable.

"Here, sit. So, tell me about yourself."

"Oh, I arrived two weeks ago and am looking for a job," I say with a sheepish grin.

He wrinkles his forehead and leans back into his swivel chair.

"Well, we typically don't hire freshman, and certainly not a new international student who is just gaining her footing. What have you done in the past? What is your background in special education?" He pauses, searching my eyes for an answer.

This is so embarrassing. What was I thinking? I want to dash out of the office right now!

He senses my awkwardness and tries to ease the conversation. "This job requires some basic skills in writing, computing, and library research."

He points to the computer. "Have you ever worked on one of these before?"

"Uh, no."

"This?" He points at the keyboard.

I shake my head.

"What about this?" He points at the mouse. "Do you know what this is called?"

"Uh-uh. I've never seen one before," I reply with obvious self-consciousness, shifting glances all around the room.

"This is called a mouse," he says in his consoling voice, sensing I probably don't know that either. "Look at the wire. Doesn't it look like a mouse with a tail?"

"Oh yeah, I see, it does look like a mouse!" I let out.

Of course, I know what a mouse looks like; rodents have been the bane of my existence. It's weird to compare something so technical to something so ghastly. Who on earth came up with that name? Probably wackos who think everything is cute, even rats.

"Want to touch it and see how it works?" Brother Jackson invites me.

"Okay. Uh, maybe not." All I can see is this image of disgusting rats. "Maybe you can show me how instead," I say, muscles tensing.

He moves on. "Do you know what this green symbol is?"

"Nope." I'm getting edgier with each question. I'm not doing well in this interview at all. Wish I can hide my face in my hands.

"It's a cursor. See? It moves around on the screen. This is called a monitor, and the cursor tells you where you are on the screen," he says, still smiling.

"Never heard that word before," I mutter and shift my weight from side to side of the chair.

That sounds more like *"curses"* than anything else. These computer terms are getting too foreign for me to squeeze in my non-existing electronic dictionary.

"Sorry," I finally confess defensively, "I don't know anything about anything. But I can learn."

Brother Jackson leans back again, except this time he's all the way back, almost looking like he's going to tip over. "What am I going to do with you?"

I don't know if he's expecting an answer, but he continues asking about my skills in typing, organization, communication, filing, and letter writing. I think he knows my answers by now. He looks more puzzled than before the interview, wondering how I got accepted into BYU–Hawaii in the first place. I didn't realize interviewing for a job could be so brutal, putting one on the spot to declare one's incompetence. This ten-minute feels like the Judgment Day.

"I may not know anything, Brother Jackson, but you'll never find another person more willing to work hard than me. I promise that if you hire me, I'll learn everything there's to know to get the job done. Just give me a chance to prove myself."

I don't know where that surge of confidence, or desperation, comes from, but he looks at me with full of compassion and nods, "Okay."

"OK, like you'll hire me or okay I should leave now?" still unsure what to make of it. I sit there, twisting my hands, fingers shaking.

"OK," he says a second time. "You're hired."

I jump out of my seat and hug him. I have to.

"Thank you! Thank *you*! You won't regret this! I can start tomorrow!"

I race out of his office, realizing I missed my appointment with Sister Lowe, but I feel invigorated. Only out in the hall does the reality of what just happened begin to sink in. I'm a research assistant for special education—whatever that means. Overcome with excitement and sheer unadulterated panic, I run back to my dorm and immediately kneel down to thank God.

Brother Jackson is a man with tremendous dignity. Despite his great stature, his immense head, and booming voice, he's as enthusiastic about life as a child. He's most passionate about being a teacher. In retrospect, it must have given him pause that I didn't even know such simple things as how to turn on a computer. He doesn't merely explain what I need to do, he role-plays with me through each task, from making a phone call to typing a letter, and from labeling files to using the typewriter.

"Now, watch, Barbara," he says, "this is how you call someone to request for something."

Dialing an imaginary phone number, he changes his voice to vaguely resemble mine. "Good morning. I'm Barbara Hong, Research Assistant for Professor Jackson at BYU–Hawaii." I picture Brother Jackson looming over his desk piled with papers, beaming down at me with a phone receiver in his hand. I certainly did not feel like an employee at all. I was his student, and he was my teacher.

That first semester, we compile a national list of all the disability-related services on Oahu and all the current special education materials at BYU–Hawaii's Joseph Fielding Smith Library. Our goal is to create the first comprehensive guide for disability services in Hawaii. He explains that I'm going to play an important role in getting the first special education program accredited at BYU–Hawaii. As always, every chance I get to be a first in something, I'm adrenalized!

Brother Jackson goes back to the drawing board many times to explain what accreditation entails. I take initiative and stay ahead of each task so I can be on schedule. I feel a sense of urgency to learn everything there is to know about special education in case someone asks me. I don't ever want to be caught unprepared. For the first time, I'm contributing to something important that'll have a significant impact in the future.

Brother Jackson says, "You work so fast that I have to hurry to find things for you to do. What am I going to do with you?"

I take that as a compliment. I was so worried that Brother Jackson, or anyone, might see through me and fire me. I don't allow myself any time for relaxing or hanging out with my friends. I work even when I'm not getting paid. I go to the library before and after each class and check out books and video tapes about special education. I read journals and magazines related to disabilities. I ask questions and take notes on everything Brother Jackson says, directions he gives me, and tasks I'm supposed to do. I want to get everything right.

Before long, I realize I have been researching about the children at MINDS. That was one of the most memorable times in my youth, and I often reminisce about those children. I can't believe I get to study about them now. I become more eager in my research. I learn so much about special education that sometimes, Brother Jackson refers others to me to answer questions. I have never loved learning so much.

He is very appreciative of everything I do and acknowledges my work privately and in front of others with overwhelming accolades. He values my input no matter how insignificant or irrelevant it is. I've never met a teacher so compassionate with a student, especially one who doesn't know her left hand from her right. Of all the lessons, the most lasting is the way Brother Jackson reminds me of how I should address someone with a disability.

People are persons first before they are disabled. We ought to refer to them as "a person with a disability" rather than "a disabled person," making it a person-first language. So instead of saying "I work with a down syndrome child," say "I work with a *child who has down syndrome*." Instead of saying an autistic child, say a *child with autism*. Likewise, instead of a learning-disabled boy, say a boy *who has a learning disability*.

What Stacia Tauscher declares is true: *"We worry about what a child will become tomorrow, yet we forget that he's someone today."*

Indeed, person-first language is empowering, dignifying, and not patronizing. This respectful manner of speaking has been ingrained in me since that day and helped me to develop a perspective on how I view everyone, disabled or not, and who I am as a person, an educator, and a mother.

It is not about being politically correct as it is about the way we regard another human being. Which do we see first? The condition or the person? Each of us is a person first before anything else—the profession, the disability, the wealth, the poverty, the title, or the education. Everything else is just an appendage. It's not about denying the disability or the condition; it's about acknowledging what is most important first—the individual. People with disabilities do not need pity nor do they need to be perceived as normal or average (whatever that is). Every human being wants to be treated with dignity and respect, with or without a disability. We may be different, but *we're not less*.

Chapter 17
Making 86,400 Seconds Count

Not everything that can be counted counts, and not everything that counts can be counted.

&ethinspace; *Albert Einstein*

"*B*arbara, don't tell me you're working on math again!" Nicole, my roommate, pounds on me. It's already mid-semester, but she's still homesick, and her family lives less than an hour from campus.

On weekends, Nicole begs her dad to pick her up, and then she returns to campus on Sunday night. Occasionally, though, Nicole accompanies me on weekends so we can do some fun things together, like watching a free movie on campus. Starting on Friday afternoon, Nicole would lecture me about how I need to live a little, let my hair down, smell the roses, and enjoy Aloha Friday!

Since I landed in Hawaii, I've only been to the beach a couple of times but have never touched the water. Nicole thinks this is an injustice to the island and to myself.

"We're going to the beach" declares Nicole, "Now!"

Nicole grabs my bathing suit and two towels, and we are out the Hale. What she didn't notice was I hid a sketch-book for my art class in between the towels.

"I don't believe you. For once, can't you just relax and not do anything for school?"

"I'm sorry. I am relaxing," I placate, "but I have to at least get some work done in a leisurely sort of way or else I'd feel bad later."

I can't get rid of this haunting anxiety that if I only complete what the professors assign, then I might miss out on something important. I'm not trying to get ahead; I just don't want to be the one caught unprepared if I'm being picked on. I know I do not have the most fundamental knowledge about any subject. I don't know the names of the planets, the history of the Revolutionary or Civil War, never heard of the law of relativity or what the heck is gravity. Every knowledge is a new doorway of information.

Since primary school, I was enrolled or tracked into the home economics, or non-science stream, because I was deemed the least likely to understand hard sciences. The teachers believed domestic housekeeping skills are more practical for me as a woman. I was never given the chance to take upper level science or math. At Townsville, I was again placed in the commerce stream, which was the most generic track for those least likely to excel. Consequently, at BYU–Hawaii, I now have to study twice as hard to compensate for my lack of basic knowledge.

"I have to work extra hard, don't you see?" I explain to Nicole, "I can't just survive. I have to thrive!"

How can I explain to anyone that I can't afford to be mediocre? It's not that average is bad, but I'm on a mission for myself. I have a goal to achieve; there's no turning back. This was a one-way ticket the minute I decided to leave Singapore. I cannot return home with anything less. The intense mode of studying also leads to a twinge of loneliness as I watch others laugh and chat without any worries about passing the time.

Once in a while, Nicole manages to waylay me in the Hale, saying, "No more studying for now," then grabs my textbooks out of my hands and drags me somewhere with her. These nights with Nicole always end the same. We go home, chat giddily about the evening, and then say our prayers and climb into bed.

The quiet settles around me. I hear the rustling of the palm trees and ponder about what all this studying is going to do for me. I still have no clue what I'm going to major in or what I'm going to do with my life. Then a sudden flood of guilt drowns me. I beat myself up for spending valuable time away from my study.

There are only 86,400 seconds each day, so I have to make every tick count. I'm on a freight train that never stops. I don't know where it's taking me, but I'm going along for the ride—in lightning speed. I need a day or two to talk myself out of this eruption of guilt. Still, a nagging uneasiness, even remorse, remains for weeks.

When I look back at my four years of college, I had never joined a club, never participated in a campus activity, never went to the swimming pool, never hung out in the game room (didn't even know it existed), never been to a game night, and never read a book that wasn't a textbook. I didn't have any group of Asian friends to hang out with or eat with at the cafeteria, just like back in Singapore. I rush in and rush out of mealtime, so I could get back to work or get back to my study. I deliberately avoid company and did things by myself, so I didn't have to explain to anyone what I was doing with my time. I didn't realize college has so many opportunities for building camaraderie that can last a lifetime. I didn't know part of being in college is to experience college life. Before long, I get used to being by myself and can't get out of that bind.

On Friday night when most students are off somewhere doing something fun, I lay on the grassy area by the circular field where the flags of every country represented on this campus are displayed. Because Laie is located farther north from the city, street lights are not bounced back as much into the sky, allowing infinite visibility of the glittering stars to mesmerize my soul. I recall what I had learned in astronomy class about how people in ancient times used the constellations to navigate their way. I wish the stars could direct my path right now and show me where I'm going. Maybe the stars will guide me if I stare hard enough into space. Maybe I'm not meant to go anywhere. Maybe I'm meant to be alone. Is God waiting to see if I will fail or succeed?

I have been at BYU–Hawaii for two years now, and I never grow tired of learning. I never wait more than a couple hours to review my notes. I know most of the information will fade away if I don't spend time thinking about them. I develop a habit of asking for immediate and specific feedback each time an assignment is returned, regardless of the points. I want to be clear in my understanding so there's no confusion. It's more important that I understand why I got an item wrong than why I got it correct. I pay careful attention to my errors, a lesson I learned from Julia long ago.

I take advantage of every resource available, whether it's the professors, the tutoring labs, or teaching assistants. My biology professor, Brother Anderson, teases me whenever I stand by his door.

"I stopped seeing anyone right after class because I knew you would be the one at my door."

I visit with Brother Anderson three times a week without fail since my classes are on Mondays, Wednesdays, and Fridays. We go through every question I have, and he never rushes me out the door no matter how long I take. I get into a habit that I must get an answer to my question or else I can't go to sleep. Of course, I accept *I don't know* but never *I don't want to know*.

The exciting part of this whole adventure of discovery is not so much my fanaticism about getting all the right answers but more so about knowing how to learn and how to study. It was not until years after I became a professor that I noticed there are two types of students— those who know how to learn but don't know how to study, and those who want to study but don't know what they have learned. Ideally, a combination of studying strategies and learning skills are essential in framing a disposition for achieving the optimal outcome.

Learning involves attending classes, paying close attention, thinking deeply about a topic or concept, asking follow-up questions, and clarifying one's understanding. In order to get to that point, one must build up the prerequisite knowledge for such learning to take place. This could mean reading the texts before a class or going beyond the assignment to solidify one's background information.

Sometimes, learning involves participating in relevant activities, taking careful and uncluttered notes, paying attention to errors and figuring out how not to incur them again. A key difference in why some students succeed while others don't is their ability to recognize the gap in their learning and their willingness to seek resources to close that gap. Recognizing the need to acquire the prerequisite skills or background knowledge is quintessential in furthering one's learning.

For example, it is more difficult to learn long division when one has not developed adequate fluent retrieval of multiplication facts. When one's domain knowledge is intact then learning can take place more meaningfully because old information is aligned with new information to form the next layer of knowledge.

Studying strategies, on the other hand, entail regulating one's habit to complete tasks in order to strengthen one's learning. For example, sitting at the desk for the designated duration, managing time consciously by the minutes, curbing urges that are distracting such as social media, text messages, phone calls, emails, or last-minute errands. Such avoidances should not be approached as a form of deprivation or stimuli inhibition but as a conscious and deliberate effort to achieve one's goal in learning.

Studying strategies also call for one to know why, when, and how to reward oneself for good efforts and performance as part of reinforcing a personal sense of self-efficacy. It would be unhealthy to compel oneself to study out of sheer desperation or as a punishment. Being self-directed and self-regulated in managing one's time is the hallmark of an empowered individual.

Once I discover that both learning and studying aptitudes are essential for optimal outcome, I'm excited to enroll in as many classes as I'm permitted. Nicole teases that I'm turning into an addict of knowledge. I'm not sure if that's a compliment but I'll take it. I become fixated on reading everything I can get my hands on, everything non-fictional, that is. I never have an inclination for fiction and still haven't to this day. I'm intrigued only by non-fictional topics, something which I can say, "Um, why didn't I know that? Aha, now I do!"

The excitement of gaining new understanding, whether it's history, neurology, criminal justice, economics, physics, especially astronomy, elevates my adrenaline and gets me hooked, like an addict, I guess.

As *Alice in Wonderland* experienced, the excitement of the journey through various tunnels is about more than just reaching the end of the rabbit hole. There are no boundaries to knowledge and no time limits. The power of conscious learning and deliberate practice becomes a perpetual adventure of uncovering and revelation.

BYU–Hawaii is a small campus, with fewer than 2,000 students then. Professors are incredibly personal. That comes with the common faith and shared values within the Church, not to mention the prevailing aloha spirit in the community. My encounters with professor, administrator, and staff have been complementary and encouraging—except for one.

The class is political science. The professor, whose name I have mercifully forgotten, is a brusque, energetic, balding man in his fifties. He makes jokes often, but they are always American jokes which I can't understand. Everyone is laughing, except me. My notebook is a scrawled mess of terms like *Congress, elections, senators, electorate, mandate, legislature*, blah, blah, blah. I draw pictures and check the definitions to every term and try to make sense of what Professor X is saying, but to no avail. The whole concept of America is way too complicated for a small-time Singapore girl.

The first week of class, Professor X gives us a pretest on the function of the three branches of government. I scored a big fat twenty percent and an *Inadequate* scrawled in big red marker. I'm crushed.

I went to see Professor X and let him know that I'm a diligent student and am willing to work my head off to learn the material. If only I have a little more understanding of these foreign terms, I believe I can make it and even excel in his class.

I have no background on what's the difference with words like *states, federal, cities, national, nations, countries, counties, and capitals* because Singapore has only one city, one state, one capital, and one nation. The textbook also did not delineate these differences in comparison to other countries, and of course, the Internet wasn't in place yet.

Before I can explain my confusion, Professor X blurts, "This quiz is just the basic stuff. If you can't get hold of that, there's nothing I can do."

"What can I do to learn these terms then?" I ask, fending off devastation.

"I don't have time to explain everything to everyone," Professor X turns to his student assistant to solicit agreement. "If I had to explain to one student, then I'd probably have to explain to everyone else. I don't have time for that, do I?"

I leave his office in tears and feeling helpless. I have to drop the class. Dropping a class is a strange concept. I didn't know students can add and drop a class. I find this whole *dropping* notion outlandish for a learning institution. It's like admitting defeat and I can't have any ounce of that in my pursuit. What kind of a student will that make me? I can't shake the feeling that I'm a failure. I have started something I can't finish. I cry for a full day and vow I will never drop another class, whether I like it or not.

I don't know the idiosyncrasies of American professors. Professor X may have his rationale for the way he responded, I just don't get him or the way he teaches. Each time I run into him on campus, the color on my cheeks rises—a reminder that I'm a loser, a failure, and a dropout. I wish he had taken a little time to get to know me, to understand where I'm coming from, and why I asked those stupid questions. I think I could have found a way to make it through A little bit of background was all I needed to clarify the structure of the American government.

I didn't know it then, but my quiet, simmering indignation was an important moment, as a teacher and now as a professor. I promised myself that I'd never let a single student walk out of my class feeling the way I felt. My experience with Professor X instilled in me the centrality of explaining concepts in context. I never take any students' background for granted.

On the first day of class, I let my students know that no question is ever too shallow, too stupid, or too redundant. If one student does not understand, it'll be worth the time to explain until the whole class gets it. There's no point proceeding when each piece of information is cumulative and leads to a more complex idea. Unlike traditional illustrations where learning is explained as an extended vertical or horizontal line, it is better described as a circular spiral twister, interwoven into various forms of meaning. I'm often confounded by the simplest questions from my students.

The following semester, I sign up to retake the class from another instructor, Sister Debi Hartmann. She is a part-time instructor working on her master's degree at the University of Hawaii, but extremely knowledgeable about the subject matter and approach to delivery. For a foreign student like myself, I understand everything she teaches. It's the way she makes connections fathomable and coherent.

What is surprising is at the end of the semester, Sister Hartmann suggests that I should consider majoring in political science. I'm flattered, but what's defining is the power one teacher has on a student because she is willing to reframe the content from an outsider's perspective looking in. That's what I call empathetic teaching.

I keep my promise and never drop another class because I never have to. I stick it out no matter how out-of-this-world the subject is for me, like tennis, keyboarding, visual arts, psychology, piano, or American literature. The price of staying on course is finally coming to fruition.

I enrolled in Physical Science—a subject I know absolutely nothing about. A retired instructor from BYU–Provo taught the class. About fifty-five students signed up.

Brother G. is a brilliant professor. His depth of knowledge about how the world works mesmerizes me. He makes connections between temporal and spiritual theories and enlightens us about God's fingerprints in the universe.

The only problem is that he speaks in a low, monotone, inflectionless voice, and lectures to an overhead projector. By the second week, only half of the class is showing up. By the following week, it has dwindled to fewer than ten.

"How can anyone deny there's a God?" he poses to himself. "Look at all the marvelous creations and how everything is in its perfect place. No one can do that except a supreme being. He is the master of our universe."

I don't understand why anyone would want to miss such an inspiring class, even if the instructor is stale.

"I don't want to hear him talk about God every ten minutes," a student grieves, "I get enough of that in Sunday School."

"It's a waste of time; fifty minutes feel like fifty hours," another complains.

"You can skip class and still pass the class" another one fesses up, "that's what I heard from previous students."

I don't try to understand where these students are coming from. I thoroughly enjoy seeing how Brother G. reveals God's workings in the universe. I feel a deep reverence and humility learning from someone who possesses such immense knowledge. While some may think that this parallel comparison between temporal and spiritual matters is irrelevant, or even inappropriate, in higher education, I have come to appreciate the power of knowledge from my heart and not my head alone.

Instead of moaning about professors who are boring, I choose to be intrigued by the subject. Through Brother G., I now see the universe as more than patches of black holes and empty spaces. Till this day, I'm particularly obsessed with anything physics-related because Brother G. has instilled in me a thirsty fascination about the universe. I am curious about everything around, above, and below me. I know I'm not alone.

Chapter 18
"ONE" MATTERS

⸺⸺⸺⸺⸺⸺⸺⸺⸺

There are people who live their whole lives on the default
settings, never realizing you can customize.
☙ *Robert Brault*

I grow intensely passionate about special education
after my second year as a research assistant. I think
I'm going to declare that as my major. Of course, none of
my Asian friends think that's a good idea, given that
Singapore doesn't have that field of study and the lack of
demand for that kind of teachers.

"What are you going to do with that major?" Fen,
the most outspoken Singaporean asks. "You'll never find a
job in Singapore if you study that. I guarantee you. You're
going to regret it."

"This is not a major for Singaporeans," says Julian,
another Singaporean who arrived the same year as me.
"Asians don't study that kind of thing. Besides, you don't

need a degree to teach those sorts of kids. They don't know anything you say anyway."

Fen's sister chimes in, "Let's stick with the plan. Don't waste your time. If you choose to study whatever this thing is called, you're not going to be the same as us."

Before long, my major in special education becomes a topic of gossip on the small campus. One student after another vocalizes his or her disapproval and concern. I know they mean well, but I want to follow my heart even if everything in my head says otherwise.

Life is full of choices, and sometimes I have to take the next step regardless of whether I can see the path or not. I'm reminded of the scene in *Indiana Jones and the Last Crusade* where Harrison Ford has to take a leap of faith to walk across an impassable ravine on the edge of a canyon. The only problem is he couldn't see the path from where he was standing because it was hidden; nevertheless, he relied on faith, took the first step, and walked through the void to complete his quest for the Holy Grail. He did it not by convincing his head, but by following his heart because getting the Grail was the only way to save his dying father.

I try to disregard what I know with my logical, human mind and see with my heart instead. I'm standing on mortal ground, so sometimes it's hard to leave the camouflaged footing and take that leap of faith. I could dwell on the *better-not-try-this* notion, but I prefer the *what if* and just take the chance.

Jim Rohn, the American entrepreneur, said, *"If you are not willing to risk the unusual, you'll have to settle for the ordinary."*

When I decided on my major in special education, many of my Singaporean friends disowned me for defying their advice. I want to be part of the crowd, but I also want to do what I came here to do, which is to define myself. I didn't come all this way to please others and am certainly not going to change that now. I'm the only one who is responsible for my destiny. I'm going to move forward with my decision, whether I float or sink, I'm going to swim with it.

Oscar Wilde said, *"Be yourself. Everyone else is already taken."* I believe there are alchemists and angels in my midst who are helping me walk the obscured path to the other side of the ravine. I may be alone momentarily, but I'm going to be fine.

అఞఞ

Dr. Sherman Han has been teaching English and Chinese literature at BYU–Hawaii for twenty or more years by the time I arrive. I don't know why but students address him more formally as "Doctor" or "Professor," maybe because he's not a member of the Church. Nevertheless, he's a devout Taoist, very docile, clement, and soft-spoken. A typical Taiwanese gentleman, Dr. Han is of small stature and dresses simply, usually wearing a short-sleeved polo shirt with a cap to keep the sun off his face.

We meet for the first time in an introductory Chinese class. I don't think he likes me, or maybe I don't like the subject. I feel victimized by his scrutiny. Dr. Han asks a question then peers across the room to zeroes in on me.

"How would you use this word in a sentence, Barbara?" he calls me out, "who's that character?"

I can only shake my head. He knows I'm weak in Chinese, very weak; yet he calls on me incessantly, as if to embarrass me openly.

"I don't know. I DON'T know," I react grouchily.

"You don't know or you're not trying?" Dr. Han asks, always with a broad smile.

"I honestly don't know any of these words."

I hate the class. I hate the professor even more. I thought I got over this whining and complaining as a junior now, but I guessed wrongly. I have never disliked a course so much. Since he's the only instructor teaching it, I have no choice but to take it from him. I have made a promise to never drop another class, so I'm stuck with this one.

Whenever I see Dr. Han strolling down the McKay hallway, I duck and run. One afternoon, as I am doing my duck and run act, he spots me and calls me out—in Chinese, of course, "Barbara, come to my office, I want to talk to you."

Urghhhh, now what does he want from me?

His office is perfectly arranged. Side walls raised all the way to the ceiling, piled with books; Chinese literature on one side and English literature on the other. His oversized window overlooks a huge bush of ferns and some rusty bicycles. I bet one of them is his.

Sitting on the opposite side of the shelves is a long black leather couch. It looks so inviting, so I help myself to it and sit down. I gaze out the window longingly. Another perfect, seventy-degree Fahrenheit Hawaiian day—no rain, just blue-whitish sky with a brisk breeze swaying the palm trees from side to side. I'm reminded of something I learned about Sigmund Freud in a psychology class from Sister Jackson. The comfort of the therapy couch relaxes me and invites me to lay bare my soul, but I catch myself quickly and sit right up.

"Yes, Dr. Han? What is it that you want to talk about? Am I failing?" I stay polite without showing my true annoyance.

Dr. Han starts to laugh, the kind that's out loud when you hear a funny joke, yet genuine. "Do you think I'm hard on you?"

I open my mouth but then close it again. I don't know how to answer him.

"Do you know why?" He doesn't wait for an answer. "Because I believe in you. I can tell you want to do well in school. Sometimes the hardest thing about learning is learning about yourself."

He got me.

Dr. Han leans forward. "What do you want to do when you graduate? Where do you see yourself ten years from now?"

All I've been doing so far is teach. I don't know what else there is. I try not to let him read my thoughts even though his Freudian couch is hypnotizing me.

"Be a mother, I guess," I say it half-flippantly, half-truthfully. Then, more modestly, I reveal, "When I was on my mission, I enjoyed teaching."

"So, what kind of teacher do you want to be?"

"Special education, I guess. That's what I've been doing with Brother Jackson, but my friends think I'll never find a job."

With the charismatic laughter, Dr. Han continues, "Never mind what others think. What do *you* want to do every morning when you wake up? And how do you want to feel at the end of the day?"

Hmm ... good questions. "I know I love to work with children with special needs, but I don't know if I'd be any good at it."

I don't want to sound naïve. I know it takes a lot more than passion to work with these children, and I don't know if I have what it takes. Volunteering at MINDS is one thing, working full time with these children is quite another. I hear it's a very demanding job.

"I can see you being a teacher and maybe more," Dr. Han says. I didn't ask what *more* means.

I wasn't expecting this response from a professor who knew I hated his class. I thought he was going to laugh at my first mention of being a teacher, given my drudgery about learning in his class.

I step out of his office that day with a different impression of Dr. Han. I think he's quite nice even though he appears traditional and strict, like many Asian teachers. I wasn't majoring in English or Chinese literature, so he didn't need to spend the time chatting with me. The fact that he chose to do that for an undeserving student says a lot about the person he is. It took me a few months, after the semester was over, to realize that Dr. Han was not picking on me, but he cared about me. I feel remorseful that I had thought he was mean and spiteful. He is a very kind teacher and sees in me more than what I see in myself.

It wasn't about the subject, and it certainly wasn't about the grade. It was always about me. I didn't recognize that because I was so consumed with finding faults about the class. Dr. Han never judged me on whether I finally mastered Chinese literature or not. He simply cared about my learning.

It is possible to dislike a subject without disliking the teacher. Likewise, it's possible to like a subject but dislike the teacher. I assume the latter will result in a less-than-optimal learning atmosphere. The antithesis of learning is to love the knowledge but hate the giver of that knowledge. It takes two to build a relationship—the learner and the learned. The prize for learning is the reciprocity of this synergy between both parties.[4]

As the famous saying goes: *"They may forget what you said, but they'll never forget how you made them feel."* That day, I make myself another promise—I have to find out what I want to be and dream bigger.

Dr. Han goes above and beyond to make me feel safe, continuing to advise me throughout my years at BYU–Hawaii, even after I complete the required Chinese and English classes. He never lets me out of sight each time I pass by the McKay hallway. We become very close, like family.

---

[4] Hong, Barbara S. S., and Peter J. Shull. "Impact of Teacher Dispositions on Student Self-determination." The International Journal of Learning: Annual Review 16, no. 1 (2009): 261-71.

Nicole is bewildered because she knows how much I hate Chinese, but Dr. Han and his wife continue to invite me over for dinner, especially on the weekends when Nicole goes back home, and I'm by myself in the Hale. During Chinese festivities, such as New Year's or lantern festivals, the Hans make sure I hang out with them and their two children and celebrate together, like a family.

෨ൟ

To get over my homesickness the first few days upon arriving in Hawaii, the Matsuzakis insist that I attend the single adult conference dance where unmarried members between eighteen and thirty, socialize together. Throughout the night, I stand in the hallway and peer in and out to listen to the songs, not particularly interested in talking to anyone.

On the last song of the night, a young man walks up to me, as if I was the only woman in the room, and invites me to dance with him, but I refuse. Instead, we sit on a bench outside and chat for about ten minutes. I avoid eye contact, but he keeps glaring at me as if to figure out if I understand English or not. He introduces himself as Steve, a US Naval officer here on his first assignment at Pearl Harbor.

Māma warns me about American guys and says that they are all notorious for being flirtatious and untrustworthy. She also warns me never to trust a man who drives a Jeep, wears dark sunglasses, and is in the military—the exact description of Steve. I know Māma gets these whimsical ideas about *white* people, from TV shows that Bàba watches, but I've no clue how she understands because she can't speak a word of English. Steve continues to write me every week for the next six months, and I continued to rip up every letter.

"Just go out with me for one month. And, if you feel I'm not the guy, then I'll leave you alone and never bother you again."

Why are men so stubborn? It's a good thing I am as well.

One Saturday afternoon in February, while Nicole and I are on our way to a church event called, *Especially for Youth*, we bump into Steve on campus. Even though this event is meant for the youth, ages fourteen to seventeen, Nicole got tickets from her father, who is a bishop, and we think it'll be fun to attend. Coincidentally, Steve's bishop had also encouraged him to attend even though he's twenty-eight. Nicole and I try to avoid him, but he already spots us from his parked hunter-green Jeep Wrangler. Now I have to say "hi," so I don't appear to be rude.

"Hi, Steve. Are you here for EFY too? Aren't you too old for this?"

I can't resist, but Steve is too mature and gracious to engage in this sort of rhetoric. Even after that sarcasm, he asks, "Would you like to go out after EFY? Lunch or something."

What's the harm? I think to myself. Not wanting to be perceived as rude again, I agree to go out.

It turns out that Steve is very serious about me from the first time we met at the dance. The next day, he told his racquetball buddy that he had found the girl he is going to marry. I don't know how on earth he possesses such gallant optimism after just one encounter. I still don't have a clue who he is, and neither does he about me. After dating for merely two months, which is equivalent of about eight dates since I only see him once a week, and only on the weekend, Steve proposes. That summer, we got married, but none of our families came, not even a distant relative.

As Steve and I stroll into the BYU–Hawaii ballroom, six tall naval officers, dressed in their summer dress-white chokers, lift their swords in unison and form the

Arch of Sabers. We pass underneath the swords into the reception hall, not knowing what to expect because the entire banquet is put together by Steve's ward members.

Every inch of that room is perfectly decorated, and the food is exquisite—all homemade. We have over two hundred guests from the five branches of the military—Air Force, Army, Coast Guard, Marine Corps, and Navy; all dressed in their smart number-one uniform.

A Korean student, who lives in my Hale, volunteers to play George Winston's version of Canon in D Major on the piano. Steve and I take our place by the enchanting, home-made, three-tiered, peach-colored, wedding cake. A saber is passed to us to slice the cake. This is the grandest gesture of nobility and elegance of the reception.

We step in the front of the ballroom and dance to our wedding song. Of course, it has to be *You Look Wonderful Tonight*—the song which I refused to dance with him the first time we met.

As I look around the ballroom, I feel the love of friends, classmates, professors, ward members, and strangers. But through all the congratulatory smiles and heartwarming jubilance, my only wish is for Māma and Bàba to be here.

ॐॐ

Brother Jackson is transferred to the psychology department across campus, and a new faculty member, Brother William Phillips, joins the School of Education. I'm worried that we might not get along. *What if he doesn't like me? What if he fires me? What if he sees through me?*

Oh, boy was I wrong. Brother Phillips is more than a typical professor; he's a natural-born teacher. Each time I observe him, I learn what being genuine is all about. The way he talks, greets, smiles, encourages, and teaches, there is no lingering thought of guile or hypocrisy. He is a transparent and caring person.

"Teaching," Brother Phillips says, "is not a one-stop fast-food restaurant, where you grab everything you want in a quick fashion and then gulp them down. Teaching is a learning curve."

Brother Phillips always seems to have something wise to say that confounds me and leaves me in awe, sometimes for days. He's like a spiritual teacher but in a pedagogical way. He teaches me that I must never forget to bring in the spirit when I teach. It's not the religious part but the moral consciousness inside each of us.

"If teachers are constantly focusing on the standards, homework, tests, grades, or curriculum," he says, "then they are missing the very quintessential subject of teaching—the students. The power of teaching comes in knowing that *C* stands for *Children*, not *Curriculum*.

It's hard to describe Brother Phillips except to say he's composed, jolly, and ridiculously nice. Even amid a chaotic situation, either people grumbling about the photocopying machine being jammed or the air-conditioner not working, he has a way of putting a smile on their faces.

Whenever he greets people, whether they are faculty, students, or the secretary, he will say, "How are you doing today?" and wait for a reply. He doesn't rush off to what he was doing and treat the remark like a passing thing. He truly wants to know how you're doing.

An American-born British businessman, John Templeton once said, *"It's nice to be important, but it's more important to be nice."*

I have never seen Brother Phillips get upset, ever. He seems to be in control of his temperament no matter what the situation is. "At the end of the day," he counsels, "the only thing that matters is the people."

Despite his somewhat casual and peculiar mannerisms, Brother Phillips has a mind as organized as a perfectly shelved library. He knows everything about special education and can cite research and who wrote the articles right off the top of his head as if he just read them a few minutes ago. I wish I could do that one day. I bet he reads a lot and reflects on what he reads to achieve that deep learning.

Brother Phillips is a brilliant man, but what's most impressive is his humility. As C. S. Lewis says, *"Humility is not thinking less of yourself, it's thinking of yourself less."* Brother Phillips does not like to be in the limelight of any conversations. He'd rather listen and let others showcase themselves than butt in to say what he wants.

Brother Phillips is also trusting of people but not in a gullible or naïve sort of way. He believes people are genuine if you're genuine with them.

"People are born good, but sometimes, experience changes them," he continues, "it's a wonderful thing when you can bring out the best in people."

Brother Phillips is the kind of person who takes a chance on people without reservation. Rather than expect me to do things the more efficient way or his way, he encourages me to figure things out on my own, often at the expense of his time. He doesn't hurry or remind me of the urgency of the timeline. If I get impatient with myself, he'll say, "Don't rush. It's harder to think when you're rushing. The process of completing a task can be more important than the task itself."

He compliments me for the tiniest things— preparing his slides, correcting typos, opening his mail, tidying his desk, filing his papers, answering the phone, even closing the door behind him. I've never been around someone so appreciative of every small act someone does.

An inherent character trait he possesses is standing up for the underdog, whether it's the custodian, the secretary, the delivery man, or anyone that others may deem insignificant. The *people factor* is the constant denominator, and no monetary reward can compensate for failure in our relationship with people.

"Everyone deserves to be respected no matter how they dress, how much money they make, or what title they hold," he says. "We work with people, not projects. We communicate with people, not objects. No matter what priority you have, remember that behind the desk is another human being."

I learned not to take anyone for granted, thinking he or she'll never have anything to do with me or my work. No one is insignificant. Everyone is someone, and no one is dispensable. Likewise, a teacher's first and foremost lesson to the class is the lesson of self. The way I talk, the things I say, how I behave, what I do or do not do, are the most powerful lessons my students will learn from me. Brother Phillips may be one person, like a drop in the vast Pacific Ocean, but the lessons he taught me have rippled through the lives of those I come in contact with, not only as an educator but as a mother, a wife, a daughter, and a sister.

After four enriching years, I graduated from BYU–Hawaii with the highest honor, completing twenty-six extra credits simply because I enjoy learning. It is no longer a burden but a joyous experience. I am challenged by Mark Twain's ethos: *"Never let your education interfere with your learning."* I'm not against public education; I'm against the mundane approach to learning.

I may have astounded myself, but I know I didn't do it on my own. "It takes a whole village to raise a child," says an Igbo and Yoruba proverb. Indeed, BYU–Hawaii is that village in more ways than one, and even though I wasn't a child, I became the child, learning at the feet of master teachers. Not only was my mind opened, but my heart was penetrated. I learned to see the goodness in people and, I hope, to radiate that same goodness to the world one day.

Walt Disney said, *"You can design and create, and build the most wonderful place in the world. But it takes people to make the dream a reality."*

The bond I had with these mentors at BYU–Hawaii ignited an unquenchable fire within me. They were not just playing their roles as cheerleaders on the sidelines while I complete my schooling. They were the synergy of the power of ONE—one opportunity, one candid talk, one exemplar, one act of kindness, one listening heart—all making a mark on how I will steer myself from this point on. Truly, this was more than an education I have gained. These lessons define who I am, what I stand for, and why I do what I do.

That spring, I gave birth to Elijah. It is the breathtaking phenomenon of a lifetime. I wish Māma could be here to hold my hands and wrap her arms around her first grandson. I'm a Māma now.

That summer, I marched proudly across the stage to receive my diploma, but Māma and Bàba were not there.

Chapter 19
FACING THE CROSSROADS

Consider the postage stamp: its usefulness consists in the ability to stick to one thing till it gets there.

⊱ Josh Billings

There are moments when you are about to begin a new journey and you panic, *Am I ready for this?* Then trying not to choke, you move into action.

I start teaching at Aikahi Elementary School right after graduating. This is my chance to put everything I've learned into practice, a chance to see what I can do with my students.

My class is a special education resource room for elementary students with mild to moderate disabilities. While the main school building is housed in a lovely concrete structure with large windows, contemporary lighting, and landscaped with palm trees and hibiscus bushes, my special education students are enclosed in a portable unit at the end of the field, away from everybody. My students have varying levels of ability, some with learning difficulties, others with attention concerns, and still others with cognitive challenges.

After three months, Mrs. Arakawa, the principal, a petite lady with a low husky voice, heard the rumors about the remarkable progress of my students. She decides to check out what I'm doing. She never steps inside, but I can tell she's inspecting from the windows. In the weeks that follow, Mrs. Arakawa invites teachers from other schools, including those on the Leeward side, to come and observe my class.

My students are distracted by the regular visitors coming to the class, but as time passes, they get used to it and openly share about why they love coming to Mrs. Foster's (my married name) special education class.

"What's your magic with these kids, Ms. Hong?" one teacher whispers to Rhys, my second grader who has severe learning disability.

"Magic? There's no magic, magic," Jordan overheard, another second grader who has attention deficits. "All we do is just enjoy learning together."

Teachers are whispering to each other, I assume, about how on earth do students with disabilities get so excited about learning. Something is unusual in this room, perhaps.

Everything we do, we ought to start by building a good relationship of trust first, something I learned on my mission and from my mentors at BYU–Hawaii. Students are often strangely skeptical because they don't expect teachers to be "nice" to them for some reason, but as soon as I open up to them, they start feeling at ease and trusting.

I have no problem sharing with students about my fears, strengths, limitations, interests, dreams and goals. This is not the same as confessing weaknesses or exposing vulnerabilities to weaken one's authority as a teacher. The last thing you want to do is to have students lose confidence in their teacher.

I personify learning as humanly as possible, letting students see that it's all right to learn from scratch, to make mistakes and to correct oneself, to articulate how we solve problems out loud, to use our fingers to count, and to say, *"I don't know the answer, but let's find out together."*

This reciprocal dialoguing in teaching is what builds a mutual relationship of trust. The more transparent I am about how I learn a concept; the more likely students will mirror my thought process with their own thinking. The science of teaching is not in the hiding but the revealing of how one thinks. If teachers do not know how they arrive at a concept, then how are they supposed to delineate each step of the process in order to teach their students?

I don't want to instill in them the fear of a teacher who thinks she knows-it-all or an authoritarian figure whom students cannot approach and ask why, how, when, or what takes place in the mind as one learns. Students are more likely to respect your knowledge if you respect their processes of developing that knowledge. When students see how a teacher picks up precept by precept, much like themselves, they feel safer and more confident to think that they, too, can get to that point. They become more willing to explore, more prepared to assimilate, and more anxious to engage.

The visitors continue coming each week and take notes throughout the lesson while browsing through every novelty around the room.

One teacher asks, "How do you get students to want to learn?"

Learning itself is the reward. I don't go into school thinking what I should do to entice students. Curiosity about the world is already a part of everyone's instinct. My job is to not mess it up!

I agree with Einstein, *"I never teach my pupils. I only attempt to provide the conditions in which they can learn."*

The first task is to ensure students feels safe. Safe enough to open up, to ask questions, to make mistakes, and to expect to learn every day when they come to school. I spend a good amount of time getting to know my students on an individual basis. It is the most rewarding of all the things I do. Between students and teacher, there is no second guessing as to what the one party is like or what their classmates might think of them. We even pin down each other's facial expressions and nonverbal cues. We know when one is tired, frustrated, confused, or overly excited to chat. We learn about each other's hobbies, favorite movies and TV shows, most- and least-liked food, favorite games, hidden phobias, and more. We discover that we're more alike than we are different, and we enjoy hanging out with each other and learning together.

There is no need for reward charts or warnings on the board. No need to raise my voice or remind students to get on task. No need to use bribes or threats. Almost a dream classroom I would say. I can't believe it myself! There is a natural atmosphere of reverence and hominess saturating the room. Each of the students is like my own child. We become a close-knit family where being respectful and kind to each other is part of the learning.

One of the fun ways we learn together is in how I pronounce Hawaiian names and words. We laugh out loud as I attempt it again and again. Another special way we learn is when I can't figure out how to get through to a student, and somehow one of them always steps up and offers a better example or explanation than I can. Those are some of my most precious moments as I see students care about each other and not judge anyone for something that may seem easy to them.

It is easy to forget that teaching is, fundamentally, a human interaction and should not be reduced to some quantifiable lesson sequence. Getting to know my students is key to everything I do because not knowing them connotes not knowing my audience. How can I be an effective deliverer if I cannot relate to the people I teach? Getting to know my students enables me to walk in their shoes and to draw upon their experiences to make learning meaningful and relatable. I called this *empathetic teaching*.

Teachers may have their subject matter pat down, but to effectively get the materials across to students is another matter altogether. A curriculum is *not* a living thing, but my students are. As a teacher, I may be their thought-provoker, connector, mediator, and motivator, but there are countless instances when the roles are reversed and my students become the teacher, and I, their student.

I think of a teacher like a playwright director who turns the script into a live performance, transforming learning into a personalized and contextualized living experience. My role is to maneuver that script to enable students to bridge the gap on their own terms and to ignite a spark in their own minds.

As the children are dismissed, a shimmering radiance lights their countenances. Today, I get to put a smile on their faces. I can't wait to see them tomorrow.

The term is coming to an end, I hug each student goodbye with a "*Mahalo*, I love you." As happy as I am at Aikahi, my gut tells me that I need to do more about my life. Just as my thoughts are lingering, Mrs. Arakawa invites me into her office.

"Have you thought about doing your master's?"

"No, not really," I pretend to know what she's talking about.

"You've impressed me so much with your first teaching position," Mrs. Arakawa raises her eyebrows, "even more so than some of my long-time teachers. I know you'll touch many more lives if you go on and do your master's."

"Thank you, I'll think about it," I patronize.

I don't know what's a master's degree. Do I want to take on another schooling challenge?

⧉⧉⧉

"Teachers College, Columbia University," Dr. Han says without a blink. "If you want to do a master's in teaching, then you have to go to the best college for teachers."

"Is it like BYU–Hawaii?" I ask ignorantly, not having heard of that school before.

Dr. Han shakes his head. "No, it's not like BYU–Hawaii. But I can promise if you put in the same effort as you did here, you'll do fine. It's not about the place; it's about your attitude and effort."

I think I've heard of that school once when my political science professor, Sister Debbie Hartmann, mentioned it. She talked about how grandeur the historical architectures were and the liveliness of the city.

I never question Dr. Han and went ahead and applied to Teachers College. He knows me better than I know myself. I don't know anything about Teachers College—where it is located, how much tuition cost, what's the cost of living, or where on earth is New York City!

Several months later, I learned that I could have applied to a few more schools, but it's too late now. I never knew America has several hundreds of universities, unlike Singapore. I try to be positive and console myself that applying to only one school has saved me a few hundreds of dollars.

June approaches and a letter comes in the mail—I got accepted! I can't believe it. I didn't think it was going to happen. It's official. I'm going to start graduate school. This is going to be the real test now. No one is going to coddle me anymore like in a church school. It's the survival of the fittest. I'm either to be refined or resign to fate. Only three months away and I will be moving to the Big Apple. It feels so surreal.

Applying for graduate housing is a strange experience. My choices are between roadside view or courtyard view. Steve thinks it would be more pleasant to look out the courtyard and see some bushes, flowers, benches, tables, and maybe even a barbeque pit than watching cars go by. At least that was what we thought we were signing up for.

Walking into our 900-square foot apartment, my eyes are drawn to the dark linoleum-flooring and a dozen rusty bicycles chained outside to an even rustier pipe. I burst into tears.

"Why did we leave our ocean-view house on the Marine Corps Base in paradise Hawaii for this!"

"Mom," Elijah, almost two and a half, consoles me, "it's ok, I like this place."

We hug each other and begin unpacking our new lives in New York City. It takes more than three months before all the boxes are emptied. About two-thirds of the stuff had to be stored some two hours' drive away.

The life-altering city is so monumental and uncharacteristic to anything I've known. Everything is a first for me—First train ride in the smelliest subway, planets away from the sanitary, unstained Singapore Mass Rapid Transit. First time seeing such rampant, but impressive, graffiti on buildings, bathrooms, walls, and of course, the subway. First time blasting my ears off to the boisterous sirens, honking, and screeching noises. Worst of all, first time living inside of an icebox. Now I know what snow feels like! It sure looks prettier from inside the window. I feel the sharp pain piercing through my ears. Winter is not what I expect, so it's going to be some long and torturous years.

Dr. Han was right. Columbia is nothing like BYU–Hawaii. My first month is inconceivable. I don't understand why people admire those who live in

Manhattan. It's only incredible for those who have tons of money. I mean the historical structures surrounding the urbanized skyscrapers warrant some architectural merits, but I am abandoned in the middle of a battleground without even a plastic knife to defend myself. There's nothing to envy about being a poor, pathetic student-family, living in student housing.

What on earth does *uptown* and *downtown* mean? It took me a year to figure out uptown means the subway number goes up whereas downtown means the number goes down. Why can't someone just spell these nuances out in a survival guide for NYC greenhorns like me?

I have to learn which way to look when I cross the street because Singaporeans drive on the opposite side of the road. I did not have this confusion in Hawaii because I was the driver more than the pedestrian. I instinctively look on the wrong side every time I cross the street. These New York taxi drivers are the most unforgivable road maniacs. They practically weigh their palm on the horns to make sure I get the message. When that happens, I freeze. As soon I make it to the other side of the road, vendors start yelling at me from all directions.

"Buy one, get one half off. Genuine handbags, belts, wallets!"

Before I can turn my head to avoid contact, a flyer is shoved in my face—One Day Sale. Don't Miss It!

Normal walking is new. Almost every day, I slip and fall. I didn't know that if there's no snow on a spot, it doesn't mean it's easier to walk, because it could be icy.

Dr. Han keeps his promise and continues to mentor me via emails and phone calls, but I'm still mad at him. Of the hundreds of schools that I could have attended, he thinks this one in NYC is for me.

While the Morningside Heights brownstone at Bancroft has an eclectic façade of a Vienna Secessionist style, featuring copper-clad bay windows, I'm most paranoid about getting robbed. My next fear is being lost in this nocturnal city or being raped by an insane man. Most frightening of all, I'm raising my son in a city that I'm barely surviving.

I spend my days running between classes and the library, going to practicum in Harlem, dropping and picking Elijah up from childcare, and the stinky subway. I'm constantly exhausted, nervous, and worried.

"What am I doing here, Dr. Han? Why did you have me come here? I have to get out of here!" I call him every two weeks.

Having gone from a tiny campus of 2,000 students to one of over 30,000, I am besieged from all angles.

"Hi, I'm from Berkley," a girl to my right introduces herself.

"I'm from Boston College," another girl interrupts.

"I'm from Stanford," the girl in front announces.

All I can say is, "I'm from Brigham Young University in Hawaii."

"From … where?" Phyllis wrinkles her face and tries to conceal her ignorance.

"Brigham—what?"

"Brigham—Young—University—in Hawaii," I enunciate each word, thinking maybe it's my accent.

"Never heard of that school before, but Hawaii is nice," she flashes a fake smile and turns around.

"It's a lot warmer for sure." I nod but no one is listening.

Teachers College is not the place where the aloha spirit prevails. Students are not bad; they are just preoccupied with their own agenda. There's no room for someone like me. It's better to keep to myself than be friendly. I revert back to my college days and immerse myself in school while trying to repress the noise of the sleepless habitat.

After two semesters, I'm back on the phone with Dr. Han. He only has the same advice for me, "Hang in there. As long as you put in the same effort you did at BYU–Hawaii, you'll do fine."

"I can't take it any longer," I protest. "What were you thinking? This place is dreadful! Stinky! Noisy! Not to mention, expensive. The Apple is too *big* for me."

"You can do this," Dr. Han urges in his hoarse laughter. It'll be over before you know it."

"Easy for you to say. You've never lived here," I retort. I still hear his voice echoing—*You can do this! You have to do this for yourself!*

My head is half in the water and half above. I feel like I'm trying to breathe while drowning. The good thing that comes from unanticipated adventures is that I'm more determined than ever to finish up school as quickly as possible. I need to break out of this urban jungle soon.

Within two semesters, I complete all my credits, including internship, and write up my master's thesis. I am set to leave, except my advisor is not ready to let me go. He wants me to consider embarking on another master's.

"Are you kidding me? I shock myself, "I didn't know there are any more degrees after a master's.

Now that the thought is planted in my mind, I can't help but brood over the quandary of doing another master's. We're practically living from paycheck to paycheck. Can we afford to live another year in the city and raise a child? Is pursuing another piece of paper worth it?

This whole ordeal has been a nightmare for me and, I believe, for Elijah too. I can never afford treats for him, whether it's food, toys, a candy bar, or simply a cup of Italian ice. On very rare occasion when we can't resist the smell of the roasted honey peanuts or glazed almond sold on the street corner for a dollar, we buy a packet to split three-ways with daddy. I feel selfish asking my family to hang in for another round of battling and financial suicide.

One Friday, I receive an invitation to attend a ceremony in Main Hall the next day. When I step into the auditorium, I notice a group of students, kempt and dressed in formal attire, sitting to the right of the stage. I suspect they are the reason for this special gathering. Everyone seems to be staring in that direction. Friends and families are in the middle section, waving surreptitiously to this special group. I quietly sneak myself into an empty chair at the farthest back row.

The President of Teachers College pleasurably strolls to the podium and congratulates these students seated. They have just passed their doctorate exams and are now officially doctoral candidates. I can't help but envy them for having taken on this challenge to arrive at where they are. I wish I can be one of them.

My special education professor from BYU–Hawaii, Sister Kari Gali, once told me she earned her doctorate at thirty and became the youngest professor at BYU–Hawaii. I can never catch up to be like her for the mere fact that I started college at twenty-four, but maybe, just maybe I can make it at thirty-one.

"Steve, I think I'm ready to take my education to the next level." I proclaim right when I reach home.

He supports me wholeheartedly. It is also at this time that we welcome our second child into the family. Since she was born in Manhattan, we named her Audrey after the 1961 movie, *Breakfast at Tiffany's* starring Audrey Hepburn.

Before I know it, my studies become an ongoing trajectory into the depth of Special Education. I continue on with my third master's while raising two children in the city that's beginning to recognize me—and I it.

Chapter 20
INSIDE OUT

Sometimes you put walls up not to keep people out, but to
see who cares enough to break them down.

⤷ *Socrates*

*E*ach night at five, Steve and I trade places. He gets
home from work to watch the kids while I run across
the street to my classes. As I wander hurriedly through the
hallway at Teachers College, I am surrounded by
elaborative gold-framed portraits of founding educators
such as Thorndike, Macy, Horace Mann, Grace Dodge,
and other legends. These images are haunting and
daunting in some respect because I feel intimidated and
privileged at the same time to be here.

Teachers College, established in 1887, is the first
and largest graduate school of education in the United
States and is ranked among the nation's best. Looking back,

I think it would help if I had known something about this school before I applied.

I try to take advantage of every free talk given on this campus so I can learn from the experts. Many textbook names now become real—Howard Gardner, Maxine Green, Lucy Calkins, Michael Apple, William Bennett.

After completing three master's degrees, I'm ready to embark on my doctorate. The sight of those candidates I set my eyes on just a few years back hasn't left me. I want to be one of them.

Of all the mentors I had at Teachers College, Dr. Thomas Sobol and I have the least in common. From the outset, he amazes me. A man of few words, people are confounded by his sage wisdom. Everything he says matters. His nickname at Teachers College is the "Rock Star." I have never heard this expression before. I picture a rock star as a punk with colored, spiked hair, don with metal chains and clothing, or no clothing, and piecing from ear to nose to belly, but that's not Dr. Sobol.

His office is on the second floor of Main Hall. I see a faculty member wheel him into the office each morning and help him get settled into a deep burgundy leather recliner. I don't know why he can't walk. There's more to that than his age.

Even in his wheelchair, Dr. Sobol stands taller than anyone else. I see him frequently being surrounded by visitors who want to interview him or ask for advice.

Dr. Dennis Mithaug, my advisor, suggests I take a class, any class, from Dr. Sobol.

"How about 'Ethical Issues in Educational Leadership,'" he points to the catalog.

"Why can't I take a more relevant class?" I defy.

I don't understand why I need to take a course from a professor who is not even in special education. I try to convince Dr. Mithaug to consider another class but to no avail.

"If you leave TC without taking a course from Sobol, you would be remiss," he forewarns.

"Okay, fine," I give in.

I have never heard Dr. Mithaug asserts himself like this before. He was not joking. I hope he's not sabotaging me. He seems to have a reputation for that from what I've heard.

On the first day of Sobol's class, a school principal sits next to me.

"Dr. Sobol is brilliant. Listen to every word he says. He's not interested in superficial comments," he advises.

"Ok, I'll bear that in mind," I mumble.

For half the semester, I say nothing, not a single word. I do not want to make a fool of myself in front of these administrators, and certainly not in front of Dr. Sobol.

He is a down-to-earth practitioner who spent most of his life in the public schools, not the ivory tower, as a superintendent of the Scarsdale District, New York. A graduate from the Boston Latin School, he held a degree in English from Harvard.

Born the son of a railroad worker, Thomas Sobol is a self-made man. He told a high school graduating class in a speech I came across later in *The New York Times*[5]:

> *I remember my father when I was a child: home by streetcar from work in the railroads, the smell of creosote on his boots and pants; on his breath, beer; the huge workman's hands, the shortness of temper at whining voices in small rooms. I'll transcend this, I dream.*

He carried this feeling with him into all his distinguished positions, a lasting sense that he had to do more, that his real mission was to help children who did not have access to education; children like himself.

---

[5] Carmody, Deirdre. "A Practical Administrator: Dr. Thomas Sobol." *The New York Times.* March 25, 1987. Accessed June 5, 2015.

The more I read about him, the more I feel he's going to see through me and fail me. I panic, suspecting that my advisor has set me up.

Mid-semester comes and Dr. Sobol asks to see me in his office. He is known for seeking out outliers. My hands are sweating a hundred times worse than when Dr. Han called me in. Why would a high flyer like Dr. Sobol want to see me, the mutest student in his class?

I knock on the antique-looking wooden door, inevitably glancing over the eye-level panel—*Professor of Outstanding Education Practice.* Good grief, I'm in trouble.

"Good afternoon, Dr. Sobol, I'm Barbara. You wanted to see me?"

"Have a seat. Let me finish this email," he says without making eye contact.

His office looks like an old library. Every corner is lined with thick binding books filled to the brim of the ceiling at the back wall. Reminds me of Dr. Han's office, except five times larger. The expresso-brown window panes have no curtains, so lights from outside penetrate freely into the dark-floored space. On his oversized executive, cherry desk are stacks of papers and notes, unopened letters, and more books, neatly piled in some mysteriously systematic way that only the owner can find what he needs. On the edge of the bookcases are various artifacts and curios from a variety of cultures, probably gifts from students and colleagues. I recognize an old velvety black calendar with embroidered zodiac animals that reads *Singapore* hung next to the desk. The walls are filled with plaques of recognition and award.

Dr. Sobol has served with *great distinction* in Scarsdale public schools. During his tenure, the district was among the top performing in the nation. When he became the New York State Commissioner of Education, he led the authorship of *A New Compact for Learning: Improving Public Elementary, Middle, and Secondary Education Results in the 1990s.*

This was among the first documents to lay out the terms in which states are accountable for providing a good education to all children.

It is almost impossible to imagine our current educational system without this work, which raised awareness not only of every child's right to a decent public education but also of how that education might be structured to deliver on its promises.

Dr. Sobol has been a true hero, showing commitment to the cause of educating all children in an even more dramatic way. When plaintiffs sued the State of New York, arguing that districts had not sufficiently met the challenge of providing an adequate education due to the size of their tax base, Dr. Sobol changed sides, mounted a winning argument on behalf of the plaintiffs. No superintendent, and certainly no education commissioner, had ever done anything like this before, risking their own popularity and their career for the cause of the children.

Dr. Sobol's sense of responsibility and courage to speak up for the rights of children and their future is not something I take lightly. I study in depth what it takes to become an advocate for something you believe is right, even if it makes you unpopular or have to risk your career, relationships, and sometimes, your life.

Dr. Sobol never boasts about these landmark cases. He's about as low-key a gentleman as one can be. I have not yet realized who Dr. Sobol is—this could be a good thing. That way I am not bedazzled by his magnificence and profundity. Hanging out with him was like visiting your grandpa.

"How are you doing? Barbara, right?" he turns around from his computer to address me.

"Yes, I'm Barbara. I'm in your class. I enjoy everything I'm learning though I haven't spoken in class," I said, hoping this is not about my participation. "I'm learning so much, I don't want to interrupt."

"What topic are you going to do for your dissertation?"

"What?" I am caught by surprise because this is usually the role of the advisor, not an elective faculty.

"I'm not sure yet," I admit thoughtfully.

"How do you see yourself having an effect in the world?" he queries further.

No one ever asked me that before. I don't know what to tell him. Dr. Sobol meets my gaze head-on, leaning forward with one hand knuckling over the other hand, waiting for a reply. His complete attention is disquieting. He wants a truthful response.

Socrates says, *"Understanding a question is half an answer."*

What exactly is he trying to get out of me? I have to utter my next words carefully.

"Teach, uh … I want to teach children with special needs," I stammer but seeing a look of slight disappointment flash across his face, I square my shoulders, sit up straight, and try to give another shot at my response.

"Barbara," he says in his posh New York accent, "in everything we do, there must be a sense of caring about why we're doing it; otherwise, it's a waste. What effect do you care to have on others?"

Dr. Sobol gazes at me while I'm still simmering in my thoughts on the word *care.* I do care about teaching. I do care about children with special needs. I do care about learning everything I can about disability, but I'm just one person. How am I supposed to have any effect on others?

I leave his office with my mind magnified one-hundred-fold. For the first time, I envision my education doing more good than what I have in mind within the four walls of a classroom. For the first time, I understand that getting an education can't just be about what I want. I have to give something back. I have to make a difference;

however small it may be. I have to do something good with this knowledge. I have to touch lives.

Dr. Sobol assigns the class to read Dr. Nel Noddings's *Caring: A Feminine Approach to Ethics and Moral Education*.[6] Dr. Noddings is a professor emeritus at Stanford and is at Teachers College as a visiting faculty.

Her research seeks to revive John Dewey's ethos of how teacher-student relationships ought to be. She maintains that a teacher must care enough about the students and truly seek to understand each of them as a whole person, encompassing his or her physical, social, psychological, and cultural self. Only then can the teacher grasp what ways of learning are most appropriate for that individual. Only then is a teacher truly impacting the community for good.

As I lay awake late into the night in that two-hundred-year-old run-down student housing, I ponder over Dr. Noddings's words. One quote stops me in my tracks: *"The structure of current schooling works against care, and at the same time, the need for care is perhaps greater than ever."*[7]

I haven't quite put together how I'm going to respond to Dr. Sobol's challenge, but Dr. Noddings's words awaken me to a new understanding of the power of caring that I've never considered before. I've been a recipient of such caring to get to where I am today, whether intentionally or accidentally. Cultivating such an attribute is quintessential in the teaching profession. But there's more to that. I've never considered caring as a catalyst for change. I got into this field thinking more like a job, or a career perhaps, and nothing more. But that's not what Dr. Sobol was instigating. He wants me to think of making

---

[6] Noddings, Nel. *Caring: A Feminine Approach to Ethics and Moral Education.* Berkeley, CA: University of California Press, 1984.
[7] Noddings, Nel. *The Challenge to Care in Schools: An Alternative Approach to Education.* New York, NY: Teachers College Press, 1992.

changes in people's lives, not just any changes but changes that have a positive, prosocial effect.

I didn't get much sleep that night. I ease into the living room and stare out the rusty steel window panes, watching strangers in the street roving around under the orange glow of the streetlights. My mind drifts into nostalgic moments in Aikahi. I miss my students so much. Why can't I just be a teacher in my quiet classroom and do my thing? That's the only picture I've painted in my mind this whole time.

Time stood still while I picture the endless star-filled sky of Oahu, void of city traffic and Chinatown noise, and treat myself to a melancholic state of mindfulness about all the people who have touched my life.

The most powerful, yet intangible, curriculum is neither the textbook nor the content, but rather the caring of a teacher. This conscious act alone can have a greater potential to morph self-determination, self-confidence, and self-empowerment in a student than any subject matter a teacher could deliver. A person who is educated and self-determined, but does not care about anyone else, can be a danger to society.

History is full of such individuals. Take Theodore John "Ted" Kaczynski, the Unabomber and math prodigy, as an example. He was accepted into Harvard at sixteen and became a professor at the University of California, Berkeley at twenty-five. Instead of using his talents, education, and passion to benefit the world, he turned against it.

I think I was no different for the longest time, apathetic, selfish, prideful, and determined. I would stop at nothing to get whatever I wanted, mostly for selfish reasons. It was always about me, me, me and what *I* want, even getting an education at the top university, pursuing my passion, securing a job, and doing whatever I desired.

"The true value of wisdom," Dr. Sobol once said in class, "lies in our ability to refine who we are and then extend that refinement toward society through our good deeds."

I thought about what refining oneself means. I can be self-determined to achieve all my goals, but if I did nothing good with it, I am of little worth and value. Of course, I'm not planning to use my knowledge to hurt any children, but I can easily fall prey to stressful or burnout situations and turn abusive. This is why I need to constantly remind myself the purpose of my learning and my role as a teacher, and valiantly use this knowledge to refine society into a better place.

When my attitude molds from being competitive to being ambitious, my perspective also takes a detour. Grades are no longer my top priority. I become more introspective about the relational aspects of human interactions. I'm no more ambitious than an infant taking her time to crawl, walk, and talk.

I stepped into Columbia with one unequivocal goal—get in and get out. Many of my friends went to college so they could make a career out of it. That's not me. I had always wanted to stay home and have children— eight to be exact. I'll teach if I have to, but fortunately, Steve can support us. There is no need for me to work if I so choose. I have no intention of pursuing a full-time job at any time. I'm happy with what I've been blessed, and if I ended up being a homemaker, I'd be equally satisfied. I know I can teach my children, which was my original intent when I pursued the education field.

I'd love to return to my first love in card-making or even flower arrangement, and simply hanging out with my kids. But life has a way of making you change lanes as you try to maneuver the lumps and bumps of the labyrinthine world, which is often neither good nor bad. It just happens.

I finally have a response for Dr. Sobol.

"I think a self-determined soul without a heart can be a dangerous weapon because he is like a walking bomb," I utter with a eureka jubilance! "I need to use my learning to do more than teaching. To advocate for the voiceless, even if it means one child, one parent, one stranger at a time."

"Then that's what you'll have to keep in mind no matter what the challenges are," Dr. Sobol smiles, "otherwise you might easily lose sight one day of what you're doing."

Slowly but surely, I frame my dissertation along this line of research. Since the day when Dr. Sobol and I met in his office, he promised that if I kept to this line of inquiry, he would get the best sponsor for my dissertation.

At Teachers College, a doctoral sponsor has to be someone in the academia with a high scholarly profile. Since Dr. Sobol spent most of his career as a practitioner, he is unable to sponsor me. However, he kept his promise and requested an expert on caring, Dr. Nel Noddings, to be my sponsor.

"Why did you agree to be my sponsor even though I have never taken a class from you?" I ask out of curiosity.

Dr. Noddings kindly replies, "Because Tom asked."

Wow, that was quite the honor and privilege! Indeed, in Nel Noddings, I found another great mentor. Like Sobol, Noddings comes from a first-generation American family where her father was a blue-collar industrial worker in Northern New Jersey, and like Sobol, she discovered early on the value of a good education and became a mathematics teacher.

Dr. Noddings is one patient woman. Whenever I am agonizing over my writing, she reminds me that a dissertation is not about shooting for the stars.

"Enjoy what you do," she says, "but don't forget the people you love. Spend time with those that matter most."

Each time I walk into Dr. Sobol and Dr. Noddings's offices, it's like entering a master's chamber. I inhale every word they have to say. I leave their presence feeling renewed, rejuvenated, and revived, ready to embrace not only their knowledge and teaching, but also their exemplars of caring. I hope I do not disappoint them.

This is what's so amazing about the ethic of caring. We care because we want to care. It's part of our being and intuition. Caring should not be driven by position or power or one's title, stature, convenience, wealth, or bias.

My dissertation is slowly becoming a full discourse. I am so grateful that in the process of helping me to frame my secular learning, Dr. Sobol and Dr. Noddings also helped me to frame my inner sense of who I am and what I want to become, which to this day has been my ethos, *"No one cares how much you know, until they know how much you care."* (*Theodore Roosevelt*).

Chapter 21
FINDING HOME

———————————◦≡◦———————————

I may not have gone where I intended to go, but I think I have ended up where I intended to be.
≈ *Douglas Adams*

$\mathcal{I}$t is another four months before I defend my dissertation, I can't wait to finally get out of this hell jungle. I swear I'll never miss the repulsive noise of that hum of traffic and non-stop sirens and honking. Since I have finished all my coursework, we move into suburban Westchester, located on the outskirts of Manhattan, where Steve's mom resides. I still commute to the city once a week to meet with my mentors.

One evening, the phone rings. It's the doctor. From Singapore. Bàba is given a prognosis of one month. It's not as if I am unprepared for this day. I call home immediately.

"Don't bother to come home," Māma says nonchalantly. "There's nothing you can do anyway, why waste your money. Stay with the children."

"Mā, but … I want to …"

I refuse to listen and buy three tickets for the next available flight to Singapore.

From time to time when I come home to visit, I see Bàba becoming frailer and ailing. His hands and feet are unsteady and shaking. He talks to himself in some hallucination. His speech is stammering. I no longer understand what he's saying. His body shrinks, he's fleeing timidly right before my eyes.

I no longer feel angry or disgusted but more sympathetic to him. I want to hold him, but there is always a bottle in one hand and a cigarette in the other. I can never get close enough to kiss him. Even though he cuts down on his drinking and smoking, it's too late. His body deteriorates faster than it can repair itself.

The last time I remember Bàba smiling a lot was when my sister got married a couple of years earlier. Bàba was in a dark suit with a crisp white shirt and a masculine boutonnière orchid pinned on his lapel buttonhole. He was drinking but in a celebratory way rather than to drown his sorrow. He looked handsome, somber, and with us, a sense of composure I had never seen before, nor ever again.

Up in the air, the tranquility of the midnight sky across the Atlantic Ocean blows a serenity to calm me. The twenty-five-hour flight seems twice as long, like going from the north pole to the south pole. I manage to rest my eyes with Audrey, ten months, in one arm, and Elijah, five, leaning on the other. The lethargy and heaviness of flying overtake me.

Suddenly I have an influx of memories, mostly good ones. I wish I had spent more time with Bàba instead of pursuing my self-interest. I wish I had flown home more often instead of worrying about money. I wish I had told him more often how much I enjoyed the pork buns he brought home for me, the time he drove us to the airport or to Whampoa to eat my favorite noodles, I wish, I wish …

I remember one Sunday afternoon, Bàba drives home an old red convertible Mercedes. A cigarette hangs from the corner of his mouth. He smells of beer. Even if he has to return the car the next day, Bàba wants us to know what it feels like to have something grand, something notoriously luxurious.

He waves through the chaotic two-lane traffic to bring us to the other side of town at Punggol Beach. I skip my feet over the fiery polluted sand, wearing Phillip's discarded T-shirts and shorts. Bàba lies on a ragged towel holding a beer bottle over his blown-up belly. Jennifer and I make strange faces at Bàba, shouting for him to notice us, but he couldn't. He didn't see us dancing in the waves. He didn't see us being so happy with him.

On the last leg, ascending from Tokyo, I sense a change in the color of the sky. The orangey light spreads across the whole sphere, like the painting of a large brush stroke. I lean forward to see what the painter is going to do next. He glides over another droplet of gold paint, and the whole sky is now amber red, shimmering across the bleeding sky, surrendering to the painter, like a canvas of cotton candy, illuminating radiantly. But I don't feel the heat. My hope is fainting. My feeble mind whispers—I may not get to see Bàba anymore.

Upon landing at Singapore Changi Airport, I frantically search for the closest courtesy phone and dial for Māma.

"He's gone … He's finally gone," Māma says in her solemn voice. No tears, not even a crack in her voice.

Bàba is gone.

I missed saying one last good-bye. I'm too late, too late.

God gave me this Bàba for a reason, but I still don't know why. I don't know if I want to be my Māma's daughter or my Bàba's. I don't know if I belong to this family anymore.

Jennifer is the only one who has been taking care of Bàba and Māma since we all moved out; Winston to Hong Kong and Phillip to his own apartment. Only Jennifer remains to care for our aging parents. I never see her take a break or do anything for herself. She is our steel magnolia, our fortress, our breath, and practically our Bàba and Māma.

I maintained that Jennifer loves Bàba the most. She sacrificed her education and career without ever asking any one of us to give up ours. She stayed by Bàba's bedside and at the hospital day and night while also caring for her daughter and husband.

In the last months of his diagnosis of liver cirrhosis, Jennifer cleaned and washed and cooked, running back and forth between the hospital. Nobody will ever know what she went through all those nights and days when Bàba couldn't eat, sleep, walk, or use the bathroom on his own. Jennifer did it all, without complaint. There's no question she loved Bàba. Now that he has passed on, it's as if a part of her has died too.

Bàba's body has to be embalmed right away after the autopsy because it's corroding too rapidly due to his liver and kidney failure. For the viewing, Māma spends a little on food—rice and curry, some peanuts, and tea. Relatives send a couple of wreaths for burial, nothing big.

"It's good that he's gone," someone says, "now you all can have a life and be happy."

I stare back at the woman, in disgust. I have a life. We all have a life. It wasn't like Bà took that away from us. We may not have gone on vacations and cruises or lived in a bungalow and wore name brand clothes, but we had a decent life. Good moments may have been rare, but we have our shares of laughter, at least enough for me, to treasure up in memory. No one has a right to say if Bàba gave us a life or not. How dare they judge my Bàba when they never lived with him and saw what he went through. They were not there in our lowest moments, and they certainly were not there in our happier times.

I've learned early in life never to hinge my happiness on whether I have a good upbringing or not, or whether I have a good Bàba or not. I'm insulted that anyone, especially my aunties and uncles, would think that my siblings and I cannot work out our lives unless Bàba is gone.

We don't need families to come in a nicely wrapped package. My parents, my environment, even my genes may define who I am, but these do not define my outcome and what I make of myself. I am my own destiny. I went on my mission, left for America, and graduated from college. I got married, had kids, and established a home. I did everything I wanted and never felt deprived of my pursuit of happiness.

"Would any of you like to speak about your Bàba on behalf of your family?" the pastor from the Hinghwa Methodist Church walks up and asks.

I don't know if this is a good time to ask me to speak. I'm still burning with fury about the remarks of Bàba. Being the youngest, it is not customary for me to be giving the eulogy, but Winston and Phillip are reluctant to do it. Jennifer is in an inconsolable state and is in no position to speak. Māma gives me that look, widening her eyes but in a pleading manner.

"You are better at speaking. You do it for Bà. Show everyone what kind of Bàba you had."

"That's right," Jennifer concurs. "You speak for Bàba, for all of us. Don't let anyone insult our Bàba."

I quickly jot down some thoughts and step up to the microphone. People look at me oddly, wondering why the youngest child is speaking.

"What good can she dig out of this man?" another aunt mumbles.

Ignoring my jet lag, which is making my mouth dry and everything else slightly unreal, I deliver what I have scribbled.

"Bà loves cars. He can tell you the make and year of a car from the smallest clues. He can tell the make of the car just by browsing for one second. He especially loves odd European cars—Alfa Romeos, Peugeots. He knows the ins and outs of an engine the way you know your children. He can tell what's wrong with a car just by hearing the engine rumbles or a glance inside the hood. One coughing sound and he can snap his fingers and tell you, 'It's the fan belt, alternator, transmission, gear, whatever it may be.' Like an emergency doctor, Bà can diagnose any vehicle ailment just like that. It's his gift."

"When we were very small, Bà tells us he is a car whisperer. 'The car speaks to me,' he says."

He drives home different cars to take us out for a ride. Bà is always full of surprises, that's what makes life so unpredictable.

I look at the crowd and see faces that are now mildly amused. This is not what everyone was expecting. I did not give the ceremonial sob about his drunkenness and gambling addiction.

"Bàba loves the ocean. He is never happier than on the days when he takes us to the East Coast Beach. We only go there a handful of times, but we have the most un-forgettable moments as a family. He is a joker. He makes us laugh so hard that we start tearing up. He makes funny faces and noise like a gorilla and chases us around."

"Bà loves food so every chance he gets he buys us some satays, Hokkien noodles, durians, ice-creams, cakes, and barbeque pork buns. When he gets home from his midnight shift, even at four in the morning, he wakes us up and brings us to the Whampoa hawker center. We get to order whatever we want to eat. We go home so full."

The crowd becomes a little annoyed by now, gossiping some audible remarks so I can hear them. I clear my throat and continue.

"Bà is the kind of person who would initiate a conversation with a stranger. If he sees you in the elevator, he will talk to you first. There is something about Bà that is so charismatic, but more than that, Bà is a simple, honest man, without guile or hypocrisy."

Tears flood my eyes. I choke. I can't continue anymore. I find myself begging everyone within the sound of my voice to please remember our Bàba, their brother, as a decent man, not the monster they make him out to be. To us, Bàba was real. He showed his love in different ways. He drove for miles to find Phillip his favorite remote-control spaceship. He dressed up to attend Winston's art competition where he won first prize.

I talk about how Jennifer and I loved hearing Bàba's stories over and over again and laughing out loud. The few things we did with Baba may appear insignificant to others, but to us, he was and is very much alive in our lives. He did the best he knew how.

"So, let our hearts be resolved," I conclude. "Let our souls rejoice. Let our spirits be reunited at least for this brief moment while we remember all the good about my Bàba."

"No one could have said it better," Jennifer says while nursing her newborn daughter.

I don't mind funerals, but some things my mother said crept me out. For example, it is a Chinese belief that during the night, someone has to keep watch on the coffin to prevent a black cat from jumping over the corpse. If this happens, the corpse might come alive with the nine lives from the cat. Of course, the job mostly falls on Jennifer and me.

Many relatives and Bàba's so-called beer buddies don't talk much to us. Funerals tend to make people pretentious. Everywhere I look, people are either avoiding me or giving me that when-is-this-going-to-be-over grin. Even when you're present, you're not really there as if the person who died has taken a part of your life with them too.

I lift my head and see Māma across the room. She finds, who knows where, a cardboard box, and begins sweeping and picking up waste and crumbs from the floor. I move toward her to tell her to stop, but Jennifer puts her hand on my arm.

"Leave her," she whispers. "It makes her happy when she's cleaning."

That's the way Māma is. If Bàba was home drunk, she would be sweeping the floor. If Bàba was mad, she would mop or hang up clothes. That's how Māma copes with or escapes the emotions trapped inside her.

Death has a way of making one appreciate the little things in life more. I want so much for Bàba to see me walk across the stage to receive my doctorate and be hooded in front of hundreds of people, even if he does not understand what those rituals mean. I'll never know if he's proud of me. He never said one word about my schooling since sixth grade when he wanted me to drop out.

"Bà can't make it there because he's too weak," Jennifer says as if she hears my thoughts, "but he'll be there in spirit. You're the one who made him most proud."

I want to believe her. I hope Bàba is smiling down on me. No matter what kind of a Bàba he was or wasn't, he matters to me.

I know I should be sleeping off this awful jet lag that has dogged me for days, but strangely, I feel wide awake. I don't know how many more years or months or days Māma will be with us.

I miss my family.

I miss our tears and laughters.

I miss our fights and arguments.

I believe I was born to this family for a reason. I'm proud to be part of them. Of course, it's always easier to say all these things in retrospect when I'm grown now. In large part, that's why I'm writing this book.

I'm not ashamed of my family anymore. I picture Bàba as a cop when he looks young and handsome and full of life. Maybe the tragedy is not that he was poor, but for whatever reason, never became the person he wanted to be. That larger, kinder, more open person was somehow stunted and erased.

The same can be said of Māma. I picture Māma as a seamstress so elegant and talented and beautiful. She tried to survive for everyone else that she never lived for herself. I see my sister doing the same right now.

Whenever there are roots, there will be branches. Whenever there are seasons, there will be blooms. Wherever there's resistance, there'll be strength. Whether by design or by fate, I am who I am because of my lived experiences.

ॐ

It has been almost eight years since I made that fateful decision to leave home and come to America. I blended in, acculturated myself, and become more Americanized in one way or another. A year later, after Bàba's passing, Jasmyn came into our lives.

As mercy would have it, during the final semester of my doctorate, I was offered a job on Long Island. We were able to buy our first house. It's on a quarter acre of land and has a front porch, a bay window, a cathedral sunroof kitchen, even a swimming pool. I buy my first new car and a brand-new piano. This home is where we will raise our three children and build another generation of futures.

That fall, I sit in the front row of the Cathedral of St. John the Divine, hardly believing that I am finally graduating at thirty. When I first arrived in Manhattan, I marveled at the revived architecture of this thirteenth century gothic Cathedral. I heard a tour guide proclaiming that this is the world's largest Anglican cathedral and the fourth largest church in the world.

The rose window foreshadows a youthful revival of the spirited with its multitudes of stained-glass pieces. From the iron door to the dark floor, from the granite columns to the vaulted ceiling, there are sculptures of religious figures and birds of creation at every perimeter of the area. The verticality gives the majestic space a strategic sense of unity and sacredness that's collectively breathtaking and reverent. One cannot help but pray.

Seated in the front row, dressed in my heavy grayish-blue gown and octagonal tasseled cap, I try not to fidget. I spent the whole night ironing my gown and did not want to wrinkle it like when I was going to school in Singapore with only one set of uniform.

The Dean of the College of Arts and Sciences calls my name, "*Barbara Siew Swan Hong.*" I walk across the richly carved chancel where the officiating clergy and choir typically sit, except this time there are dozens of faculty members, the board of the trustees, political officials, and distinguished guests, all dressed in formal regalia, and none of whom I recognize.

I drape my satin light blue hood over my right arm like a freshman butler and hand it to the Dean. He and his associates loop the hood over my head and present me with a plaque.

"Congratulations, Doctor Barbara Hong," the dean solemnly pronounces.

The photographers snap away while I calmly make my way back to my seat. Multitudes of congratulatory praises sound from every parameter—but only one voice stands out.

"I'm so proud of you," a voice all too familiar from a class I took not too long ago.

Dr. Han and his wife had flown from Hawaii to witness this momentous occasion because he knew no one from my family would be there. He embraces me and presents me with a fresh ginger lei all the way from Honolulu. No one else from my family came.

I did not begin my odyssey with an education in mind, but along the way, caring teachers, friends, and even strangers taught me to love myself, love others, and love learning. The footsteps of this expedition have not always been mine alone. The imprints before me, behind me, and mostly beside me have left indelible marks of faith, patience, and fortitude. Likewise, the foundation of my upbringing may not have been all that stable, at times difficult, at times unpredictable. But it was the very *caring* of those around me that lit up a path I never knew existed.

I didn't have the foresight into what my life was going to be like when I was ten, twenty, thirty, or even now. Sometimes I make it at the first shot, sometimes at the fifteenth shot. But most of the time, I stumble through unknowingly, bruised and battled along the way, not understanding why my expedition is exceptionally onerous while everyone seems to breeze through like a walk in the park. All I know is that if I keep failing forward, lifting my head up towards God, somehow a caring hand will come along the way and lift me up.

And today ... I land on both feet.

Don't compare your life to others.
There is no comparison between
the sun, the moon, and the stars.
They shine when it's their time.
⁓ Author Unknown ⁓

Meet the Author

*D*r. Hong obtained her Ph.D. from Columbia University in Special Education in addition to three master's degrees in instructional practices, policy and leadership, and as a learning specialist from the same institution. She was a three-time recipient of the prestigious Senior Fulbright Scholar, Senior Fulbright Specialist, and Fulbright Hays Fellow. Hong was also the First Honorable Visiting Scholar to Taiwan Municipal University.

Hong has been a professor for almost sixteen years at the time of this publication and has taught in New York, Texas, Pennsylvania, Virginia, and Hawaii. She is certified as a special educator, school principal, and district administrator.

In 2014, Hong was appointed by the US State Department, Bureau of International and Information Programs, as a *Speaker Specialist & Expert on Disability* where she consults with governmental agencies around the world. Her research examines the cognitive science of teaching and learning and the development of self-determination through the ethics of caring.

Hong is recognized as the *International Teacher-of-Honor* by the education honor society and the *University Exemplary Faculty* at BYU–Hawaii. She serves on the Advisory Council for the Oxford Education Research Symposium, Board of Directors for the Council for Exceptional Children (Past), President of BYU–Hawaii Honor Society (Past) and is the Founder of *P.A.C.E.*™– Parents as Advocates for Change in Education.

Hong worked as the education specialist for the Virginia Fairfax County Government, Department of Family Services, and Institute for Early Learning. In 2015, Hong returned to BYU–Hawaii as Professor and Coordinator of Special Education and later as Special Assistant to the Academic Vice-President on *A.I.D.E.*—Access, Inclusion, Diversity, & Equity. Currently Hong is a Dean of University College and Professor of Special Education at Texas A&M International University.

For more information, visit barbarahong.com or email contact@barbarahong.com.

Find her on Facebook at "Dr Barbara Hong."

Made in the USA
Coppell, TX
03 July 2021